ALASKA
TRAVEL ✦ SMART®

W9-CHC-321

ICE CLIMBING NEAR ANCHORAGE

ALASKA
TRAVEL ✦ SMART®

Second Edition

Paul Otteson

John Muir Publications
A Division of Avalon Travel Publishing

Dedication

As always, this book is dedicated to my wonderful wife, Mary, who is my anchor and my spark. And just this once, I'll add a very small dedication to the one we know affectionately as "Little Dot."

Acknowledgments

Thanks to the following businesses for their support: the Alaska Marine Highway System, the Alaska Railroad, Alaska Airlines, Northwest Airlines, Cruise West, Reeve Aleutian Airways, Era Aviation, Temsco Helicopters, Uyak Air, Homer Air, Baker Aviation, Alaska Flyers, Westmark Hotels, the Nugget Inn in Nome, the Nullagvik Hotel in Kotzebue, the unexpectedly nice Pacifica Guest House in Bethel.

Thanks to the many fine folks who make my Alaska journeys wonderful: the Dippes, Denmans, and Heapheys—my family in Anchorage; Cheri King—our Ruth Glacier leader; Mike Doncaster and David Endicott—for their help and friendship in Deadhorse; Walt and the Waldo Arms in Kaktovik; Richard Beneville—Nome's greatest asset; and many others.

And thanks to all my Denali friends—Tony, Gooch, Cliff, Jersey, Gary, Randy, Page, and so many more; Ross Houghton—my travel partner, all around good guy, and photographer par excellence; and Todd Stritter—for starting it all.

John Muir Publications
A Division of Avalon Travel Publishing
5855 Beaudry Street
Emeryville, CA 94608

Printed in the United States of America.
Second edition. First printing February 2000.

ISSN: 1520-9113
ISBN: 1-56261-448-7

Editors: Dianna Delling, Elizabeth Wolf
Graphics Editor: Bunny Wong
Production: Scott Fowler
Design: Marie J.T. Vigil
Cover Design: Janine Lehmann, Marie J.T. Vigil
Map Style Development: American Maps—Jemez Springs, NM, USA
Map Illustration: Kathleen Sparkes, White Hart Design
Printer: Publishers Press
Front cover photos: small—© Howard Folsom/Photo Network (Hammer Slough, Petersburg, Alaska)
large—© Mike Jones/Photo Network (Mount McKinley, Denali State Park)
Back cover photo: © Mike Jones/Photo Network (Fly Fishing, Denali State Park)

Distributed to the book trade by
Publishers Group West
Berkeley, California

ALASKA TRAVEL·SMART: A GUIDE THAT GUIDES

Most guidebooks are basically directories, providing information but very little help in making choices—you have to guess how to make the most of your time and money. *Alaska Travel·Smart* is different: By highlighting the very best of the state and offering various planning features, it acts like a personal tour guide rather than a directory.

TAKE THE STRESS OUT OF TRAVEL

Sometimes traveling causes more stress than it relieves. Sorting through information, figuring out the best routes, determining what to see and where to eat and stay, scheduling each day—all of this can make a vacation feel daunting rather than fun. Relax. We've done a lot of the legwork for you. This book helps you plan a trip that suits *you*—whatever your time frame, budget, and interests.

SEE THE BEST OF THE STATE

Author Paul Otteson, a San Francisco resident, considers Alaska his second home. He has hand-picked every listing in this book and gives you an insider's perspective on what makes each one worthwhile. So while you'll find many of the big tourist attractions listed here, you'll also find lots of lesser known treasures, such as the Musk Ox Farm in Palmer and the "Largest Gold Pan in Alaska"—Nome's centerpiece. Each sight is described so you'll know what's most—and sometimes least—interesting about it.

In selecting the restaurants and accommodations for this book, the author sought out unusual spots with local flavor. While in some areas of the state chains are unavoidable, wherever possible the author directs you to one-of-a-kind places. We also know that you want a range of options: One day you may crave king crab legs, while the next day you would be just as happy (as would your wallet) with fish and chips or a burger. Most of the restaurants and accommodations listed here are moderately priced, but the author also includes budget and splurge options, depending on the destination.

CREATE THE TRIP YOU WANT

We all have different travel styles. Some people like spontaneous weekend jaunts, while others plan longer, more leisurely trips. You may want to cover as much ground as possible, no matter how much time you have. Or maybe you prefer to focus your trip on one part of the state or on some special interest, such as history, nature, or art. We've taken these differences into account.

While quite a few travelers begin their Alaskan journey with a flight to Anchorage, many arrive by ferry or cruise ship via the Inside Passage of the Southeast or by driving the Alaska Highway through Canada. Chapters are conveniently arranged for surface travelers, beginning with Ketchikan in the far Southeast and proceeding region by region, northward and westward through Anchorage, Kenai, and the Southwest. The final four chapters are arranged heading northward from Anchorage to Denali and Fairbanks, then on to the remote regions of the Far North and West. If you had the time to visit every destination in this book, you'd experience a tour of the very best Alaska has to offer.

Each destination chapter offers ways of prioritizing when time is limited: In the Perfect Day section, the author suggests what to do if you have only one day to spend in the area. Also, every Sightseeing Highlight is rated, from one to four stars: ★★★★—or "must see" sights first, followed by ★★★ sights, then ★★ sights, and finally ★—or "see if you have time"—sights. At the end of each sight listing is a time recommendation in parentheses. User-friendly maps help you locate the sights, restaurants, and lodgings of your choice.

And if you're in it for the ride, so to speak, you'll want to check out the Scenic Routes described at the end of several chapters. They take you through some of the most scenic parts of state/region.

In addition to these special features, the appendix has other useful travel tools:

- The Planning Map and Mileage Chart help you determine your own route and calculate travel time.
- The Special Interest Tours show you how to design your trip around any of six favorite interests.
- The Calendar of Events provides an at-a-glance view of when and where major events occur throughout the state.
- The Resource Guide tells you where to go for more information about national and state parks, individual cities, local B&Bs, and more.

HAPPY TRAVELS

With this book in hand, you have many reliable recommendations and travel tools at your fingertips. Use it to make the most of your trip. And have a great time!

WHY VISIT ALASKA?

Alaska is in a class by itself as one of the wildest and most spectacular destinations in the world. The grandeur promised by travel videos and brochures is for real. Hundreds of glaciers relentlessly carve the tall, rugged peaks of vast mountain chains. Grizzly bears, bald eagles, and humpback whales abound. Millions of salmon run thick in spawning streams during summer and fall. You can read a newspaper by June's midnight twilight and gaze at the northern lights in wonder in the long, dark winter.

Virtually the entire state of Alaska is a scenic highlight. Rush from point A to point B and you'll miss much of the magic. The land between popular attractions and points of interest is so richly endowed with wildlife and natural beauty that you'll be tempted to stop at nearly every turn to gaze or explore. Don't hesitate to do so! After all, Alaska is America's last bastion of vast, living wilderness. Immerse yourself in it to appreciate its incomparable beauty and value.

The people of Alaska are also in a class by themselves. Their rich heritage—a tapestry of native, Russian, and American histories—is reflected in the art, culture, and customs of the region. Take time to explore some of the many native centers, totem parks, historic sites, and heritage museums.

You'll find Alaskans friendly, hospitable, and well informed. In fact, many residents are directly or indirectly involved with recreation and tourism, and they're ready for you. Assistance and advice are often just a question away. And despite the state's enormity and remoteness, services, basic accommodations, and hearty food are readily available on travel routes.

Why visit Alaska? Because it embodies some of the best the planet has to offer—it is welcoming, wild, and utterly amazing.

LAY OF THE LAND

The majority of travelers journey among the islands, waterways, and peaks of the geologically young mountain ranges that stretch along Alaska's south coast, from the Southeast through the Aleutians. Nearly all of Alaska's glaciers are found within this belt, as are all Alaskan summits over 10,000 feet, including Denali—North America's tallest, at 20,320 feet. About 70 active volcanoes dot the coastline, most in the Aleutian Range west of Cook Inlet. Earthquakes are common; the strongest ever recorded in the Western Hemisphere occurred here on March 27, 1964.

The five main areas of Alaska are the Southeast (the "panhandle"), Southcentral, Southwest, Interior, and Far North.

Alaska's **Southeast**, or "panhandle," is characterized by lushly forested isles, countless bays, fjords and passages, and stunning ice-crested peaks. Cruise ships, ferries, tour boats, and kayaks carry visitors to view calving glaciers and feeding whales. When the skies are clear and the glittering coast mountains exposed, the Southeast is beautiful beyond compare.

Two great mountain chains dominate **Southcentral** and **Southwest** Alaska. The Kenai/Chugach/St. Elias mountain system wraps the Gulf of Alaska, while the Aleutian/Alaska/Wrangell system runs inland to the east, then far to the south and west through the Aleutian island chain. Between the ranges are the valleys of the Matanuska and Susitna Rivers (the "MatSu"), Cook Inlet, the Kenai lowlands, the Copper River Basin, and the Talkeetna Mountains—all areas of great economic and recreational interest.

North of these mountains and south of the older Brooks Range sprawls Alaska's vast **Interior**, dominated by the 1,800-mile Yukon River, which flows from Canada to the Bering Sea. The Interior receives substantially less precipitation than the coast. Winter low temperatures dip to −70 degrees (F) while summer highs can reach into the 80s. The region features a seemingly endless carpet of spruce forest, broken by sprawling, brushy wetlands and by high hills that appear as tundra-covered islands in a sea of evergreen.

The treeless landscapes of the **Far North** and Bering Sea coast are heavily influenced by permafrost. In permafrost areas, groundwater is frozen to a depth of as much as 2,000 feet. Summer surface thawing enables a thin and fragile soil layer to support plant life. Almost all of the state located north of the maritime-influenced coastal mountains has areas of permafrost. In the Far North, the layer is continuous.

FLORA AND FAUNA

Four main vegetation zones are common in Alaska: **tundra, taiga** (boreal forest), **coastal forest**, and **wetlands**. The treeless tundra features mosses, lichens, grasses, and dwarf shrubs. Alpine tundra—famous for splendid wildflower displays—is found above treeline throughout the state, while arctic tundra overlies permafrost in the Arctic and Bering coastal regions. Taiga, found throughout the Interior and Copper River Basin, is characterized by extensive forests of short spruce, aspen, and birch, often interspersed with muskeg—a peaty, tufty bog that may support scraggly black spruce. Sitka spruce and western hemlock dominate Southeast and Southcentral coastal forests, where old-growth trees can reach great size. Vast wetland flats spread through the Interior and delta regions, hosting millions of migratory birds in summer.

All three North American bear species are found in abundance in Alaska. Observing any of them browsing, preying, fishing, or mating can be the highlight of a visit. Black bears grow to six feet from nose to tail and reach 400 pounds. Often distinctly black, they can range from dark to medium and "cinnamon" brown. More than 50,000 live throughout Alaska's forests. Look for them in clearings and at the forest's edge. Polar bears, rarely seen by visitors, live solitary lives on the pack ice off the Arctic coast, coming ashore in the summer to mate, then returning to the ice when the ocean margins freeze in November.

The Alaska brown bear is the world's largest land carnivore, feasting on nutritious salmon for much of the feeding season. It can weigh more than 1,500 pounds. Premier viewing areas include Admiralty Island, Kodiak Island, and Katmai National Park. Inland grizzlies usually are recognized as the same species as the brown bears of the coast, though they are smaller and may have lighter, almost blond fur. They face a harsher climate and consume mainly berries, roots, and plants, plus the occasional ground squirrel, moose calf, or caribou. There are about 40,000 browns and grizzlies in the state.

Approximately 7,000 timber wolves live in Alaska in packs of up to 35 individuals. Territories range from perhaps 50 to 5,000 square miles. These animals mate for life. They are rarely spotted, though a pack has been active in Denali National Park recently. Other common land mammals include beaver, fox, lynx, marmot, porcupine, river otter, and wolverine.

DON'T MESS WITH THE MOOSE

Moose injure more heedless observers than any other animal in Alaska—a big bull moose can weigh 1,500 pounds and sport antlers six feet across. Don't approach them, and if they charge, run!

Moose are common in boggy, forested areas, where they dine on willow shoots. Many live in basins south of the Alaska Range and on the Kenai Peninsula, though they are common elsewhere. Other hoofers include nearly 1 million caribou, which live in about 30 separate herds, each with a distinct migratory route. They are commonly seen in open terrain. Dall sheep—close relatives of the bighorns—usually stay up high, but are often spotted from the Denali Park Road, along Turnagain Arm, and at Sheep Mountain on the Glenn Highway. Snow-white mountain goats reach their northern limit in the high crags of the southeastern ranges. Reindeer (essentially domesticated caribou), musk ox, bison, and elk are found in certain spots.

Both gray and humpback whales migrate to Alaska for the summer. Humpbacks are frequently seen in the Southeast, their dorsal fins rolling through the water, mist spouting from their blowholes. The lucky traveler will see one breach, rising to lift its bulk completely from the water before crashing again into the sea. Other cetaceans include minke whales, killer whales (also called orcas), and white beluga whales. Bowhead whales are found in far northern waters. Porpoises are sometimes seen racing along in the bow waves of ferry and tour boats.

Seals and sea lions are often spotted bobbing in a harbor or lying about on rocks or beaches. Once-threatened fur seals live in large numbers on the remarkable Pribilof Islands. Walruses can be viewed on special tours to a remote southwestern preserve. Look for sea otters along the south coast, floating on their backs in the waves, preening or cracking shellfish.

Bald eagles are common throughout the Southeast, Prince William Sound, Kenai Fjords, and well into the Interior. Nearly 4,000 gather in the Chilkat Bald Eagle Reserve north of Haines from late September into December. Other birds of prey include golden eagles, peregrine falcons, gyrfalcons, hawks, and snowy owls.

The willow ptarmigan is the chief state game bird. Its feathers turn from mottled brown to pure white in winter. If you spot one, you might witness a mock broken-wing diversion or a puffed-chest courtship dance.

Fantastic populations of migratory waterbirds summer in Alaska. Several types of geese are common, including Canada, snow, emperor, and the once-rare Aleutian Canada goose. White trumpeter swans are a splendid and not uncommon sight. Many species of ducks are often observed, including the spectacled eider. Seabird species include gulls, terns, murres, kittiwakes, and cormorants. With their colorful triangular beaks, bright orange feet, and wave-dodging flight, puffins are popular with viewers.

HISTORY

The humans who became the first North Americans probably reached Alaska from Asia between 30,000 and 10,000 years ago. When cold periods lowered the sea level to expose the Bering Sea bottom, the continents were joined, allowing land passage. Today, the Eskimo, Aleut, Athabascan, Eyak, Tlingit, Tsimshian, and Haida descendants of these original settlers have a combined Alaskan population of about 83,000. Traditionally, Eskimos have lived in coastal regions, Aleuts on the Aleutian Islands, and Indian peoples in the Interior and Southeast.

Danish explorer Vitus Bering may have been Alaska's first European visitor. Sailing for the Russians, he landed on St. Lawrence Island in 1728 and again in 1741 on Kayak Island in Prince William Sound. Bering died on the latter journey, but others returned to Russia with otter pelts. Russian trappers were soon at work throughout the coastal waters, rapidly depleting the otter population.

Alexander Baranov, appointed by the czar to secure Alaska for Russia, established a settlement at the present site of Kodiak, then moved on in 1799 to found New Archangel, later renamed Sitka. Tlingit Indians burned Sitka in 1802, but it was rebuilt and served as the capital of Russian Alaska until the territory was sold to the United States. The Russians founded a number of settlements, surveyed mineral wealth, and established trade routes.

On October 18, 1867, the American purchase of Alaska negotiated by Secretary of State William H. Seward was made official in a ceremony on Sitka's Castle Hill. Because the secretary's critics saw the purchase as a waste of money, it became known as "Seward's Folly." Salmon fishing, whaling, and seal and otter hunting expanded, but development was slow and the derisive moniker stuck.

The discovery of gold in the Yukon in 1896 changed things in a big way. Miners had been working claims in Alaska for several years, but this strike was different. The Klondike Gold Rush drew some 30,000 gold seekers to the region in 1897–1898. Arriving via the instant boom towns of Skagway and Dyea, the first prospectors crossed the mountains on the famous Chilkoot Trail, then floated along the Yukon River to the gold fields.

When the Klondike rush slowed, newcomers and Yukon veterans took their tools elsewhere. Gold was discovered again in 1899, on a beach on the Seward Peninsula; Nome became the new boom town. Fairbanks was the hub of the next rush, in 1902. Juneau became Alaska's capital in 1900, and in 1912, Alaska became an official U.S. territory. By then, the label "Seward's Folly" had been turned on its head.

During the 1920s, aircraft began to supplement riverboats and dogsleds as modes of transportation into the bush. The Alaska Railroad from Seward to Fairbanks was completed in 1923. The thirties saw the establishment of agriculture in the Matanuska Valley. Still, development was slow, limited by isolation and a hard climate.

Alaska's modern era began when the Japanese attacked the Aleutian Islands in 1942. In a breathtaking effort, workers built the Alaska, Haines, and Glenn Highways within one year. With the military build-up, the state's population nearly doubled by 1950, reaching 130,000.

Since then, the state has grown in fits and starts in response to economic cycles of boom and bust. New corridors of commerce opened with the completion of the George Parks Highway in 1971 and the Dalton Highway and Trans-Alaska Pipeline in 1977. Major land use issues were resolved through the 1971 Alaska Native Claims Settlement Act (ANSCA), the 1980 Alaska National Interest Lands Conservation Act (ANILCA), and the 1999 finalization of the Tongass National Forest Management Plan. Resource exploitation still dominates the state economy. As a visitor, you will participate in perhaps the biggest boom of all—tourism.

CULTURE

Alaska's cultural attraction lies not in urban ambiance or highbrow arts, but in the character of the people. While the trappings of modern homogeneity abound here, many Alaskans are in touch with a deep and vital cultural heritage.

Alaska's native peoples represent no fewer than 20 distinct language groups. Beyond this, cultural variety relates to regional ways of life. The use of fish wheels by Athabascans dwelling along the Yukon; the totem-carving arts of Tlingits who reside in a coastal rain forest; the subsistence engineering of Eskimos who once built homes of sod, driftwood, and whalebone—all express cultures intimately connected to the local environment. Today, you'll find in Alaska's native centers a modern people who are close to their roots.

Alaska is also peopled by the descendants of pioneers, adventurers, and fortune seekers—and by their present-day counterparts. These resilient folks are also tied to a rich heritage. And though parts of Anchorage look like Akron or

Omaha or L.A., leave that suburban bastion and you'll meet plenty of people who put the rugged in "rugged individualist." Even so, Alaskans are among the friendliest, most mutually supportive folks in the world.

Indeed, an interesting feature of Alaskan culture is the prevalence of barter as an accepted and valued form of economic exchange. Folks often exchange goods and services—not just dollars—for mutual benefit. In addition, many Alaskans "make hay" while the sun shines—that is, they work, sell, hunt, fish, and harvest in season to gather supplies and money, then go into partial economic hibernation during the long, dark winter.

THE ARTS

Alaskan native arts are excellent and accessible. Traditional dances and music are demonstrated for visitors in tourist centers such as Juneau, Haines, Anchorage, and Barrow. The remarkable totems of the Tlingit and Haida Indians stand in totem parks and elsewhere throughout the Southeast; particularly good examples are found in Ketchikan, Hydaburg, and Sitka. Excellent heritage museums and modern gift shops feature the ivory carvings, baleen baskets, jewelry, and other creations of coast-dwelling Eskimo and Aleut people.

If you're driving the Richardson Highway east of Fairbanks, stop at Mile 332.3 to see the spruce gall sculptures at the Knotty Shop. Inside, in addition to the usual tourist items you'll find an bountiful sample of nature-inspired Alaskan folk arts. Shops like this abound along Alaskan roadways and often feature exceptional work by local artists and craftspeople.

Don't miss the works of the outstanding photographers, videographers, and painters who capture images of Alaskan culture, wilderness, wildlife, and natural wonders. Their offerings are available in shops, galleries, and cafés in tourist centers such as downtown Anchorage, Juneau, and Denali National Park. Communities renowned as artist colonies include Nome, Homer, Halibut Cove, and Haines.

Anchorage supports an admirable slate of fine arts offerings, including a symphony, local and touring theater, and an opera. Fairbanks and Juneau offer a smaller range of fine arts, while college and arts towns such as Homer, Sitka, Ketchikan, Kenai, Kodiak, Bethel, Seward, Nome, and Valdez rely mainly on local talent, some of it excellent. Check out one of the hokey "Alaskana" melodramas that play in the tourist centers—they're a blast!

CUISINE

"Cuisine? What cuisine?" you may ask after sampling the fare in Alaska. Those hoping for an intriguing regional twist on the culinary arts may come away disappointed. At most roadhouse and small town restaurants, expect hearty, filling, and very basic food that's just right for a family with an appetite. Fortunately, this prosaic backdrop makes the exceptions stand out.

Alaskans are blessed when it comes to fish and seafood. Although the dishes in many restaurants are unimaginative, the quality and freshness are top notch. Fine restaurants like the Perch near Denali and the Saltry in Halibut Cove are rare islands in the hinterland where chefs do justice to salmon, halibut, and crab. Similar results can be enjoyed in fine restaurants found in Princess and Westmark hotels.

Alaska's larger cities certainly offer a greater variety and higher caliber of dining options. Anchorage hosts several excellent restaurants, including top ethnic choices—particularly Japanese, Chinese, and Korean. Juneau and Fairbanks boast a few good spots, while Homer, Sitka, and Ketchikan are blessed with a pleasant surprise or two.

But who needs fine cuisine when you can sample such genuine Alaskan treats as a caribou steak, moose burger, or the world's best smoked salmon? A salad of the "fiddleheads" from fiddlehead ferns might satisfy, or a bowl of plump blueberries fresh-picked on the tundra. And a rare taste of muktuk will leave you with a memory, if not a smile.

OUTDOOR ACTIVITIES

Without a doubt, the favorite recreation of Alaskans and visitors alike is fishing. Trout, grayling, arctic char, and Dolly Varden are popular sport fish, while deep-sea halibut fishing is enjoyed by the bold and strong of stomach. Topping the list is the pursuit of salmon. Five types of salmon (each with two names) return by the millions on a clockwork schedule to clear-running coastal streams to spawn. Alaskans line the shores of the Kenai River in June to haul in king (Chinook) salmon. Silver (coho) salmon can be caught from the beach in Seward and elsewhere. Pinks (humpack or "humpies") are the mainstay of the canned-salmon industry, while chum salmon are a staple of subsistence fishers of the Interior. Reds (sockeye) are prized for their taste. If you elect to join the bears, birds, and people of Alaska in their favored pursuit, you can obtain a fishing license at bait shops.

Hikers and backpackers can choose from hundreds of lonely valleys and trackless ridges for everything from half-day hikes to summer-long treks. Developed trails are numerous near Anchorage, Palmer, Fairbanks, Cordova, Juneau, elsewhere in the Southeast, and on the Kenai Peninsula. Areas with one or two trails or old roads of note include the Wrangell Mountains, Denali State Park, and the White Mountains near Fairbanks. The Chilkoot Trail follows the historic gold rush route near Skagway. Huge parks like Denali National Park and Gates of the Arctic are virtually pathless, though the treeless ridges offer routes into the wild. Access to remote areas can involve an expensive flight.

River running is a wonderful choice, whether you want a two-hour excursion or a multiday trip. Rafting companies serve all suitable rivers accessible by road, as well as many that aren't. Great canoe routes are found on Admiralty Island, the Kenai Peninsula, and Nancy Lake Recreation Area north of Wasilla. A number of longer rivers offer outstanding white water for the kayaker, as well as calmer stretches appropriate for canoes. Rivers with road access and outfitter support include the Fortymile, Delta, Tanana, Gulkana, Copper, Chitina, Nenana, Susitna, Little Susitna, Kenai, and Yukon.

Sea kayaking is an adventurous way to explore the coastline. The larger towns of the Kenai Peninsula, Prince William Sound, and the Southeast all have guides and outfitters that serve kayakers of varying interests and abilities.

"Flightseeing" is a must for anyone with $100 or more to spare. Fixed-wing and helicopter flying services take visitors over icefields, along glaciers, and around high peaks for incomparable views. Some flights offer glacier landings, while others take you to "guaranteed" bear-viewing spots. Flightseeing can be combined with a drop-off or pickup so you can enjoy a float, hike, or a few nights in a remote cabin or lodge.

Some visitors book stays in wilderness lodges and cabins, enjoying outdoor activities by day and comforts from primitive to luxurious come evening. Full-service backcountry lodges offer package deals that include transport, meals, and a range of recreational activities. Remote rental cabins typically are rustic boxes near a water source that feature bunks, an outhouse, and a wood or fuel stove. Most can be reserved through the Public Lands Information Centers in Tok, Anchorage, or Fairbanks, or at National Forest offices.

Horsepacking and trail ride outfits are found in several locations, often near tourist centers such as Denali. Most available rides are guided, though renting horses may be possible. Remember that riding a horse is not like riding a bus. If you're not used to horses, explain your novice status to the outfitter.

For information about outfitters, see the Fitness and Recreation section in each chapter.

PLANNING YOUR TRIP

Before you set out on your trip, you'll need to do some planning. Use this chapter in conjunction with the tools in the appendix to answer some basic questions. First of all, when are you going? You may already have specific dates in mind; if not, various factors will probably influence your timing. Either way you'll want to know about local events, the weather, and other seasonal considerations. This chapter discusses all of that, while the Calendar of Events in the appendix provides a month-by-month view of major area events.

How much should you expect to spend on your trip? This chapter addresses various regional factors you'll want to consider in estimating your travel expenses. How will you get around? Check out the section on local transportation. If you decide to travel by car, the Planning Map and Mileage Chart in the appendix can help you figure out exact routes and driving times, while the Special Interest Tours section provides several focused itineraries. The chapter concludes with some reading recommendations, both fiction and nonfiction, to give you various perspectives on the area. If you want specific information about individual cities or counties, see the Resources section in the appendix.

WHEN TO GO

Summer is the travel time of choice for the great majority of Alaska visitors. Bookings for cruises, tours, flights, ferries, and rooms rise and fall in a bell curve, starting from near zero in early May, peaking to sold-out in July and August, and dipping again by late September. June, July, and August are the big months for fishing, bear viewing, backcountry access, and long daylight hours. They are also peak season for the insatiable Alaskan mosquito.

Off-season travel can be a challenge. Although most Alaskan highways remain open year-round, ferry and rail service declines from fall through spring. Many tour companies, lodges, and roadside businesses shut down, the long nights limit viewing hours, and the weather turns wintry indeed. On the other hand, ski resorts such as Alyeska, near Anchorage, bustle with activity. Several lodges specialize in viewing of the northern lights and snow-machine trips. The lingering sunrises, sunsets, and twilight hours imbue the winter landscape with a rare beauty. Popular events like the Iditarod and Yukon Challenge dogsled races attract many visitors to Nome and Fairbanks.

Loose clothing, long sleeves, and long pants offer some protection against the insatiable Alaskan mosquito—as does a liberal dose of repellent. The insects typically pester no more after Labor Day.

My favorite time to visit is late summer, from the last week in August through mid-September. Berries are ripe, the fall colors splendid, several salmon runs still in progress, and the bears and whales still active. Availability improves for rooms, tours, flights, and ferry tickets, while prices may drop—plan carefully, however; some businesses shut down after Labor Day. Best of all, the mosquitoes are gone, and the northern lights reappear with the lengthening nights.

No matter when you visit, pack layers that will keep you comfortable when it's chilly and wet. Casual dress is appropriate just about everywhere.

HOW MUCH WILL IT COST?

A trip to Alaska can be expensive—in part because goods and services cost more in this remote state, but mainly because it's pricey to get here. Drivers heading to Anchorage from the lower 48 will cover from 2,500 miles (Seattle) to 5,500 miles (Miami) and will spend from four days to two weeks on the road—each way! At $1.25 per gallon of gas, a one-way, 4,000-mile trip in a car getting 25 miles per gallon will cost about $200. A trip in an RV traveling the same route could cost $800. Double that for a round trip and add in food and lodging . . . suddenly, a flight to Anchorage and car rental might seem an attractive alternative!

TRAINS, PLANES, AND AUTOMOBILES

Alaska is vast, and traveling it takes time. Combining modes of transport enables you to see as much of this beautiful state as possible. For example, you could fly to Juneau to join a cruise. Or fly to Anchorage, rail to Denali and back, then rent a car for a week on the Kenai Peninsula. You could drive the magnificent Alaska Highway to Fairbanks, then fly to Nome. Your options are numerous.

Fortunately, some road-accessible food and lodging options may be cheaper than those at home because many are no-frills, even rustic. Along major highways, motel and B&B rooms range from $40 to $70, camping is cheap or free, and gas and groceries run just 10 to 20 percent above average U.S. prices. Once in the state, a family of four that sticks to the roads, drives 300 miles a day, camps, cooks for themselves, and enjoys low-cost attractions can get by on less than $100 a day. If the same family stays in motels, eats basic restaurant meals, and spends more on activities, $200 to $250 per day is the more likely figure.

Leave the road system for remote towns and the local cost of living can double. Prices for both scheduled and charter air transport are very high—an Anchorage–Nome round trip costs $350, while four-passenger bush charters run $300 per hour and up. Wilderness lodge stays can cost as much as $1,000 a night. A six-day cruise on a small ship can run over $2,000.

No matter what your budget, remember: Your Alaska trip offers you and your travel companions a rare opportunity for extraordinary experiences. Plan carefully so you have a few hundred extra dollars to spend on unique adventures such as bear viewing, flightseeing, a short cruise, or a stay in the backcountry.

ORIENTATION AND TRANSPORTATION

Alaska is as big as six Nevadas, yet has fewer than 600,000 residents. It's 2,500 miles from the southeast tip of the panhandle to the end of the Aleutian chain—as far as it is from South Carolina to San Francisco. To reach the closest point in the Southeast from Seattle, it takes 20 hours of driving or a 36-hour ferry trip. It's nearly triple that to reach Anchorage. If you plan to cover much of this state, you'll want to budget plenty of time. Consider the options below.

Alaska by Land

The main land route to Alaska is the lonely and beautiful Alaska Highway. It starts in Dawson Creek, British Columbia, then runs 1,486 miles to Fairbanks. Virtually the entire route is paved, and services are available at regular intervals. A scenic, slightly shorter alternative follows the Yellowhead Highway west from Prince George, then the Cassiar Highway north to its junction with the Alaska Highway near the Yukon border. The Cassiar has long gravel stretches but is well maintained. A third alternative involves driving to Prince Rupert or Hyder to connect with the Southeastern ferries.

	Depart Vanc.	Arrive PG	Depart PG	Arrive PR
B.C. Rail:	Sun, Wed, Fri, 7 a.m.	8:30 p.m.		
VIA Rail:			Mon, Thu, Sat, 7:45 a.m.	8 p.m.
	Depart PR	**Arrive PG**	**Depart PG**	**Arrive Vanc.**
VIA Rail:	Sun, Wed, Fri, 8 a.m.	8:10 p.m.		
B.C. Rail:			Mon, Thu, Sat, 7 a.m.	8:45 p.m.

Entering Alaska, you'll find all main routes paved, with plenty of campgrounds, accommodations, and services along the way. Carry a good map or an atlas such as Delorme Mapping's *Alaska Atlas and Gazetteer.*

Greyhound (800/231-2222, www.greyhound.com) offers bus service to Prince Rupert for ferry connections, or as far as Whitehorse in the Yukon. **Gray Line** (800/478-6388, 907/277-5581, www.grayline.com) runs the Alaskon Express with bus service along all main Alaskan highway routes from Haines, Skagway, and Whitehorse. Gray Line also sponsors many bus tours throughout the state.

It's possible to take the **B.C. Rail** Caribou Prospector (800/663-8238 outside B.C., 800/339-8752 in B.C., www.bcrail.com/bcr) between North Vancouver and Prince George. Trains leave at 7 a.m. in both directions, arriving at 8:30 p.m. Adult one-way fare is $200 (Canadian), including meals. In addition to its famous trans-Canada route, **VIA Rail** (888/842-7245 in U.S., various phone numbers in Canada, www.viarail.ca/en.index.html) runs a train between Prince George and Prince Rupert; fares cost $70 to $90 (Canadian) economy class, $190 "totem class," including meals. Both trains run only three days a week in each direction, but the schedules are well coordinated, allowing timely passage with a comfortable, 10-hour overnight in Prince George—not to mention all-daylight travel through splendid British Columbia.

In Alaska, the **Alaska Railroad** (800/544-0552, 907/265-2494, www.akrr.com/index.html) runs four trains daily in summer: Anchorage–Seward–Anchorage, Anchorage–Whittier–Anchorage, Anchorage–Denali–Fairbanks, and Fairbanks–Denali–Anchorage. These beautiful routes, a great choice for independent travelers, are included in many tour packages, including those offered by Cruise West, Princess, and Westours. You can connect with the ferry in Seward and with Alaskon Express buses in Anchorage and Fairbanks.

Ferries

The best way to travel to and through coastal Alaska is via the ferries of the **Alaska Marine Highway System** (A.M.H.S., 800/642-0066, www.akferry.com). A weekly ferry departs Bellingham, Washington, for the three-day ride to the highway connections in Haines or Skagway. You can meet the route halfway by driving, railing, or taking a bus to Prince Rupert, British Columbia. Smaller ferries access Southeastern communities off the beaten track.

The day-and-a-half Prince Rupert–Haines trip costs about $175 for those over age 12, $95 for children. Passage for an average-sized vehicle costs about as much as a single adult fare; the cost rises rapidly with vehicle size. Staterooms are similarly expensive. Double the total for the three-day Bellingham–Haines trip.

Ferries operate regularly in Prince William Sound and the Southwest, accessing roadheads in Valdez, Whittier, Seward, and Homer. Once a month, a ferry links Juneau and Valdez, while another monthly run sails from Homer to Dutch Harbor in the Aleutians. With enough money and time, it is thus possible to sail the entire coast from Seattle to Dutch Harbor.

British Columbia's **B.C. Ferries** (250/386-3431, www.bcferries.com) run from Port Hardy at the north end of Vancouver Island to Prince Rupert every other day throughout the travel season. Contact Greyhound (see above) about bus connections between Port Hardy, Vancouver, and points east and south.

Cruising

Each summer, thousands of tourists board the gargantuan ships of **Princess**, **Holland America**, **Carnival**, and other cruise lines for an Alaska package tour. Southeastern cruises feature calving glaciers, whale watching, and port stops in the tourist hearts of Juneau, Sitka, Ketchikan, and Skagway. Other packages hook up with the train in Seward for tours of Anchorage and Denali. Cruising, it's hard to remove oneself any further from Alaskan reality—this is the tourist shuffle at its best and worst.

Small-ship cruising, on the other hand, offers the advantages of a package deal at a more personal level. Smaller ships, like the excellent **Cruise West** fleet (800/888-9378, www.smallship.com), typically carry a hundred or fewer passengers. You're eight feet above those racing porpoises and rolling whales—rather than eight stories. For glacier viewing, small ships can enter the narrower, more beautiful inlets such as Tracy Arm. And when you arrive in a port of call, you're off the ship in moments and feel like a traveler, not an invader. Small-ship cruising is usually more expensive than passage on the big-line behemoths, but if it's quality of experience you want, the choice is clear.

Air Travel

Flying to Alaska is the fastest and cheapest way to go. Flying *in* Alaska is often the only way to go. Fares reflect this distinction, with bargains available from the lower 48 but unavailable for in-state routes.

Alaska Airlines (800/426-0333, www.alaskaair.com) is the carrier of choice to reach Alaska from the western United States and Canada, teaming with partner Horizon Air to provide excellent schedule and routing options. Alaska Airlines is also the premier carrier throughout the state, serving Alaska's top 20 communities from Ketchikan to Dutch Harbor and Barrow to Anchorage. They offer a variety of tour options, including excellent off-season trips that feature celebrations, dogsled races, or northern lights viewing.

For travel from the southern, eastern, midwestern, and Rocky Mountain states, **Northwest Airlines** (800/225-2525, www.nwa.com) is the top choice. They offer great direct flight options, featuring eight Alaska arrivals daily from three hub cities, as well as routing coordination with Alaska Airlines for flights via Seattle. Partner KLM adds numerous international routing options. As an added bonus, frequent flyer miles are transferable between Alaska Airlines and Northwest.

Other airlines with at least summer service to Anchorage include Delta, United, Continental, and American. Major regional carriers such as Era Air (800/866-8394) and Reeve Aleutian Airways (800/544-2248) provide more in-state options at the same fare levels. Smaller companies offer flightseeing, charters, and scheduled service to remote villages.

RECOMMENDED READING

Jack London's stories of the Far North and Klondike were published at the turn of the century. Perhaps his most famous tale, "To Build a Fire," which appeared in the 1910 collection *Lost Face*, is today widely anthologized. London's two renowned novels of the north are *White Fang* and *The Call of the Wild*.

Robert Service immortalized life in the Yukon in such poems as "The Cremation of Sam McGee" and "The Land God Forgot." For a collection that gathers his best work, look for *Best Tales of the Yukon*.

John Muir's classic *Travels in Alaska* details his journeys to the Southeast in the late 1800s. Muir's vivid narrative style evokes splendid images of the land and people. *Letters from Alaska*, edited by Robert Engberg and Bruce Merrell, is a collection of columns the naturalist wrote for the *San Francisco Daily Evening Bulletin* in 1879–1880.

For a broad selection of tales from different eras, pick *The Readers Companion to Alaska*, edited by Alan Ryan. Included are adventure stories by John Muir, Charles Kuralt, Tim Cahill, John Krakauer, Anne Morrow Lindbergh, and a dozen others.

Scores of wonderful photography collections and photo essays suggest travel destinations and inspire activities. A fine recent entry, *Untamed Alaska*, by Steve and Yogi Kaufman, with an introduction by Margaret Murie, entices with classic images of Denali, salmon-fishing bears, the Far North, and more.

Two good books offer rich information on where and when to find Alaskan fish, which species you'll find, and how to catch them. *Alaska Fishing*, by Rene Limeres with Gunnar Pedersen, is a comprehensive resource; the slimmer *Fishing Alaska*, by Alaska legends Evan and Margaret Swensen, points you to the best spots. Flyfishers will appreciate *Flyfishing Alaska* by Anthony J. Route.

Particularly impressive is Jan Halliday's *Native Peoples of Alaska*. A great supplement to the book you're reading now, it not only offers a wealth of information on native Alaskan history and culture, but also describes many native towns and lists native businesses and tour providers.

For a slim, clear guide to Alaska's plants and animals, *The Nature of Alaska* is a good choice. Edited by James Kavanagh, this Waterford Field Guide identifies native fish, land and marine mammals, birds, wildflowers, trees, and more.

For more extensive information on eco-travel, hiking trails, rafting routes, wilderness areas, and wildlife refuges, look for my book *Alaska: Adventures in Nature*. It also is published by John Muir Publications.

City•Smart Anchorage, by Donna Freedman, features complete listings for Alaska's largest city. If you plan to explore Anchorage in depth, this is a must-have resource.

Want something fun and educational to read on the long trip north? *The Alaska Almanac* (21st edition)—featuring the "Wacky Wisdom of Mister Whitekeys"—will tease you with tidbits and trivia about the country's largest state.

1
KETCHIKAN AND THE SOUTHERN PANHANDLE

Alaska's Southeast, or "panhandle," stretching from Canada to Yakutat Bay on the St. Elias coast, is one of the loveliest areas in the state. Bald eagles perch on the tops of the tall evergreens, humpback whales roll through the waters, and glaciers drop from jagged peaks to calve bergs into hidden fjords.

Many visitors come to Alaska via the Southeast, arriving on cruise ships and ferries from Seattle and other points. For most, their first Alaskan port of call is the town of Ketchikan, which sits beside the Tongass Narrows on the southwest shores of Revillagigedo Island. Tongass and Cape Fox Tlingit Indians long used the area near the mouth of the Ketchikan Creek as a fish camp, naming it Kitschk-him, or "thundering wings of an eagle." Undaunted by rainfall in excess of 200 inches per year, settlers began arriving in the 1800s to harvest the region's abundant fish and timber.

Today, Ketchikan is the second-largest community in the Southeast and the chief town of the southern panhandle. You'll enjoy strolling through the compact town center and visiting important native sites. A small road system provides access to points of interest, Forest Service roads, and hiking trails. Ketchikan is also the region's best base for excursions. Tour boats and flying services take visitors to the sinuous waterways of Misty Fiords National Monument, while visitors with vehicles may wish to ferry to Prince of Wales Island and take advantage of the Southeast's most extensive road system to reach less-visited sights.

KETCHIKAN

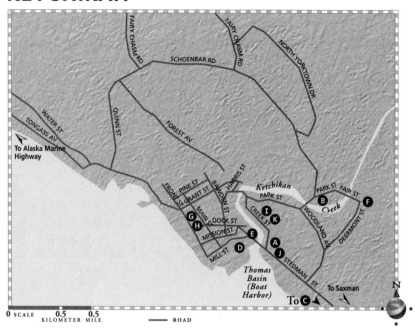

SIGHTS

A Creek Street
B Deer Mountain Tribal Hatchery
C Saxman
D Southeast Alaska Visitor Center
E Tongass Historical Museum and Public Library

SIGHTS *(continued)*

F Totem Heritage Center

FOOD

G Annabelle's Keg & Chowder House
H Papa's Ketchikan Cafe and Pizza

LODGING

G The Gilmore Hotel
I Inside Passage Bed & Breakfast
J The New York Hotel and Cafe
K Westmark Cape Fox Lodge

Note: Items with the same letter are located in the same area.

A PERFECT DAY IN KETCHIKAN

Take a walking tour of Ketchikan's fine central sights, including Creek Street, the Southeast Alaska Visitors Center, and the Totem Heritage Center. Book a short and easy kayak tour with Southeast Sea Kayaks to enjoy the waterfront and historic Ketchikan Creek. Consider a local guided tour, such as a Perseverance Trail Hike (Alaska Travel Adventures, 800/791-2673), a trip to see the totems and clan house at Totem Bight State Park (City Tour, 907/247-9465), or a custom tour with Lois Munch in her '55 Chevy (Classic Tours, 907/225-3091). If you're more ambitious, a day trip to Metlakatla or a boat/flight adventure to Misty Fiords might fit the bill.

ORIENTATION

Ketchikan stretches a short way along the Tongass Narrows at the mouth of Ketchikan Creek. The Tongass Highway, which extends a few miles north and south of town, serves as Ketchikan's main street. Forested mountains rise behind Ketchikan, while rain-forested valleys extend inland from the coast.

KETCHIKAN SIGHTSEEING HIGHLIGHTS

★★★★ CREEK STREET
Downtown Ketchikan
Running between the small boat harbor and Park Avenue, this boardwalk lane on raised pilings follows Ketchikan Creek and is the town's signature attraction. Once the red-light district, Creek Street now affords visitors pleasant strolling, photo opportunities, gift shops, and a café or two. For fun and a good view, ride the short, free tram that climbs up to the Westmark Hotel above town.
Details: (30 minutes—1 hour)

★★★ SAXMAN
Information, 907/225-5163
Ketchikan's native heritage is alive and well just three miles southeast of downtown in the largely Tlingit community of Saxman. A good totem park sits just above the road. At the nearby tribal house—a tribal cultural center and gathering place—you can observe master totem carvers at work or perhaps see performers tell stories and demonstrate traditional Tlingit dances. Stop at the Cape

Fox store and Saxman Arts Co-op for fine art and craft objects. Saxman is a regular stop on town bus tours.

Details: *(1 1/2 hours)*

★★★ **SOUTHEAST ALASKA VISITOR CENTER**
50 Main St., 907/228-6214
My favorite Ketchikan attraction, this interagency, public lands information center is much more than a place to grab pamphlets. Excellent exhibits relating to area nature and culture are featured, while in-depth planning assistance is available for wilderness travel and backcountry cabin rentals. It's located right in the heart of town.

Details: *(30 minutes)*

★★★ **TOTEM HERITAGE CENTER**
601 Deermont St., 907/225-5900
A designated National Landmark, this beautiful, modern facility features original and replica totem poles, indoors and out. Several other exhibits and presentations display the arts and culture of the Haida, Tlingit, and Tsimshian peoples; highlights include exhibits on life at a fish camp and the many styles of drums made on Alaska's Northwest Coast.

Details: *A 10-minute walk from downtown Ketchikan. Open May 15–Sept 30 daily 8–5; winter Tue–Fri 1–5. $3 admission, $5 for Totem Center and Deer Mountain Tribal Hatchery (see below) together. (1 hour)*

★★ **DEER MOUNTAIN TRIBAL HATCHERY**
429 Deermont St., 907/225-5158
Salmon and steelhead trout are raised at this facility, located next to the city park and the Totem Heritage Center. The hatchery has added a small raptor center with birds that can't be returned to the wild.

Details: *A 10-minute walk from downtown Ketchikan. Open May 15–Sept 30 daily 8–4:30. $3 admission, $5 for Totem Center and hatchery together. (30 minutes)*

★★ **TONGASS HISTORICAL MUSEUM AND PUBLIC LIBRARY**
629 Dock St., Ketchikan, 907/225-3331
Located with the library downtown, this small museum features regional and local heritage displays. Of special interest is the exhibit on the town of Loring, Ketchikan's predecessor. You can't miss the three

historic Tlingit totems outside, including the Chief Johnson Totem Pole, an exact replica of a turn-of-the-century pole raised by Tlingit Chief Johnson.

   Details: *Open May 15–Sept 30 daily 8–5; winter Wed–Fri 1–5 and Sat–Sun 1–4. $2. (1 hour)*

SIGHTSEEING HIGHLIGHTS NEAR KETCHIKAN

★★ **HYDER, ALASKA, AND STEWART, BRITISH COLUMBIA**
Hyder Information Center and Museum, 250/636-9148; Stewart Chamber of Commerce, 250/636-9224
Though no longer accessible by ferry from Ketchikan, Hyder and Stewart are a good choice for a side trip from British Columbia's Cassier Highway via BC Route 37A. Stewart is the real town of the two, with a population of 2,300. Hyder, with only 138 official residents, bills itself as "the friendliest ghost town in Alaska." Both are located at the head of beautiful Portland Canal, part of a 100-mile

CREEK STREET, KETCHIKAN

© Paul Otteson

fjord system along the eastern boundary of Misty Fiords National Monument. If you drive Highway 37A between Stewart and the Cassiar Highway, stop for a long look at **Bear River Glacier**, 23 miles east of town. **Fish Creek**, four miles north of Hyder by road, offers fishing for record-size chum salmon along with bear-viewing opportunities. In town, you can enjoy mining heritage exhibits and receive area information at the **Stewart Museum** (Sixth Street at Columbia, Stewart, 250/636-2568; open daily in summer 10–4, Sat–Sun noon–5).

Details: (half day minimum)

★★ **METLAKATLA TOUR AND SALMON BAKE**
Metlakatla, 800/643-4898, 907/247-8737
You can visit the native village of Metlakatla on a half-day tour that begins and ends in Ketchikan. The trip includes a short floatplane flight, a local tour, an all-you-can-eat salmon bake, a tribal dance performance, and the chance to meet Tsimshian artists and craftspeople. It's a great way to sample native life in the Southeast, both modern and historical. The A.M.H.S. also offers regular ferry service between Ketchikan and Metlakatla. Overnight stays are possible.

Details: Reservations are required; tours provided throughout the summer. (3 hours)

★★ **MISTY FIORDS NATIONAL MONUMENT**
Headquarters: 3031 Tongass Ave., Ketchikan, 907/225-2148, www.fs.fed.us/r10/tongass
Misty Fiords, more than 2 million acres in area, is the largest national monument in the United States. This is a land of steep ridges, long valleys, and deep, winding fjords. Several lakeside cabins in the popular west-central portion of the huge monument can be reserved for backcountry stays. The ferry that once connected Hyder and Ketchikan via the monument's southern boundary no longer operates.

Misty Fiords National Monument is spelled with an "i," not the more usual "j." Most other Alaskan fjords are spelled with a "j."

Organized visits to Misty Fiords are offered by Alaska Cruises (Ketchikan, 907/225-6044, boat/flight tours and drop-offs), Taquan

Air (Ketchikan, 907/225-1010, flightseeing), and Promech (Ketchikan, 907/225-3845, flightseeing, charters).

Details: *For complete information on Misty Fiords and the Tongass National Forest, stop at the Southeast Alaska Visitor Center (50 Main St., Ketchikan, 907/228-6214). (half day–several days)*

★★ PRINCE OF WALES ISLAND
Prince of Wales Chamber of Commerce, Craig, 907/826-3870

America's third-largest island has more miles of drivable roads than any other region in the Southeast and is thus of particular interest to vehicle travelers. An A.M.H.S. ferry links Ketchikan with Hollis, usually making the crossing at least once daily. The island features interesting native communities, forest and coastal scenery, and recreational opportunities.

Craig, the island's chief town and home to about 2,000 residents, features three hotels and a variety of travel services. The largely native community of Hydaburg boasts a fine totem park. Inquire at the Southeast Alaska Visitor Center (see above) regarding primitive tours of El Capitan Cave, one of many limestone caves found on the island.

Details: *Access by ferry from Ketchikan. (1 day minimum)*

FITNESS AND RECREATION

Hiking and sea kayaking are top activities in the region, while the road system makes cycling another good option. Eight miles north of town, turn up the Ward Lake Road a short way to reach the 2.3-mile **Perseverance Trail**, a moderately easy, largely boardwalk route through mixed muskeg and forest. The **Deer Mountain Trail** climbs straight from town 2.5 miles

WHY NOT TRY A WALKING TOUR?

A walking-tour map of Ketchikan is available at the Ketchikan Visitor Information Center (131 Front St., 800/770-3300, 907/225-6166, www.ketchikan.com) and the Southeast Alaska Visitor Center (50 Main St., 907/228-6214).

SOUTHERN PANHANDLE

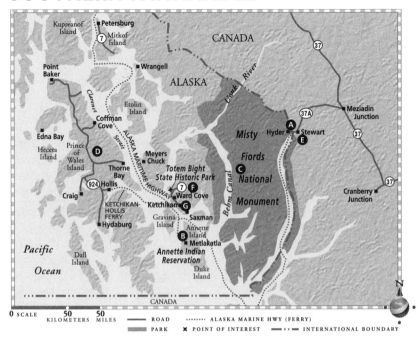

SIGHTS
A Hyder, Alaska
B Metlakatla Tour and Salmon Bake
C Misty Fiords National Monument
D Prince of Wales Island
E Stewart, British Columbia

FOOD
E Bitter Creek Cafe
E Brother's Bakery

LODGING
A Grand View Inn
E King Edward Motel

CAMPING
D Eagle's Nest
D Exchange Cove
D Horseshoe Hole
D Lake Number 3
F Settler's Cove State Recreation Site
G Signal Creek and Three C's
D Staney Creek Bridge

Note: Items with the same letter are located in the same area.

to a rentable Forest Service cabin, then continues southeastward through open, high terrain. Good overnights are possible. For guided kayak trips of varying levels, try **Alaskan Aquamarine Experience, Inc.** (Ketchikan, 907/225-8886), or **Southeast Sea Kayaks** (Ketchikan, 907/225-1258). Bike rentals are available at **The Pedalers** (Ketchikan, 907/723-1088).

FOOD

Ketchikan has plenty of good places to grab a bite. Several of the lodging options listed below also feature restaurants.

For a tasty and moderately priced lunch or dinner, try **Annabelle's Keg & Chowder House** (326 Front St., Ketchikan, 907/225-9423). Seafood, pasta, chowder, salad, sandwiches, and espresso are on the menu. **Papa's Ketchikan Cafe & Pizza** (316 Front St., Ketchikan, 907/247-7272) opens at 11 a.m. for lunches and dinners featuring pasta, sandwiches, burgers, and of course, pizza.

If you pass through Stewart and Hyder, try the **Bitter Creek Cafe** (Fifth Avenue, Stewart, 250/636-2166), where a varied menu includes salads, pasta, seafood, pizza, and Mexican dishes. For a quicker bite, **Rainy Mountain Bakery and Deli** (Stewart, 250/636-2777) is a coffee shop and deli with a pleasant courtyard.

LODGING

Listed on the National Historic Register, the **Gilmore Hotel** (326 Front St., Ketchikan, 907/225-9423) offers waterfront views, private baths, cable TV, and good food and drink at Annabelle's Keg & Chowder House (see above) for $64 to $74 (winter) or $70 to $130 (summer). For a small, charming option near the tourist attractions along Creek Street, consider the **New York Hotel and Cafe** (207 Stedman St., Ketchikan, 907/225-0246). This restored hotel features full baths, cable, and 1920s decor for $70 and up (winter), $80 and up (summer). Ride the tram from Creek Street to reach the **Westmark Cape Fox Lodge** (800 Venetia Way, Ketchikan, 800/544-0970, 907/225-8001). Part of the Westmark chain, this is the nicest hotel in town, featuring a beautiful lobby and all modern amenities starting at $109 (winter) and $131 (summer).

The small **Inside Passage Bed & Breakfast** (114 Elliot St., Ketchikan, 907/247-3700) is located on the stairway, offering great views of town and harbor for $70 to $100. Stay in one of two rooms (shared bath) or a one-bedroom apartment and enjoy a full breakfast in the morning. The **Ketchikan**

Reservation Service (800/987-5337, 907/247-5337) can find you a spot in other B&Bs and hotels, as well as book rental cars, charters, and tours.

Visitors to Stewart and Hyder can opt for the **Grand View Inn** (Hyder, 250/636-9174), a basic motel with kitchenettes, or the **King Edward Motel** (Fifth and Columbia, Stewart, 250/636-2244), which offers a coffee shop, dining room, kitchenettes, TV, and phones. Rooms are $70 to $250 (Canadian dollars)

CAMPING

About 15 miles northwest of town at the end of the North Tongass Highway is the campground at **Settler's Cove State Recreation Site**. Two national Forest Service Campgrounds—**Signal Creek and Three C's**—are found along Ward Lake Road, which meets the North Tongass Highway at Ward Cove, about seven miles northwest of Ketchikan.

Five National Forest campgrounds are accessible by road on Prince of Wales Island. They are **Exchange Cove** in the far northeast on National Forest Road #30, **Eagle's Nest** on Thorne Bay Road just east of the Prince of Wales Road junction, **Lake Number 3** near Salt Chuck on National Forest Road #2030, **Staney Creek Bridge** on National Forest Road #2050 west of Prince of Wales Road, and nearby **Horseshoe Hole** at the ocean end of National Forest Road #5034.

Scenic Route: The Inside Passage and Tongass National Forest

Almost all visitors reach Ketchikan via the ferries and cruise ships that ply the beautiful, calm waters of the Inside Passage—the main water route from Prince Rupert, British Columbia, in the south to Skagway in the north. The passage is sheltered from the waves and weather by the Southeast's many islands.

*Most of the Inside Passage is within the **Tongass National Forest**, America's largest at 17 million acres. The forest features tree-carpeted isles, sparkling peaks, massive glaciers, and windblown waterfalls. The Tongass hosts brown and black bears, Sitka black-tailed deer, moose, lynx, mountain goats—even bald eagles. Humpback whales share the waters with seals, otters, and porpoises.*

*Ferries and cruise ships trace a main route that links Ketchikan, Wrangell, Petersburg, Juneau, Haines, and Skagway. **Sitka** is a common alternate, while the cruise ships frequent **Glacier Bay National Park**. To sample the quieter towns, shallower passages, and narrower fjords you'll have to book passage on the smaller ferries, tour boats, and small-ship cruises—or head out in your kayak, well supplied and ready for adventure.*

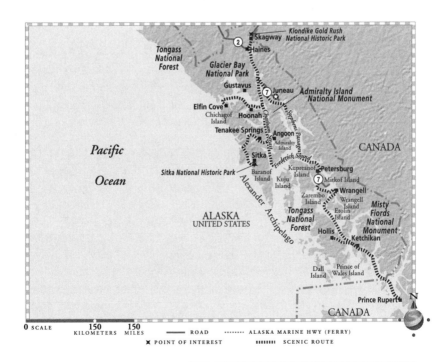

2
WRANGELL AND PETERSBURG

These working towns comprise a not-too-touristy pair that attract travelers because they're located along the main waterway of the Inside Passage. Important as bases for tours and side trips, both Wrangell and Petersburg are worth a visit in and of themselves.

Wrangell claims to be the third-oldest Alaskan community and the only Alaska town to have been ruled by four different peoples: Tlingit, Russian, British, and American. Logging, commercial fishing, fish processing and transport, and tourism are the primary sources of employment. Visitors to this friendly, genuine Alaskan town enjoy such attractions as pleasant short hikes and a local history museum.

Wrangell is also home to a garnet business engaged in by local scouts. The Boy Scouts of America owns Garnet Ledge, a geologic formation at the mouth of the Stikine River where garnets are found in abundance. The scouts sell garnets to arriving passengers at the ferry terminal.

The Wrangell Chamber of Commerce and Visitor Center (907/874-2010, www.wrangell.com) is located in the Stikine Inn, one block from the ferry dock. It's open when cruise ships and ferries are in port.

Thirty miles northwest, Petersburg sits at the northern end of the Wrangell Narrows, an amazingly slender stretch of the Inside Passage. Named for town father Peter Buschmann, Petersburg has a rich Norwegian heritage embodied by its Sons of Norway Hall. The Petersburg harbor hosts Alaska's largest

WRANGELL

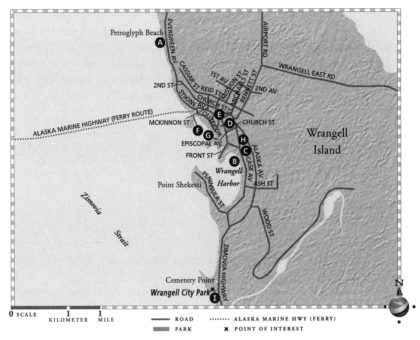

SIGHTS

A Petroglyph Beach
B Shakes Island and Tribal House
C Wrangell Museum

FOOD

D Diamond C Cafe
E Jitterbugs

LODGING

F Stikine Inn
G Thunderbird Hotel
H Wrangell Hostel

CAMPING

I Wrangell City Park

---

halibut-fishing fleet. If you like fishing, several local charter captains can take you to where the big ones are biting.

Both Wrangell and Petersburg have short road systems that allow access to sights, beaches, trailheads, parks, and kayak put-ins. Both offer flightseeing and boat tour options, as well as guides and rental services. Wrangell is the best base for excursions up the Stikine River or to the Anan Bear Observatory, while water or air trips to LeConte Glacier are best begun in Petersburg.

A PERFECT DAY IN THE WRANGELL/PETERSBURG REGION

Although it's entirely possible to spend a day enjoying the simple pleasures of these friendly towns, an excursion to a nearby attraction adds variety to your stay. A jetboat trip to Shakes Hot Springs on the Stikine River will bring you closer to the glacier-carved heights of the Coast Range, as well as offer the chance for a warm soak. A side trip to the Anan Bear Observatory could provide a not-too-close encounter with Alaskan bears. To view LeConte Glacier and the berg-dotted waters of LeConte Bay, book a charter boat or flight. You'd rather be fishing? Hire a charter captain to take you to where the halibut are biting.

ORIENTATION

Wrangell sits on the northern tip of Wrangell Island, opposite the sprawling tidal flats of the Stikine River delta. The town's buildings hug the small harbor, easily navigated on foot. The Zimovia Highway runs south along the shores of Zimovia Strait, enabling access to remote parts of the island.

Petersburg, situated at the far northern tip of Mitkof Island, is tucked back into the narrow harbor at the head of the Wrangell Narrows. A few residential blocks and the airport back the small but busy waterfront. Most sights and the heart of town lie along a five-block stretch of Sing Lee Alley and Nordic Drive. You can't get lost. The 35-mile Mitkof Highway runs south from town along the narrows to the island's southeast shore and Blaquiere Point.

WRANGELL SIGHTSEEING HIGHLIGHTS

★★ PETROGLYPH BEACH
Stikine Avenue

A boardwalk provides access to the 40 or so petroglyphs that face the water above the high-tide line at Petroglyph Beach. The origins of the carvings are unknown; they may be as much as 8,000 years old.

Details: Just over 0.5 mile north of the ferry terminal on Stikine Avenue; a small parking area and shore access mark the location. (1 hour)

★★ SHAKES ISLAND AND TRIBAL HOUSE
Wrangell Harbor, 907/874-3747

A boardwalk leads out onto Shakes Island, where you'll find a re-stored Tlingit tribal house displaying interesting artifacts. Usually open only to groups by appointment, you may be able to enter if others are present. Several fine totem poles stand outside. The original interior carved house posts can be seen at the Wrangell Museum (see below). Chief Shakes Tribal House is listed on the National Register of Historic Places.

Details: *At the south end of Front Street near the floatplane harbor. Open in summer; call for hours. $1. (1 hour)*

★★ WRANGELL MUSEUM
318 Church St., 907/874-3770

Regional heritage exhibits and artifacts include 200-year-old Tlingit doorposts and a great collection of historic photographs.

Details: *Down the street from the ferry dock. Open Mon–Fri 10–5, Sat 1–6, and Sun when the ferry is in port. $2 adults, under 16 free. (1 hour)*

PETERSBURG SIGHTSEEING HIGHLIGHTS

★★ CLAUSEN MEMORIAL MUSEUM
Second and Fram Streets, Petersburg, 907/772-3598, www.alaska.net/~cmm

Step in if only to see the world's largest king salmon (126.5 pounds) and the world's largest chum salmon (36 pounds), both now stuffed and handsomely displayed. Local heritage items are also exhibited.

Details: *Open 10–4 daily, may be closed Sat. (1 hour)*

★★ SAILING/KAYAKING TRIP
Sea Wind Sail/Yak Charters, Petersburg, 907/772-4389, www.petersburg.org/seawind

This unique offering pairs sailing with kayaking. A six-berth sailboat is your floating base for exploration, while you'll climb into a kayak to investigate the coastline. Sleep on the boat, camp on the shore, stay in coastal cabins, or mix it up. Custom packages of one or more days include meals and kayak rentals.

Guided van tours of Petersburg are offered by See Alaska, Petersburg (907/772-4656).

Details: *About $200–$250 per day per person. (1 day minimum)*

PETERSBURG

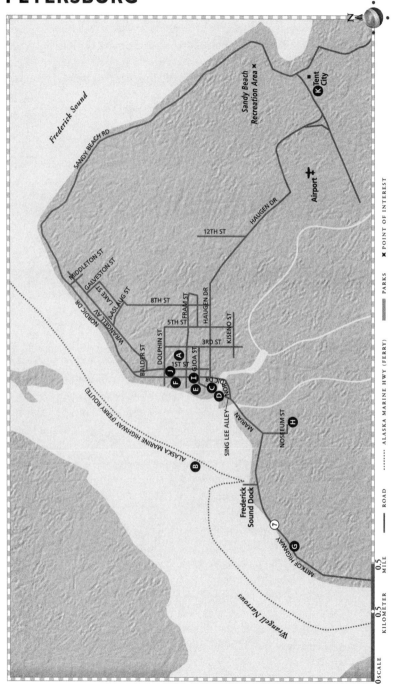

★ **SONS OF NORWAY HALL**
Sing Lee Alley, Petersburg
You'll pass this gathering place, which speaks to the town's Norwegian heritage, on your walkabout. Built in 1912, it sits on pilings over Hammer Slough on Sing Lee Alley, which begins and ends at Nordic Drive, Petersburg's main street.
Details: *View from the outside only; usually closed to the public.* (5 minutes)

SIGHTSEEING HIGHLIGHTS AROUND WRANGELL AND PETERSBURG

★★★ **ANAN BEAR OBSERVATORY**
35 miles SE of Wrangell
c/o Wrangell Ranger District office, 525 Bennett St., Wrangell, 907/874-2323
Accessible by boat or floatplane, this is perhaps the best place to view bears in the Southeast. The observatory consists of a hut and wooden platforms near a waterfall on Anan Creek, where black and brown bears come to feed on Alaska's largest run of pink salmon (also called humpbacks or "humpies"). Watch for bald eagles and the seals that frequent the lagoon near the stream mouth. A half-mile trail links the boat and plane landing to the observatory.

Boat tours, lasting about five hours each, are offered by Alaska Waters, Inc. (Wrangell, 800/347-4462) and Breakaway Adventures (Wrangell, 907/874-2488).
Details: *June 22–Sept 2 8–6; reservations unnecessary.* (half to full day)

SIGHTS
Ⓐ Clausen Memorial Museum
Ⓑ Sailing/Kayaking Trip
Ⓒ Sons of Norway Hall

FOOD
Ⓓ Harbor Lights Pizza
Ⓔ Helse Cafe
Ⓕ Homestead Cafe
Ⓖ Joan Mei Restaurant

LODGING
Ⓗ Harbor Day Bed & Breakfast
Ⓘ Scandia House
Ⓙ Tides Inn

CAMPING
Ⓚ Tent City

WRANGELL/PETERSBURG REGION

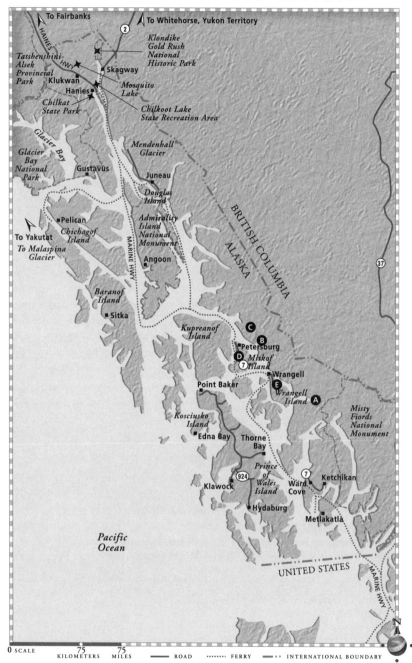

To Fairbanks

To Whitehorse, Yukon Territory

2

Klondike
Gold Rush
National
Historic Park

Tatshenshini-
Alsek
Provincial
Park

Skagway

Klukwan

Hanies

Mosquito
Lake

Chilkat
State Park

Chilkoot Lake
State Recreation Area

Mendenhall
Glacier

Glacier
Bay
National
Park

Glacier Bay

Gustavus

Juneau

Douglas
Island

Pelican

Chichagof
Island

To Yakutat

To Malaspina
Glacier

Admirality
Island
National
Monument

MARINE HWY

BRITISH COLUMBIA

ALASKA

37

Angoon

Baranof
Island

Sitka

Kupreanof
Island

C

Petersburg

B

D

Mitkof
Island

7

Point Baker

Wrangell

E

Wrangell
Island

A

Misty
Fiords
National
Monument

Kosciusko
Island

Edna Bay

Thorne
Bay

924

Prince
of
Wales
Island

Klawock

Ward
Cove

7

Ketchikan

Hydaburg

Metlakatlà

Pacific
Ocean

UNITED STATES

MARINE HWY

N

0 SCALE   75   75
KILOMETERS   MILES   ━━━ ROAD   ······· FERRY   ━━ ·· INTERNATIONAL BOUNDARY
                              ✗ POINT OF INTEREST

★★ LECONTE GLACIER
LeConte Bay

About 25 miles southeast of Petersburg, at the head of LeConte Bay, America's southernmost tidewater glacier calves chunks of ice into the sea. The glacier is long and winding, blending into vast icefields among the high, sharp peaks of the Coast Range. Icebergs often litter the bay, sometimes deterring large powerboats from disrupting the quiet.

Boat tours are offered by See Alaska (Petersburg, 907/772-4656) and Alaska Passages (Petersburg, 907/772-3967).

Details: (half day)

★ CHIEF SHAKES HOT SPRINGS
North Shore of the Stikine River, 25 miles north of Wrangell by boat

The 120-degree (F) waters of this spring, located about 20 miles upstream from the mouth of the Stikine River, are distributed to indoor and outdoor tubs. About three miles upriver from the springs, Shakes Slough offers access to a lovely, steep-walled bay at the foot of Shakes Glacier. Several reservable cabins sit along the river. It should be noted that partying is not uncommon at the springs, and the area around the pools may not be found in pristine condition.

Jetboat tours are offered from Wrangell by Alaska Waters, Inc. (800/347-4462) and Breakaway Adventures (907/874-2488).

Details: (5 hours)

FITNESS AND RECREATION

Several hiking trails are accessible from Wrangell and the Zimovia Highway, including a pleasant, four-mile biking and jogging path that runs along Zimovia Strait. For those wanting to explore LeConte Bay the quiet way, **Tongass Kayak Adventures** (Petersburg, 907/772-4600) offers kayak outfitting, base

---

SIGHTS
Ⓐ Anan Bear Observatory
Ⓑ Chief Shakes Hot Springs
Ⓒ LeConte Glacier

CAMPING
Ⓓ Ohmer Creek National Forest
Ⓔ Shoemaker Bay Park
Ⓕ Shoemaker Bay RV Park
Ⓓ Twin Creek RV Park

Note: Items with the same letter are located in the same area.

---

camps, and drop-offs. At **Three Lakes Recreation Area** (Three Lakes Loop Road, 27 miles from Petersburg via Mitkof Highway), three miles of boardwalk trails connect four small mountain lakes. You can enjoy fishing, berry picking, wildlife, and more. A rowboat is available for use at each lake. The moderately difficult **Raven Trail** (four miles, about a thousand-foot gain) climbs a ridge behind the Petersburg airport to a Forest Service cabin and affords marvelous views of Petersburg and nearby islands.

FOOD

In Wrangell, the **Diamond C Cafe** (223 Front St., Wrangell, 907/874-3677) offers a family-style menu. It's open daily for breakfast and lunch. For a good cup of coffee or espresso, stop in at **Jitterbugs** (309 Front St., 907/874-3350).

In Petersburg, try the **Helse Cafe** (Sing Lee Alley and Goja Street, Petersburg, 907/772-3444). The **Homestead Cafe** (217 Nordic Dr., Petersburg, 907/772-3900) is open 24 hours every day except Sunday. Among the standard fare are local seafoods, espresso drinks, ice cream, and desserts. **Harbor Lights Pizza** (201 Sing Lee Alley, Petersburg, 907/772-3424) features pressure-fried chicken and a salad bar. For breakfast, lunch, and dinner, seven days a week, stop at the **Joan Mei Restaurant** (300 Nordic Dr., Petersburg, 907/772-4222), which serves Chinese and American cuisine.

For additional eateries, check the Lodging listings below.

LODGING

In Wrangell, the **Stikine Inn** (one block from ferry terminal, right on the water, 907/874-3388) houses the Wrangell Visitor Center, the Chamber of Commerce, and Stickeen Wilderness Adventures, along with a decent motel and restaurant. Try the **Thunderbird Hotel** (223 Front St., Wrangell, 907/874-3322) for a basic motel with clean rooms. Consider the **Wrangell Hostel** (First Presbyterian Church, 220 Church St., Wrangell, 907/874-3534) if you're on a budget and looking to meet some like-minded souls. Bunks run $10.

Petersburg has several accommodations, including the **Harbor Day Bed & Breakfast** (404 Noseeum St., Petersburg, 907/772-3971). The two rooms (shared bath) run from $60 to $70, including breakfast, and offer good town access. Petersburg's newest hotel is the **Scandia House** (110 Nordic Dr., Petersburg, 800/722-5006, 907/772-4281), featuring a central downtown location, courtesy shuttle, and continental breakfast. Rooms and suites run $80 to

$165. Also right in town is the **Tides Inn** (First and Dolphin Streets, Petersburg, 907/772-4286), offering cable TV and continental breakfast; some rooms have kitchenettes.

CAMPING

Tent camping is allowed at **Wrangell City Park**, on the water about a mile south of town. **Shoemaker Bay Park**, five miles south of town on the Zimovia Highway, has tentsites, and nearby **Shoemaker Bay RV Park** has 16 sites for vehicles and RVs ($10 with hookups, $6 without). Contact the Tongass National Forest ranger regarding sites on Forest Service roads (525 Bennett St., Wrangell, 907/874-2323).

In Petersburg, **Twin Creek RV Park** (907/772-3282) has full or partial hookups, laundry, showers, groceries, and more. **Tent City** (907/772-4224), about two miles from town, features showers and wooden platforms for tents. The **Ohmer Creek National Forest Campground**, 22 miles south of Petersburg on the Mitkof Highway, offers nice sites near Blind Slough and south coast access. For information on campsites along the Forest Service roads on Mitkof Island, contact the Petersburg Ranger District (above the post office in Petersburg, 907/772-3871).

3
JUNEAU

Alaska's capital is perhaps the most beautiful capital in America—not because of its buildings and monuments, but because of its marvelous setting. No capitol dome graces the town's meager skyline. No sprawling commons surrounds a stately government complex. Instead, a capitol building resembling an old bank is crowded among similarly undistinguished structures on a narrow back street. But just behind downtown rise the high peaks of the Coast Range, while beyond the waterfront are the sparkling waters of the Inside Passage.

Long the site of a fish camp for Tlingit Indians, Juneau came into existence in 1880 when Joe Juneau and Richard Harris discovered gold in Gold Creek. The town became the state capital in 1906. Though mining dwindled in the 1930s and 1940s, modern technologies have revived the industry in the area.

As the chief city of the Southeast, a major regional transportation hub, and host to some 750,000 travelers annually, Juneau is well prepared for the visitor. Travelers arrive by plane, ferry, or cruise ship. The town boasts scores of restaurants, lodging options, and minor attractions and serves as a hub for outbound adventures and side trips. Visitors can enjoy a walking tour of historic and government sites, the shops and lanes of downtown, a visit to the excellent Alaska State Museum, or a tram ride up Mount Roberts. Mendenhall Glacier, the only Southeast glacier allowing close road access, is the most popular destination for short excursions.

A PERFECT DAY IN JUNEAU

Juneau is a compact city that's easy to tour on foot. Start with a tram ride up Mount Roberts and enjoy a hike to a higher point on the ridge. Back in town, head out again to Mendenhall Glacier, either on a guided tour or via a city bus. Later, take your time exploring the shops and restaurants on or near Franklin Street, reserving at least an hour to tour the Alaska State Museum. A longer walk leads you to the capitol, past the governor's mansion, up to the House of Wickersham, and over to St. Nicholas Orthodox Church, the oldest in the Southeast.

ORIENTATION

With a west-facing harbor, mountains to the east, and a short road system stretching north and south along the coast, Juneau resembles other Southeast communities. Alaska's capital, however, is a bustling small city that spills across the harbor and Gastineau Channel onto Douglas Island. North of town, commercial, retail, and residential centers stretch along the channel for several miles. The ferry terminal is located at Auke Bay, about 112 miles from the city's center.

Most of the sights in Juneau are on the main waterfront streets, particularly Franklin Street, which anchors Juneau's small historic heart and fronts the cruise docks. Other attractions are located within a few blocks above the harbor, a moderate walk away. With the water to the west and the mountains rising quickly from the shore, it's nearly impossible to get lost, even on excursions further afield.

JUNEAU SIGHTSEEING HIGHLIGHTS

★★★★ ALASKA STATE MUSEUM
395 Whittier St., Juneau, 907/465-2901,
www.educ.state.ak.us/lam/museum/asmhome.html
This outstanding museum is a must-see. As you might expect, it features permanent and rotating exhibits on the natural and human history of Alaska, as well as displays of native arts. You'll find a tiny thimble basket in the Aleut Gallery, a 34-foot umiak (boat) in the Eskimo Gallery, and a life-size eagle tree in the Natural History area. Exploration artifacts date from the Russian and early American periods. The Children's Room features a one-third scale model of George Vancouver's ship, *Discovery*.

JUNEAU

To E

EAST ST
BASIN RD
HARRIS ST
GOLD ST
7TH ST
FRANKLIN ST
4TH ST
SEWARD ST
MAIN ST
2ND ST
GASTINEAU ST
S FRANKLIN ST
S SEWARD ST
S FRONT ST
S MAIN ST
MARINE WAY
To Thane

GOLDBELT AV
CALHOUN ST
7TH ST
VILLAGE ST
WILLOUGHBY AV
WHITTIER ST
W WILLOUGHBY AV
7TH ST
CAPITOL AV
A ST
15 ST
C ST
D ST
12TH ST
10TH ST

Gold Creek

Harris Harbor

EGAN DR
GLACIER AV
BEHRENDS AV
FOSS WAY

To O

Gastineau Channel

JUNEAU-DOUGLAS BRIDGE
To West Juneau, Douglas Island

SCALE
0.25 MILE
0.25 KILOMETER
ROAD

Details: Mid-May–mid-Sep Mon–Fri 9–6, Sat–Sun 10–6; winter Tue–Sat 10–4. $3 adults, kids and students free. (2 hours)

★★★★ **MENDENHALL GLACIER**
Visitors Center, 907/789-0097
This accessible glacier is Juneau's top attraction. Descending from the icefield above, the glacier ends at Mendenhall Lake, about three miles in from the coast and 11 miles north of downtown Juneau. The visitors center, at the east end of the lake, features displays, a viewing platform, and naturalist-led activities. An hourly city bus ($1.25) can take you from the cruise docks to a point about a mile from the visitors center. If you're driving, take the Glacier Highway north from town and turn right on Mendenhall Loop Road.

Several small tour companies offer van/bus trips to the glacier from town. Alaska Native Tours (114 S. Franklin St., Juneau, 907/463-3231) offers three-hour town and glacier tours. Mendenhall Glacier Transport, Ltd. (look for their buses or representatives at the cruise dock, Juneau, 907/789-5460), has town and glacier bus tours for $12.50.

Details: Public access, open always. (1 hour minimum)

★★★★ **MOUNT ROBERTS TRAMWAY**
South Franklin Street at cruise docks, Juneau,
907/463-3412, www.alaska.net/~junotram/
From the cruise ship area at the south end of downtown Juneau, the

SIGHTS
Ⓐ Alaska State Capitol
Ⓑ Alaska State Museum
Ⓒ House of Wickersham
Ⓓ Juneau-Douglas City Museum
Ⓔ Last Chance Mining Museum
Ⓕ Mount Roberts Tramway
Ⓖ Naa Kahidi Theater
Ⓗ St. Nicholas Orthodox Church

FOOD
Ⓘ Armadillo Tex-Mex Cafe
Ⓙ Fiddlehead Restaurant & Bakery
Ⓚ The Hangar on the Wharf

FOOD (continued)
Ⓛ Heritage Coffee Company
Ⓜ Pizza Verona

LODGING
Ⓝ Alaska Hotel and Bar
Ⓞ Alaska Wolf House
Ⓟ Breakwater Inn
Ⓠ Inn at the Waterfront
Ⓡ Westmark Baranof Juneau

SIDE TRIP: GLACIER BAY NATIONAL PARK AND PRESERVE

When English explore George Vancouver explored Icy Strait at the mouth of what is today Glacier Bay, he found ". . . solid mountains of ice rising perpendicularly from the waters edge. . . ." In the 200 years since his visit, the glaciers of Glacier Bay have retreated almost 60 miles inland. Today, waterborne visitors must fly, cruise, or paddle at least 40 miles from the park center at Bartlett Cove to reach one of the bay's spectacular tidewater glaciers. Rich in wildlife and recent geological history, Glacier Bay is one of the top destinations in the Southeast.

The majority of the 350,000 annual park visitors arrive via one of the 139 cruise ships permitted to enter the bay during the summer months. All follow a similar route: They cruise up the western arm, inch in through the icebergs toward each glacier face, allow passengers a long look, then cruise out again. Independent travelers can enjoy a richer experience by booking passage on one of the splendid small-ship cruises that tour the Southeast or by joining a tour aboard one of the smaller boats that frequent the bay.

*Non-cruisers commonly arrive by air in the town of **Gustavus** (information, 907/586-2201), staying in town or shuttling to **Bartlett Cove** to camp or stay at Glacier Bay Lodge, the park's only hotel.*

*The only lodging in the park is **Glacier Bay Lodge** (Bartlett Cove, 800/451-5952), with rates starting at $160 per person and tour packages from $410. It is operated by concessionaire **Glacier Bay Tours & Cruises** (Seattle, Washington, 800/451-5952), which also offers a vari-*

tram climbs steeply up the slopes of Mount Roberts, which rises 2,000 feet above the shore. The views from the tram are spectacular.

Hiking trails at the top of Mount Roberts range from easy nature loops to longer, tougher trails that return you to town or take you to the high ridges. Visitor services at the top of the mountain include a theater, restaurant, bar, and gift shop. Guided walks also are offered.

Details: *During tourist season Sun–Fri 9–9, Sat 9–10. $16 adults, $10 kids. (1–2 hours)*

ety of Glacier Bay and Southeast small-ship cruise packages, including fly-one-way/cruise-the-other options. Most cruises and tours start in Juneau. Bartlett Cove features a primitive free campground, store, gift shop, boat dock, and short trails.

There are several lodging options in Gustavus. **A Puffins Bed and Breakfast Lodge** (Gustavus, 907/697-2260) features five nice cabins, three with private baths ($85). The beautiful **Glacier Bay Country Inn** (Gustavus, 907/697-2288, winter 801/673-8481) specializes in Glacier Bay tour packages. Room, meals, and tour together run about $300. Another lovely inn, located in a large, restored 1928 home, is **Gustavus Inn at Glacier Bay** (Gustavus, 907/697-2254). The $130 rate includes private bath, meals, and the use of bikes and fishing poles. At **TRI Bed & Breakfast** (Gustavus, 907/697-2425), the $90 cabin features en suite bath and full breakfast. Free shuttle and bike usage are included. Packages, tours, and kayak rentals are available.

Cruise West (800/888-9378, www.smallship.com) offers a marvelous range of small-ship cruise packages that are worth the high ticket price. **Glacier Bay Sea Kayaks** (Gustavus, 907/697-3002, winter 907/697-2414, www.he.net/~kayakak) rents kayaks and related gear for $25 to $50 per day, depending on kayak size and length of use. Bring your own camping gear.

For park information, contact the headquarters in Gustavus (907/697-2230, www.nps.gov/glba/).

★★★ JUNEAU ICEFIELD FLIGHTSEEING

Several companies offer flights over the glaciers and icefields that cap the Coast Range east of Juneau; some include a glacier landing and a chance to walk out onto the ice. Floatplane flights depart from the waterfront downtown, while wheeled or ski planes and helicopters depart from the airport. Packages typically include shuttles to and from the airstrip or helipad and downtown.

Wings of Alaska (8421 Living-ston Way, Juneau, 907/789-0790) has scheduled and charter floatplane flights, including the Taku

Lodge trip described below. **L.A.B. Flying Service** (907/789-9160) offers a flightseeing trip over Taku Inlet and the Juneau Icefield for about $105. **Temsco Helicopters** (1650 Maplesden Way, Juneau, 907/789-9501) offers flights from 30 to 80 minutes, all with at least one glacier landing.

Details: *(1–2 hours)*

★★ LAST CHANCE MINING MUSEUM
Basin Road on Gold Creek, Juneau, 907/586-5338

Explore mining ruins and artifacts in this museum, located in the Jualapa Mine Camp National Historic District. Indoor exhibits are housed in an old compressor building. Visitors can also explore mining ruins spread across the hillside, which were left by the Alaska Juneau Gold Mining Company.

Details: *Open daily 9:30–12:30, 3:30–6:30. $3. (1 hour)*

★★ NAA KAHIDI THEATER
Cultural Arts Park, Franklin Street, Juneau, 907/463-4844

Naa Kahidi is an excellent, true-to-form native arts and dance performance troupe. In winter the theater tours major cities in the lower 48. Traditional legends are dramatized via native language, music, and song. Performances are held in the Cultural Arts Center, which is located at the cruise docks.

Details: *Performances throughout the summer; check at the visitors center or Cultural Arts Center for schedule and tickets. (1 1/2 hours)*

★★ ST. NICHOLAS ORTHODOX CHURCH
326 Fifth St., Juneau

Built in 1893 and 1894 by Tlingit Indians and Slavic immigrants using Russian blueprints and furnishings, this unique National Historic and Architectural Site is the oldest Orthodox church in the Southeast. Inside, a variety of icons and liturgical items are on display. Weekend services are held in English, Slavonic, and Tlingit, Saturday at 6 p.m. and Sunday at 10 a.m.

Details: *Mid-May–Sept daily 9–6. $1 donation. (1 hour)*

★ ALASKA STATE CAPITOL
Fourth Street between Seward and Main, Legislative Information Office 907/465-4648, www.legis.state.ak.us/home/capitol.htm

© Paul Otteson

This unremarkable building resembles an old bank more than a classic government edifice. A pamphlet-guided walking tour leads you to architectural features, history, heritage carvings, and a replica of the Liberty Bell.

Details: *Open during standard government hours. Guided tours may be offered. (30 minutes)*

★ HOUSE OF WICKERSHAM
213 Seventh St., Juneau, 907/586-9001

A famous Alaskan figure, James Wickersham was one of the first to attempt the summit of Mount McKinley. He later became a congressional delegate and district court judge. Wickersham was instrumental in developing the Alaska Railroad and Mount McKinley National Park, and he helped gain statehood for Alaska. Listed on the National Register of Historic Places, his Victorian home displays artifacts from the period.

Details: *May 15–Oct 1 daily 9–4. (1 hour)*

★ JUNEAU-DOUGLAS CITY MUSEUM
Fourth and Main Streets, Juneau, 907/586-3572

The gold mining history of old Juneau is featured in this small museum, located across Main Street from the capitol. A video, hands-on kids' stuff, and special exhibits fill out the offerings.

Details: *Summer Mon–Fri 9–6, Sat–Sun 10–6; winter Fri–Sat noon–4. $2 adults, under 18 free. (30 minutes)*

SIGHTSEEING HIGHLIGHTS NEAR JUNEAU

★★★ ADMIRALTY ISLAND NATIONAL MONUMENT/ BEAR VIEWING
Forest Service Information Center, 101 Egan Dr., Juneau, 907/586-8751, svinet2.fs.fed.us:80/r10/chatham/anm/ frmain.htm

Most of beautiful Admiralty Island is preserved in this splendid, wild monument, famous as the home of the Southeast's greatest concentration of brown bears. The top place to view a few of the island's 1,500 bears is at Pack Creek, an area closed to hunting and fishing on the west shore of Seymour Canal. Trails lead to designated observation points. You need a permit to visit Pack Creek independently, but if you go on a guided trip, permitting will be handled by the guide.

An option for the intrepid is a trip across the island via the 40-mile, four- to six-day Cross-Admiralty Canoe Route that connects Mole Harbor in Seymour Canal to Angoon. The route links eight lakes connected with maintained portage trails. Some backcountry cabins are available, along with three-sided shelters and primitive

JUNEAU: HOME BASE FOR ADVENTURE

Numerous excursions—such as flightseeing, kayak trips, boat tours, fishing trips, and cabin and lodge stays—can begin in Juneau. Just a few of the many outfitters and guide companies based in the city are listed within these Sightseeing Highlights. If you don't see what you're looking for, contact the Davis Log Cabin Visitor Center at Third and Seward, Juneau (907/586-2201, www.juneau.lib.ak.us/jcvb/jcvb.htm).

campsites. There's good fishing along the way for Dolly Varden, cut-throat trout, and char.

Alaska Discovery Tours (5449 Shaune Dr. #4, Juneau, 800/586-1911) offers day trips to Pack Creek, among other great trips. **Details**: *Public access. (full day)*

★★★ TRACY ARM CRUISE
Forest Service Information Center,
101 Egan Dr., Juneau, 907/586-8751

Tracy Arm is a spectacular, narrow fjord, inaccessible to large cruise ships. At the head of the arm, glaciers meet the water on either side of a ragged, 6,000-foot spur of the Coast Range. Visitors can observe glaciers calving and seals relaxing on the many icebergs that dot the waters. A small-ship cruise or tour-boat trip to Tracy Arm can be the highlight of a trip, especially if humpbacks are active along the way.

Walking-tour maps and other information are available at the Davis Log Cabin Visitor Center at Third and Seward, Juneau (907/586-2201, www.juneau.lib.ak.us/jcvb/jcvb.htm).

Juneau-based tours are offered by several companies. **Time-Line Cruises** (Birds Eye Charters, 907/586-4481) observes a 16-passenger maximum and serves breakfast and lunch. **Alaska Rainforest Tours** (369 S. Franklin St., Juneau, 907/463-3466) has three boats serving Tracy Arm, including the *Wilderness Swift*, recommended as their most personal. Lunch is served. **Auk Nu Tours** (76 Egan Dr., 800/820-2628) maintains two 78-foot catamarans that hold somewhat larger groups for the Tracy Arm tour. An onboard naturalist is present and a light lunch is served.

Details: *Cruises run daily through summer, usually between 9 and 5. Trips start at about $100. (9 hours)*

★★ TAKU LODGE EXCURSION
Contact Wings of Alaska, 1890 Renshaw Way, Juneau,
907/789-0790; Taku Glacier Lodge, 907/586-8258,
www.alaska-online.com/takulodge

Less than 30 air miles from Juneau, Taku Lodge sits near the head of Taku Inlet, across from the high peaks and glaciers of the Coast

JUNEAU REGION

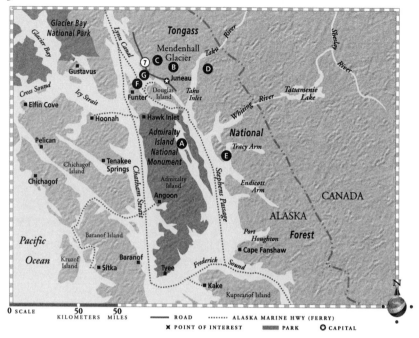

SIGHTS

A Admiralty Island National
   Monument/Bear Viewing
B Juneau Icefield Flightseeing
C Mendenhall Glacier
D Taku Lodge Excursion
E Tracy Arm Cruises

LODGING

F Huckleberry Inn Featherbed and
   Breakfast

CAMPING

G Auke Village Campground
C Mendenhall Lake Campground

Note: Items with the same letter are located in the same area.

Range. The lodge receives day trippers, most of whom sign on for a package that includes floatplane flightseeing and a classic Alaskan salmon bake. If you're looking for a short and potent adventure before your ship or ferry sails, this is a good option.

Details: *Open in summer. Packages $180 per person, $170 children under 12. (4 hours)*

FITNESS AND RECREATION

A number of excellent hiking trails are accessible from Juneau, Douglas Island, and the Glacier Highway.

Two good, short routes start right from town. Take Gold Street to Basin Street and follow it to the end to reach the trailhead of the **Perseverance Trail** (three miles, 700-foot gain) and its branches. This easy trail climbs gently to the site of old Perseverance Mine. Enjoy the views and mining ruins on this three- to four-hour round trip. Two tougher trails branch off from the Perseverance. From one mile in, the difficult **Mount Juneau Trail** (four miles, 2,900-foot gain, including the Perseverance leg) climbs steeply to the summit of Mount Juneau, which presides over the city. Certain sections require care, especially in the early summer when an ice axe may be handy. Stellar views! Two miles up the Perseverance is the junction with the **Granite Creek Trail** (3.5 miles, 1,700-foot gain, including Perseverance leg), a more difficult trail climbing to an old mining area in Granite Creek basin.

The second choice from town is the **Mount Roberts Trail** (2.5 miles, 2,500-foot gain). Steep and difficult in spots but well used, this route climbs from the upper end of Sixth Street, winding up to a possible link with the Mount Roberts Tram. Consider a tram-up/walk-down trip or vice versa. The trail continues 3.5 miles to Gastineau Peak (elevation 3,666 feet), then three additional miles to the high ridge of Mount Roberts (3,819 feet), ending nine

Alaska Bed & Breakfast Association, 907/586-2959, *represents more than 30 B&Bs, as well as a variety of tour providers and car-rental companies.*

miles from town. To make a day hike possible to the higher points, use the Mount Roberts Tram to gain the early elevation and hike on from there.

Mendenhall Glacier has trails on either side of the ice. The **East Glacier Loop** (3.5 miles, 400-foot gain), an easy trail that begins at the visitors center, features glacier views and wildlife. Take Mendenhall Loop Road to the center. One of the nicest routes in the area, the **West Glacier Trail** (3.4 miles, 1,300-foot gain) offers outstanding glacier, valley, and icefall views. Take Mendenhall Loop Road to Montana Creek Road and follow signs to campground and trailhead.

Several outfitters offer a variety of water-based recreation options. **Adventure Sport** (Juneau, 907/789-5696) rents sea kayaks. **Alaska Discovery, Inc.** (Juneau, 800/596-1911, 907/780-6226) offers custom and scheduled trips of many sorts, including kayaking, canoeing, rafting, and camping throughout the Southeast and the state. **Alaska Travel Adventures**

(800/791-2673, 800/478-0052 in Alaska only) features guided hikes, raft trips, salmon bakes, and wildlife viewing.

Birding and photography tours are offered by **Alaska Up Close** (Juneau, 907/789-9544). **Dolphin Jet Boat Tours** (Juneau, 800/770-3422, 907/463-3422) specializes in wildlife tours in the Inside Passage. For fishing, whale watching, and more, try **Kittiwake Charters** (Juneau, 907/780-4016). **Marine Adventure Sailing Tours** (Juneau, 907/789-0919) offers 4- to 10-day sail cruises with kayaking, fishing, hiking, and more during the day. A wonderful choice! **Wilderness Swift Charters** (Juneau, 907/463-4942) has a number of tour-boat, kayak, and outdoor education options for the Inside Passage, Pack Creek, Tracy Arm, and other locations.

Enough roads in the area spell good cycling. Try **Mountain Gears** (Juneau, 907/586-4327) for bike rentals in Juneau.

FOOD

Many good spots for a meal are concentrated on or near Franklin Street in the tourist heart of town. Several restaurants are associated with hotels—check the Lodging listings below.

One of my favorite spots is the **Armadillo Tex-Mex Cafe** (431 S. Franklin St., Juneau, 907/586-1880). It's a friendly place to grab a tasty lunch or dinner that harkens to a warmer clime.

The Hangar on the Wharf (#2 Marine Way, Juneau, 907/586-5018) features the largest selection of microbrews in the Southeast and lays claim to being Juneau's only waterfront restaurant. Great views!

Right around the corner from the state museum, the **Fiddlehead Restaurant & Bakery** (429 W. Willoughby, Juneau, 907/586-3150) offers gourmet natural cuisine. It's open for lunch and dinner; music is performed on the weekends.

If you hanker for a good cup of coffee, head to **Heritage Coffee Company** (174 S. Franklin St., Juneau, 907/586-1087, on the Web at www.juneau.com/heritage). It's open until 11.

Pizza Verona (256 S. Franklin St., Juneau, 907/586-2816) features good authentic Italian and Greek cuisine. Enjoy pizza, pastas, seafood, and more for lunch and dinner. Dinner reservations are advised.

LODGING

The **Breakwater Inn** (1711 Glacier Ave., Juneau, 907/586-6303, www.alaskaone.com/breakwater) features pleasant harborside rooms with views for $120 per night. The inn's waterside restaurant is a Juneau favorite for steaks and seafood. Another good choice at the higher end is the **Westmark Baranof Juneau** (127 N. Franklin St., Juneau, 800/544-0970, 907-586-6900). This plush hotel has an interesting history and attracts legislators and business-people as well as travelers. Rooms range from $110 to $140 in winter, $120 to $160 in summer.

Dating to 1913, the **Alaska Hotel & Bar** (167 Franklin St., Juneau, 800/327-9347, 907/586-1000) is listed on the National Register of Historic Places. It's charming, well-kept, rea-sonable, and right in town—though rumor has it bar noise travels to cer-tain rooms. Rooms run $45 to $55 (shared bath) or $55 to $90 (private bath or studio). Another choice with character is the historic **Inn at the Water-front** (455 S. Franklin St., Juneau, 907/586-2050). This some-what famous—or infamous; it was once a brothel—establishment has been refurbished. Rooms go for $60 and up (shared bath) or $77 and up (private bath and suites). Enjoy fine dining at the inn's Summit Restaurant.

For a current schedule of performing arts in Juneau, contact the Juneau visitors center at 907/586-2201 or www.juneau.lib.ak.us/jcvb/jcvb.htm on the Web.

A mile and a half from downtown on a quiet street is the **Alaska Wolf House** (1900 Wickersham Ave., Juneau, 907/586-2422), a B&B with several rooms, featuring cedar log construction and great views of the channel.

If you'd like to stay at a convenient wilderness lodge, consider the **Huckleberry Inn Featherbed & Breakfast** (Horse Island, seven water miles from Auke Bay, 800/549-5187). Activities include whale watching, eagle and wildlife viewing, beachcombing, and hiking; guided air, boat, kayak, and fishing tours can be arranged. Your room ($125 to $160) includes private bath, break-fast, and boat transport from the mainland.

CAMPING

Two Tongass National Forest campgrounds are found north of Juneau near Mendenhall Glacier. **Auke Village Campground** (1.5 miles west of Alaska Marine Highway, Auke Bay, 907/586-8751), located near an old Auk Tlingit vil-lage site, has 12 sites, each $8 per day. It can be reached from the Glacier Highway, approximately 15 miles from downtown Juneau. The **Mendenhall Lake Campground** (Mendenhall Lake, from Back Loop Road via Mendenhall

Loop Road, Juneau, 907/586-8751) is about 13 miles from downtown Juneau, with fees of $5 per day. Some of the 60 camping sites accommodate RVs. A dump station is on-site.

NIGHTLIFE

Head down to the waterfront and Franklin, Front, and Seward Streets to partake of Juneau's evening scene. The historic, sometimes raucous **Alaska Hotel & Bar** (see Lodging, above), the touristy **Red Dog Saloon** (241 S. Franklin St., Juneau, 907/463-3777), and the fourth-floor Thai food and dance club called the **Penthouse** (175 S. Franklin St., Juneau, 907/463-4141) are three places to cut loose or enjoy a drink.

Juneau's downtown movie house, the **20th Century Twin Theatre** (222 Front St., Juneau, 907/586-4055), features first-run films.

There are three performing arts options. The **Naa Kahidi Theater** often schedules evening shows of native dance and music (see Sightseeing Highlights, above). **Juneau's Perseverance Theater** (904 Third St., Douglas, 907/364-2421) offers a series of five plays from October to June, each with a three-week run. The shows usually have an Alaskan connection, by virtue of the story line, author, performers, or director. In the summer, the theater plays to the tourists with *The Lady Lou Review*, based on poems of Robert Service. For hokey Alaskana melodrama, enjoy the *Gold Nugget Review* at the **Thane Ore House** (4400 Thane Rd., Juneau, 907/586-3442, 907/586-1462), featuring dancing girls and gold rush characters.

4
SITKA

Rich in history and recreational opportunities, Sitka is one of my favorite destinations in the Southeast. The glacier-capped peaks of Baranof Island provide an idyllic setting for this "outer coast" community, while the near-perfect volcanic cone of Mount Edgecumbe serves as a splendid landmark on the western horizon. The students of Sheldon Jackson College and the University of Alaska add a dose of youthful energy, arts, and culture. Though frequented by large cruise ships, Sitka seems to absorb the crowds more easily than Skagway or Juneau, offering a more genuine Alaskan experience to the independent traveler.

Sitka embodies Tlingit, Russian, and American history. When the first Russians arrived at the village of Shee-Atika in 1799, they found the Kiksadi clan of Tlingit Indians established in the region. Soldiers fighting for Alexander Baranov and the Russian-America Company drove the Tlingit from their village in 1804, established a stockade and settlement, and renamed the site New Archangel. The town served as the capital of Russian America until Alaska was sold to the United States in 1867.

Sitka is an easy alternate destination for those traveling the Inside Passage by ferry. Regular air service is also available from Juneau on Alaska Airlines and smaller carriers. The area boasts numerous attractions, most easily reached on foot from the town center. Don't miss Sitka National Historic Park, the Russian Bishop's House, and the Alaska Raptor Rehabilitation Center. A hike to a high ridge behind town is well worth the effort.

SITKA

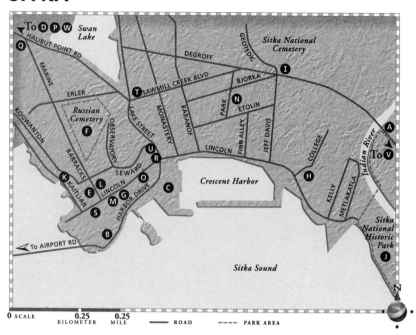

O SCALE 0.25 KILOMETER 0.25 MILE —— ROAD ---- PARK AREA

SIGHTS

Ⓐ Alaska Raptor Rehabilitation Center
Ⓑ Castle Hill State Historic Site
Ⓒ Isabel Miller Museum
Ⓓ Old Sitka Historic Site
Ⓔ Pioneers Home
Ⓕ Russian Cemetery
Ⓖ St. Michael's Russian Orthodox Church
Ⓗ Sheldon Jackson Museum
Ⓘ Sitka National Cemetery
Ⓙ Sitka National Historic Park
Ⓚ Sitka Tribe of Alaska Community House

FOOD

Ⓛ Backdoor Cafe
Ⓜ Ginny's Kitchen

FOOD (continued)

Ⓝ Highliner Coffee
Ⓞ Lane 7 Snack Bar

LODGING

Ⓟ Cascade Inn
Ⓠ Potlatch Motel
Ⓡ Raven's Fire
Ⓢ Sitka Hotel
Ⓣ Super 8 Motel
Ⓤ Westmark Shee Atika

CAMPING

Ⓥ Sawmill Creek Campground
Ⓦ Starrigavan Campground

A PERFECT DAY IN SITKA

Put on your walking shoes and do the town. Stop first at the Sitka Visitor Center to pick up a town map and inquire about events and performances. Stroll down Lincoln Drive, stopping to tour the Russian Bishop's House and Sheldon Jackson Museum. Next, hit the excellent Sitka National Historic Park Visitor Center before hiking through the forested grounds. Use your park brochure map to reach Sawmill Creek Road, then tour the raptor center.

Stop at the Sitka Visitor Center, on the cruise dock on Harbor Drive, for more information on visiting the area (907/747-5940, www.sitka.org).

Back in the town center, take refreshment at the Backdoor Cafe behind Old Harbor Books. Within the three surrounding blocks you'll find St. Michael's Church, Castle Hill, Pioneers Home, Totem Square, Sitka Tribal Cultural Center, and the Russian Blockhouse, as well as several options for a tasty dinner. End your day with a movie, a few games of bowling, or a local performance.

ORIENTATION

Perched on the coast of a mountainous isle, Sitka anchors a coastal highway that extends a few miles up and down the coast. The small town center is easy to navigate. Lincoln Drive, the town's main street, curves around the harbor from Sitka National Historic Park to Totem Square and Pioneers Home. You can't miss the suspension bridge that connects downtown Sitka with Japonski Island, which is just large enough to host the airport, high school, University of Alaska campus, and Coast Guard station.

SIGHTSEEING HIGHLIGHTS

★★★★ SITKA NATIONAL HISTORIC PARK
East end of Lincoln Drive, Sitka, 907/747-6281, www.nps.gov/sitk

Both Tlingit and Russian history are preserved in this small park, established in 1910 to commemorate the 1804 Battle of Sitka. In the battle, the Kiksadi clan of Tlingit Indians defended their village, repulsing an attack by Russians and Aleuts; they were forced to abandon the site just days later. A pleasant forest walk leads through the battleground, past a number of wonderful totems, and to the site of the Kiksadi fort held during the siege. Don't miss the excellent visitors center. At certain times, Tlingit carvers can be observed working on totems and other objects.

The beautifully restored **Russian Bishop's House** is preserved in a smaller unit of the park, located on Lincoln Drive across from the boat harbor. Completed in 1842, the house served as the center of Russian ecclesiastical authority in a vast diocese that stretched from the Kamchatka Peninsula to California. Russian bishop Ivan Veniaminov, first Bishop of Sitka, lived and worked here. Nearby is the striking St. Peter's Episcopal Church.

Details: Visitors center open daily 8–5 (closed weekends in winter). Russian Bishop's House open daily 9–1 and 2–5, by appointment in winter. $3. (2 hours)

★★★ **ALASKA RAPTOR REHABILITATION CENTER**
1101 Sawmill Creek Rd., Sitka,
800/643-9425, 907/747-8662,
www.blommers.org/ARRC/A.R.R.C.html
Dedicated staff and supporters operate this excellent facility, which aims "to provide medical treatment for bald eagles and other birds of prey in order to rehabilitate them back into the wild skies of Alaska, to educate people about birds of prey, and to conduct research on bald eagles and other raptors." Located an easy walk from the town center on Sawmill Creek Road, it's a great place to get a close look at eagles and other birds of prey.

Details: Open daily in summer; hours vary so call ahead. (1 hour)

★★★ **CASTLE HILL STATE HISTORIC SITE**
West end of Lincoln Drive, Sitka,
www.dnr.state.ak.us/parks/oha_web/castle~1.htm
Two milestone events in Alaska history took place atop this small hill: the transfer of the territory from Russia to the United States, on October 18, 1867, and the ceremony marking Alaska's statehood, on July 4, 1959. Originally the site of a Tlingit settlement, the hill is named for a Russian-built castle-like edifice that burned in 1894. Climb the steps near the Sitka Hotel on Lincoln Drive to reach this newly renovated National Historical Landmark. Good views and historic Russian cannons are found at the top.

Details: (30 minutes)

★★★ ISABEL MILLER MUSEUM
330 Harbor Dr., Sitka, 907/747-6455,
www.sitka.org/historicalmuseum
Located with the visitors center, this museum integrates the Russian, Tlingit, and American histories of the region. Of particular note is an excellent scale model of 1867 Sitka. A good collection of native spruce-root basketry and select items from the events surrounding the purchase of Alaska from Russia are on display.
Details: May 15–Oct 1 daily 9–5; winter Tue–Sat 10–4. $1 donation. (30 minutes)

★★★ SHELDON JACKSON MUSEUM
Sheldon Jackson College, 104 College Dr., Sitka,
907/747-8981,
www.educ.state.ak.us/lam/museum/sjhome.html
Reverend Dr. Sheldon Jackson, a Presbyterian missionary and first General Agent of Education for Alaska, donated and secured the funds to construct this excellent native heritage museum. The 1897 octagonal structure is modeled after a Northwest Coast native community house.
Details: Mid-May–mid-Sept daily 9–5; winter Tue–Sat 10–4. $3 adults, under 18 free. (1 hour)

★★ OLD SITKA HISTORIC SITE
North end of Halibut Point Road, Sitka
This park, located seven miles north of town, preserves the site of the original 1799 Russian settlement. Situated at the mouth of Starrigvan Creek, the park features nice boardwalk nature paths, a boat launch, and a campground (see Camping, below).
Details: Public access. (1 hour)

★★ PIONEERS HOME
Corner of Lincoln Street and Katlian Street, Sitka
This large retirement home, a Sitka landmark dating to 1934, is built on the old Russian parade ground. Stretching from building to shore, a wide plaza boasts a fine totem pole with a double-headed eagle, a Russian cannon, and old anchors. It's a great place to sit and soak in the ambiance of historic Sitka.
Details: Retirement home welcomes visitors at appropriate hours; public square. (30 minutes)

★★ ST. MICHAEL'S RUSSIAN ORTHODOX CHURCH
Lincoln Drive, downtown Sitka, 907/747-8120
The unmistakable onion-shaped domes of this Sitka landmark can be seen from many spots in town. The original 1848 church, which perhaps would have merited three or four stars, burned to the ground in 1966. Some of the wonder is missing from the exact replica built to replace it, though many original artifacts were saved from the fire and are on view.

Details: Summer Mon–Sat 11–3, open at other hours to accommodate cruise ships. $1 donation. (30 minutes)

★ RUSSIAN CEMETERY
Princess Maksoutov Grave and Russian Blockhouse
Marine Street above Seward Street, Sitka
Bask in Sitka's Russian heritage at these sites, a short stroll above the town center. The princess was the wife of Alaska's last Russian governor. The blockhouse is a replica of one built in the early 1800s to separate the Russian and Tlingit sections of town. Use a map to pinpoint graves of note. Follow Marine Street above Seward Street to begin this short tour.

Details: Public access. (30 minutes)

★ SITKA NATIONAL CEMETERY
Sawmill Creek Road at Jeff Davis Street, Sitka
The graves of military personnel are found at this site, established in 1867 as the first national cemetery west of the Mississippi. If you walk to the raptor center (see above), stop here for a look.

Details: Public access. (30 minutes)

★ SITKA TRIBE OF ALASKA COMMUNITY HOUSE
200 Katlian St., Sitka, 907/747-7290
Native dance performances, storytelling, and cultural events are offered here. A gift shop sells native artworks.

Details: Stop in or call for performance information. (30 minutes)

FITNESS AND RECREATION
A town walkabout should provide plenty of exercise for most folks, especially if you hike the route through Sitka National Historic Park, up along Indian Creek, and on via Sawmill Creek Road to the raptor center. A second in-town walk

takes in the Russian Cemetery, Maksoutov grave, and Russian Blockhouse. See the listings and map above.

There are some great short hikes around Sitka, such as the **Beaver Lake Trail** (0.8 mile, 250-foot gain). After a short climb on good trail, the route heads out to fishing spots on Beaver Lake. The marked trailhead is 5.5 miles south of town on Sawmill Creek Road, across from the old pulp mill. The **Harbor Mountain Ridge Trail** (two miles, 500-foot gain), is one of the nicest short trails with easy access. Take Harbor Mountain Road from Halibut Point Road north of town. The path climbs above treeline from road's end. The views are amazing. The trail ends at a hut, where the ambitious can continue on the **Gavan Hill Trail** (three miles, 2,500-foot gain/drop). This trail descends, sometimes steeply, back to Baranof Street in Sitka. If you're up for a quick, steep climb to a summit and spectacular views, try the **Mount Verstovia Trail** (2.5 miles, 2,500-foot gain). The trailhead is two miles south of Sitka on Sawmill Creek Road near Rookies bar.

FOOD

Sitka offers several good places to eat. Check the Lodging listings, below, for restaurants found in hotels and lodges.

Highliner Coffee (Seward Square Mall, 907/747-4924) serves espresso drinks and baked goods and offers Internet access. Nice photo display, too. **Ginny's Kitchen** (236 Lincoln Dr., Sitka, 907/747-8028) offers good soups and sandwiches, great pies, baked goods, and espresso drinks. Drop in at the bowling alley for a local favorite: the **Lane 7 Snack Bar** (331 Lincoln Dr., Sitka, 907/747-6310). It serves a classic menu of burgers, fries, and breakfasts. My favorite stop-off in town is the **Backdoor Cafe** in Old Harbor Books (201 Lincoln Dr., Sitka, 907/747-8808), an excellent bohemian retreat for book browsing, espresso drinks, and pastries.

LODGING

For a unique lodging experience, spend a night aboard a boat. Occasionally during the summer, the **Raven's Fire** (403 Lincoln Dr., Suite 233, Sitka, 907/747-6157) sets out on a 15-mile evening cruise, taking passengers to see thousands of storm petrels return to St. Lazaria Island. Stay up all night or snooze in a berth, then return in the morning. Call for the current schedule. Rates run $150 per person ($135 per person in groups of six).

The top hotel in town is the **Westmark Shee Atika** (330 Seward St., Sitka, 907/747-6241, www.westmarkhotels.com/locations/sitka/sitka.html).

Along with the usual amenities, you'll enjoy the Raven Room restaurant with its fine cuisine and great views. Rates run $119 to $131 for a double, $104 to $119 for a single.

The **Sitka Hotel** (118 Lincoln Dr., Sitka, 907/747-3288, www.sitkahotel .com), the oldest in town, had run down some before it was smartly remodeled. This well-run hotel is now a great choice for those who want a bit of history with their downtown comfort (rates $70 double, $65 single). The **Potlatch Motel** (713 Kaitlan St., Sitka, 907/747-8611) features an airport courtesy van and a cocktail lounge; rates run from $75 to $145. The **Super 8 Motel** (404 Sawmill Creek Rd., Sitka, 907/747-8804) has good standard rooms and a spa, and allows pets ($80 to $120).

Sitka's only waterfront hotel is the **Cascade Inn** (2035 Halibut Point Rd., Sitka, 800/532-0908, 907/747-6804). All rooms have balconies with a view, plus there's an oceanside deck and hot tub. Rates range from $75 to $125.

CAMPING

Two Tongass National Forest campgrounds are a short drive from town. Seven miles to the north on Halibut Point Road is **Starrigavan Campground**, located at Old Sitka Historic Site (see Sightseeing Highlights, above). For walkers, the campground is only a half-mile from the ferry terminal. Sites run $8. In the opposite direction you'll find **Sawmill Creek Campground**, seven miles east of town on Sawmill Creek Road. Sites are free, but no drinking water is available.

5
SKAGWAY AND HAINES

In 1897, gold seekers began arriving in the boom towns of Skagway and Dyea by the thousands. Seeing the need for a military presence to secure the region, the U.S. government chose the site of an 1881 Presbyterian mission settlement 15 miles to the south to build Fort Seward, now an unmistakable landmark of the town of Haines. Today, Skagway and Haines both offer outstanding opportunities for the traveler, and each anchors a great road route to the Yukon and Alaskan Interior.

Skagway, the top tourist destination in the Southeast, combines a beautiful setting with gold-rush heritage to draw visitors. It's not uncommon to see four or five cruise ships in port at once, each contributing hundreds of passengers to the bustling historic center. Many buildings on Skagway's main street date to the Klondike Gold Rush; several are preserved in the Klondike Gold Rush National Historic Park. When the cruise ships depart and winter descends, Skagway is reduced to a sleepy hamlet of about 800 souls.

Haines is the hub of a region teeming with recreational opportunities and is another one of my favorite towns. Nearby Fort Seward gives it a historical character. Visited by only five cruise ships a week, Haines is less touristy than its neighbor, and an abundance of artists and craftspeople have transformed the area into one of Alaska's regional art centers. If you visit in the fall, you can view the annual concentration of over 3,000 bald eagles along the Chilkat River.

For ferry travelers making road connections, the Haines Highway offers the

SKAGWAY

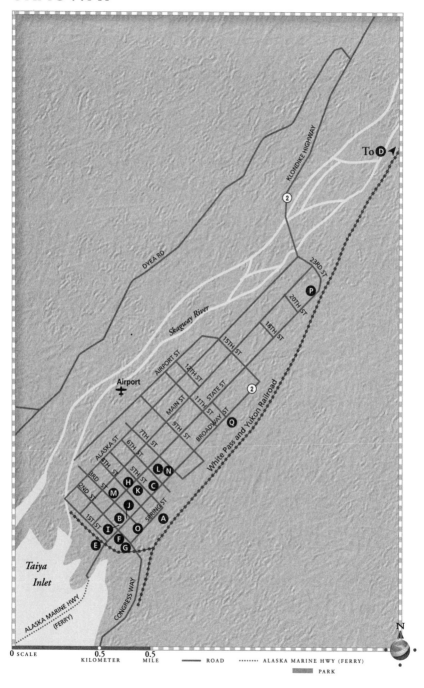

To D

KLONDIKE HIGHWAY

2

DYEA RD

Skagway River

Airport

23RD ST

P

20TH ST

18TH ST

15TH ST

12TH ST

AIRPORT ST

MAIN ST

11TH ST

STATE ST

2

9TH ST

BROADWAY ST

Q

7TH ST

White Pass and Yukon Railroad

6TH ST

ALASKA ST

4TH ST

5TH ST

L N

3RD ST

H

K

C

2ND ST

M

J

1ST ST

B

SPRING ST

I

O

A

E

F

G

Taiya
Inlet

ALASKA MARINE HWY
(FERRY)

CONGRESS WAY

N

0 SCALE

0.5
KILOMETER

0.5
MILE

ROAD   ALASKA MARINE HWY (FERRY)

PARK

most direct route to and from the rest of Alaska; those heading to Whitehorse and historic Dawson City have quicker access from Skagway.

A PERFECT DAY IN SKAGWAY AND HAINES

In Skagway, spend a little extra on one of two splendid excursions: helicopter flightseeing with a glacier landing, or a trip up to White Pass on the White Pass and Yukon Route railroad. Take your time exploring the shops, museums, and historic buildings downtown. For a little exercise and a good view over the valley, hike the moderate Dewey Lake Trail a half-mile to a nice town overlook. If you have transport or take a local tour, you can visit the site of Dyea and the head of the Chilkoot Trail.

In Haines, divide your time between the attractions at Fort Seward and those closer to the town center. At the fort, enjoy the views, tour the stately buildings, and dine at one of the eating spots. On the fort grounds, visit Alaska Indian Arts and the Chilkat Center for the Arts (inquire about performances). On the half-mile walk back to town, stop at the excellent wildlife museum of the American Bald Eagle Foundation. The highlight of the town center is the Sheldon Museum. To cap your visit, consider one of the excellent options for flightseeing, eagle viewing, and rafting offered by local guides.

ORIENTATION

You can't get lost in Skagway. The town nestles between the steep slopes that frame the Skagway River valley to the east and west. Broadway, the main street,

---

SIGHTS

- Ⓐ Alaskan Wildlife Adventure & Museum
- Ⓑ City of Skagway Museum
- Ⓒ Corrington Museum of Alaskan History
- Ⓓ Gold Rush Cemetery
- Ⓔ Helicopter Flightseeing
- Ⓕ Klondike Gold Rush National Visitors Center
- Ⓖ Yukon and White Pass Route

FOOD

- Ⓗ Korner Kafe
- Ⓘ Red Onion

LODGING

- Ⓙ Golden North Hotel
- Ⓚ Portland House
- Ⓛ Sgt. Preston's Lodge
- Ⓜ Skagway Home Hostel
- Ⓝ Skagway Inn
- Ⓞ Westmark Inn
- Ⓟ Wind Valley Lodge

CAMPING

- Ⓠ Backpack Camper & RV Park

---

runs straight north from the ferry dock. All key town sights are found on or near Broadway within five or six blocks of the waterfront.

Haines has three zones of particular interest to the visitor, all along the water. In central Haines, Main Street runs to the sea, passing by homes, shops, visitors center, small boat harbor, and Sheldon Museum. An easy half-mile walk south on Second Avenue takes you to the Fort Seward attractions and the cruise docks. Five miles north of town on Lutak Road is the A.M.H.S. ferry dock. Shuttles, van tours, and taxis can be used to link the three zones.

SKAGWAY SIGHTSEEING HIGHLIGHTS

★★★★ HELICOPTER FLIGHTSEEING
Temsco Helicopters, Broadway at the waterfront, Skagway, 907-983-2900, www.temscoair.com/tours.htm

In Skagway, stop at the Visitor Information Center in the Arctic Brotherhood Hall (Broadway between Second and Third, 907/983-2855, www.skagway.org) for information and maps.

Helicopter flightseeing easily competes for some of that money you've set aside for special activities. Flights take you up to the high peaks and glaciers in a hurry, landing at spectacular sites for a several-minute walkabout. The Temsco heliport is conveniently located in the heart of town.

Details: *Helicopters operate frequently throughout the day during tourist season. Flights last 50–80 minutes and include one or two landings. Rates $155–$230 per person. (1 1/2–2 hours)*

★★★★ KLONDIKE GOLD RUSH NATIONAL HISTORIC PARK
Visitors Center, Second and Broadway, 907/983-2921, www.nps.gov/klgo

Many of Skagway's wonderful downtown historic buildings are preserved in the park. Stop at the visitors center to view displays and pick up a park map detailing downtown history. The center's staff can provide a wealth of information. The park is thoroughly integrated into the larger town—when you tour one, you're touring the other.

The historic site of Dyea, also part of the park, is located about five miles from Skagway via the Dyea Road; few remnants of the town remain. From Dyea, the 33-mile Chilkoot Trail climbs away

THE KLONDIKE GOLD RUSH

In 1896, prospectors discovered gold in the Klondike River in the Canadian Yukon. The Klondike Gold Rush followed, capturing America's imagination just as the California rush had a half-century before. Thousands flooded northward in 1897 hoping to strike it rich, most arriving by sea from San Francisco and Seattle. The rough-and-tumble port towns of Skagway and Dyea grew up overnight at the heads of the two routes over the mountains to Lake Bennett. From the lake, miners took to the water for the 600-mile float and steamship trip down the Yukon to Dawson City and the gold fields.

The Chilkoot Trail from Dyea was the toughest on the miners. Pack animals couldn't manage the high pass, so men had to shuttle gear over Chilkoot Pass into Canada via repeated foot trips. The Canadian authorities, fearing a famine, demanded that miners come equipped with enough food to last a year. It took an average of three months for each of the 20,000 to 30,000 men to shuttle their gear over the pass to the lakes. Trams were eventually built to speed the process.

The other route to the Yukon followed the White Pass Trail from Skagway. As challenging as the Chilkoot Trail, more than 3,000 pack animals died on this route, most overloaded and unsuited to the rocky terrain. The construction of the White Pass and Yukon Route railroad established White Pass as the route of choice and secured Skagway's future. The Chilkoot Trail fell into disuse and Dyea became a ghost town.

During the first years of the rush, crime and disease took a heavy toll on the American side of the border. Although life was more orderly on the Canadian side, thanks to presiding Mounties, the majority of hopeful gold-seekers reached Dawson City only to find all the good claims already staked. Most were lucky just to land jobs working the "diggins" for others. By the end of 1898, the Klondike lode was failing and miners began to leave for home or the new strikes in Nome.

toward Chilkoot Pass, offering a three- to five-day backpacking adventure replete with gold-rush artifacts and history. Much of the White Pass Trail route is also preserved in the park, as is an area of Seattle's Pioneer Square.

Details: *Public access. Visitors center open May–July and Sept daily 8–6, August 8–8. (half day minimum)*

★★★★ WHITE PASS AND YUKON ROUTE
Station at Second Avenue and Broadway, Skagway, 800/343-7373, 907/983-2217, www.whitepassrailroad.com
Completed in 1900, this narrow-gauge railway replaced the trails as the primary mode of transport to the Yukon. Today, a diesel engine pulls the old cars into or through White Pass, offering spectacular views and historic narration to passengers.

One train takes three-hour round trips to the summit of White Pass, two or three times daily. A second train, based in Fraser, British Columbia, serves the daily train/bus run between Skagway and Whitehorse. A third train takes an all-day tour between Skagway and Lake Bennett—the point where miners took to the water for the long float to the Klondike. At Lake Bennett, Chilkoot Trail hikers can catch a Skagway-bound train at 9 a.m. They can get a ride in either direction on the Lake Bennett tour train, which arrives at the lake about noon and departs again for Skagway at 1 p.m. About six times a summer, a special train does

WHITE PASS AND YUKON ROUTE SCHEDULE

	Depart Skagway	Depart Whitehorse	Arrive Skagway	Arrive Whitehorse
A.M. summit trip	8:30 a.m.	----	11:30 a.m.	----
P.M. summit trip	1 p.m.	----	4 p.m.	----
Tue & Wed only summit	4:30 p.m.	----	7:30 p.m.	----
*To Whitehorse	12:40 p.m.	----	----	6 p.m.
*To Skagway Thu & Mon	----	8 a.m.	noon	----
Lake Bennett tour	8 a.m.	----	4:30 p.m.	----

*Bus/train transfer in Fraser 10:20 a.m. southbound, 2:40 p.m. northbound.

the Lake Bennett tour, pulled by a Mikado class 282 Baldwin steam engine. It's a must for rail buffs.

Reservations for all trains are strongly advised! Call to confirm the current schedule, which should resemble the one below:

Details: Summit trips $80; Lake Bennett tour $120 (includes coffee, lunch, Lake Bennett guide); Chilkoot Trail pickup or drop-off $65; special steam engine tours $160; children's fare half-price on all trips, under 3 free. (3 hour minimum)

★ **ALASKAN WILDLIFE ADVENTURE & MUSEUM**
480 Spring St., east end of Fourth Street at Spring, Skagway, 907/983-3600, skagway.com/adventures/
If stuffed and mounted animals appeal to you, this new museum is worth a stop. Some 70 Alaskan and Yukon animals are featured, including moose, musk ox, bear, lynx, and Dall sheep.
Details: Open daily in summer. (30 minutes)

★ **CORRINGTON MUSEUM OF ALASKAN HISTORY**
Fifth and Broadway, Skagway, 907-983-2579, www.skagway.com/sites/alaskan_history.html
Alaskan history and prehistory exhibits include a fine collection of scrimshawed walrus tusks and other original art. A gift shop features native arts, gold-nugget jewelry, and collectibles.
Details: Open summer daily 8–9. (30 minutes)

★ **GOLD RUSH CEMETERY**
Via State Street, 1.5 miles north of downtown Skagway
Notorious gold-rush crime boss Soapy Smith is buried here, along with others from the era. Lovely **Reid Falls** is a short walk from the cemetery. The falls is named for Frank Reid, the town hero who died from a wound received in the gunfight that permanently removed Soapy from the scene. Cemetery guides can be purchased at the visitors center.
Details: Public access. Take State Street north 1.5 miles from the historic district and follow the signs. (1 hour walk)

★ **CITY OF SKAGWAY MUSEUM**
Broadway between Second and Third, Skagway, 907/983-2420
This collection of gold-rush and native Alaskan artifacts is housed in

HAINES

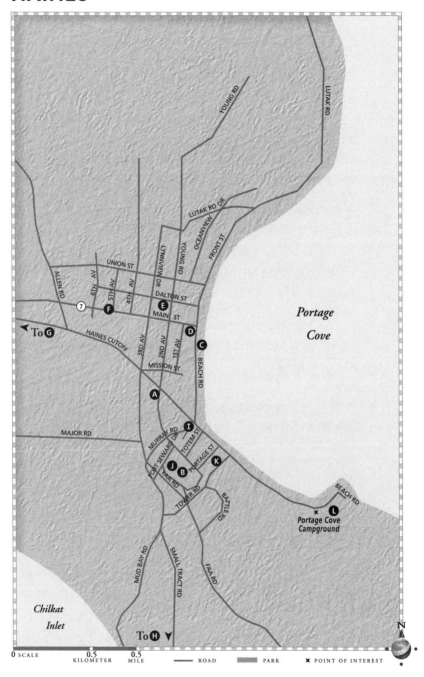

YOUNG RD

LUTAK RD

LUTAK RD DR

OCEANVIEW

YOUNG RD

FRONT ST

LYNNVIEW DR

UNION ST

ALLEN RD

5TH AV

5TH AV

4TH AV

DALTON ST

(7)

F

E

MAIN ST

D

To **G**

HAINES CUTOFF

3RD AV

2ND AV

1ST AV

C

BEACH RD

Portage Cove

MISSION ST

A

MAJOR RD

MURRAY RD

I

FORT SEWARD DR

TOTEM ST

PORTAGE ST

J

B

K

YAA RD

TOWER RD

BATTLE RD

BEACH RD

L

Portage Cove Campground

MUD BAY RD

SMALL TRACT RD

FAA RD

Chilkat Inlet

To **H**

N

0 SCALE   0.5 KILOMETER   0.5 MILE   —— ROAD   ▨ PARK   ✕ POINT OF INTEREST

the Arctic Brotherhood, or "A.B.," Hall on Broadway. Gold-rush centennial films are shown as well.

Details: Open summer daily 8–5. (30 minutes)

HAINES SIGHTSEEING HIGHLIGHTS

★★★ AMERICAN BALD EAGLE FOUNDATION
**Second Avenue and Haines Highway, Haines,
907/766-3094, www.gauntletllc.com/abef**
This internationally supported nonprofit foundation was established in 1982 to study and protect the American bald eagle. Stop in for a look at the terrific wildlife museum, featuring most of Alaska's native species. If you get the chance, sit in on the excellent naturalist presentation.

Details: Open summer Mon–Fri 9–10, Sat–Sun 9–6; winter Mon, Wed, Fri 1–4. Donation. (1 hour)

★★★ FORT SEWARD
0.5 miles south of downtown Haines
Built in 1901 to establish a military presence in the area, the stately structures of this National Historic Site are privately occupied today; some host lodging, dining, or arts businesses. The uniformly spaced buildings surround a large parade green, unmistakable to those passing by on the ferry. At the bottom of the parade ground in the totem park, replicas of a Tlingit tribal house and an early trapper's cabin can be seen.

The **Chilkat Center for the Arts** (in the old recreation hall a block south of the parade ground; call visitors center for information, 800/458-3579, 907/766-2234, www.haines.ak.us) hosts

---

SIGHTS
Ⓐ American Bald Eagle Foundation
Ⓑ Fort Seward
Ⓒ Raft, Kayak, and Motorboat Excursions
Ⓓ Sheldon Museum and Cultural Center

FOOD
Ⓔ Bamboo Room
Ⓕ Chilkat Restaurant and Bakery
Ⓖ 33 Mile Roadhouse

LODGING
Ⓗ Bear Creek Camp & International Hostel
Ⓘ Fort Seward Lodge
Ⓙ Hotel Halsingland
Ⓚ Sheltered Harbor Bed and Breakfast

CAMPING
Ⓛ Portage Cove State Recreation Site

---

performances of the Chilkat Dancers (907/766-2160) and a heritage melodrama during the summer months.

Alaska Indian Arts (907/766-2704, www.ravenswindow.com/ aia.htm) is a nonprofit center where top-notch native artisans can be observed at work creating totems, masks, blankets, and jewelry. It's located in the old base hospital on the south side of the parade grounds, open Monday through Saturday 9 to 5.

Details: Take Second Avenue a half-mile south of downtown. Public access. Sights have varying hours. (2 hours)

★★ RAFT, KAYAK, AND MOTORBOAT EXCURSIONS

Several rivers and glaciated valleys converge in the Haines area, affording a terrific range of water-based adventures. **River Adventures** (Fourth and Main, Haines, 800/478-9827, 907/766-2050) offers part-day jetboat and rafting trips through the Chilkat Bald Eagle Preserve. For a two-day fly-in/raft-out trip with a stay in a remote cabin next to a glacier, contact **Alaska Cross Country Guiding & Rafting** (Haines, 907/767-5522); the cost is $450 per person. Guided kayak trips from quarter-day to multi-day are offered by **Deishu**

The Haines Visitor Information Center is located on Second Avenue (800/458-3579, 907/766-2234, www.haines.ak.us).

Expeditions (12 Portage St., near cruise ship dock, Haines, 907/766-2427), starting at under $85 per person. They also rent kayaks: $35 for a single, $50 for a double. Several other water, air, land, and combination tour providers are based in Haines. Check with the visitors center.

Details: (2 hours minimum)

★★ SHELDON MUSEUM AND CULTURAL CENTER
11 Main St., Haines, 907/766-2366,
www.seaknet.alaska.edu/~sheldmus

Videos, library, and exhibits serve to "interpret the history and native culture of the local region while conveying unique local stories, tales and legends." Look for eagles perched in the trees outside.

Details: Open summer daily 1–5; winter Mon, Wed, Fri 1–4, Tue, Thu, Sat 3–5. $3 adults, children under 18 free. (1 hour)

SIGHTSEEING HIGHLIGHTS AROUND SKAGWAY AND HAINES

★★★★ ALASKA CHILKAT BALD EAGLE PRESERVE
907/766-2292,
www.llbean.com/parksearch/parks/html/873lls.htm
Beginning in late September, tens of thousands of chum salmon return to area rivers over a two-month period to spawn and die. Nearly 5,000 bald eagles join other wildlife for the feast; thousands of the raptors line the shores of a five-mile stretch of the Chilkat River north of Haines. The Haines Highway affords excellent access to viewing areas. Another unit of the preserve is found along the lower Chilkoot River. Do not approach or disturb the eagles in any way; stay behind binoculars and telephoto lenses, well clear of feeding areas.

Even if you won't be around for the fall Chilkat gathering, remember that eagles are visible year-round throughout the Southeast. You'll spot them perching in the treetops, fishing or scavenging near harbors, and winging along the shore. Several hundred nesting sites are located in the region.

Details: *Public access. Summer (fewer eagles, but still many) raft trips through the preserve are offered by Chilkat Guides, Ltd. (Haines, 907/766-2491). (2 hours)*

★★★ HAINES HIGHWAY/HAINES TO INTERIOR ALASKA (355 MILES)
This beautiful road climbs up the Chilkat River Valley, hugging the northeast side of the St. Elias Mountains as it passes through a corner of British Columbia and enters the Yukon Territory. The highway officially ends where it meets the Alaska Highway in Haines Junction. Stop here at the visitors center of Kluane National Park for some great information and displays. Between Haines Junction and the Alaska border, the Alaska Highway follows the shores of lovely Kluane Lake for many miles. For road and highlights information after entering Alaska, see Chapter 6, Tanana Valley and the Alaska Highway.

Details: *Good, paved road. (1 long day)*

★★★ KLONDIKE HIGHWAY / SKAGWAY TO DAWSON CITY (435 MILES)
Climbing quickly from Skagway, the Klondike Highway parallels the

route of the White Pass gold rush for many miles. Enjoy the rugged, open lake country through the pass. The road descends to Carcross, then on to its junction with the Alaska Highway and the town of Whitehorse. Stop in Whitehorse to see the old riverboat moored on the shores of the Yukon River. If you choose an alternate to the Alaska Highway, you can follow the Klondike Highway north to Dawson City. For more information on Dawson City and a description of this alternate road route and Alaska highlights, see Chapter 6, Tanana Valley and the Alaska Highway.

Details: *Good, paved road. (1 very long day)*

FITNESS AND RECREATION

Perhaps the best-developed of Alaska's relatively few long-distance trails, the **Chilkoot Trail** (33 miles, 3,700-foot gain) is the path to a wilderness experience providing scenic beauty, history, and athletic challenge, all with easy access to a gateway town. The trail begins at the abandoned town of Dyea, then climbs along the Taiya River to famous Chilkoot Pass (elevation 3,700 feet). Crossing into Canada, hikers enjoy lake country with glacier views and easier grades on their way to train connections at Lake Bennett (see Yukon and White Pass Route, above). Southbound walkers have less of a climb to reach the pass, though they won't have the pleasure of discovering the route as the miners did.

There are established campgrounds every three or four miles along the route, as well as numerous artifacts from the gold rush. Stop at the park visitors center in Skagway for detailed information on conditions, Canadian customs, north-end transport, and permits (easy to get).

FOOD

Both towns offer plenty of places to eat, including a few choices found in hotels (listed in the Lodging section, below).

For breakfast or lunch in Skagway, try the **Korner Kafe** (Fourth Avenue and State Street, Skagway). For a tasty but touristy meal in a gold rush–era gem, try to find a table at the **Red Onion** (Second and Broadway, Skagway). Offerings include pizza, nachos, beer, entertainment, and tourists. Did I mention that tourists like to eat here . . . or at least snap a picture? It's fun!

A classic choice in Haines is the **Bamboo Room Restaurant & Pioneer Bar** (Second Avenue near Main, Haines, 907/766-2800). Charles Kuralt called it "a good café bearing the unlikely name of Bamboo Room," referring indirectly to the utter lack of bamboo in the place. Ask and you

SKAGWAY/HAINES REGION

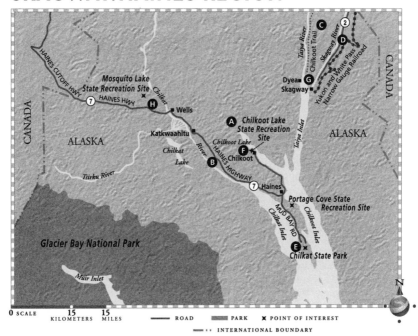

0 SCALE   15 KILOMETERS   15 MILES   ━━ ROAD   ▰▰▰ PARK   ✖ POINT OF INTEREST

━·· INTERNATIONAL BOUNDARY

SIGHTS

- **Ⓐ** Alaska Chilkat Bald Eagle Preserve
- **Ⓑ** Haines Highway/Haines to Interior Alaska
- **Ⓒ** Klondike Gold Rush National Historic Park
- **Ⓓ** Klondike Highway/Skagway to Dawson City

CAMPING

- **Ⓔ** Chilkat State Park
- **Ⓕ** Chilkoot Lake State Recreation Site
- **Ⓖ** Klondike Gold Rush National Historic Park Campground
- **Ⓗ** Mosquito Lake State Recreation Site

---

shall hear the story. It opens at 6 a.m. daily, year-round. The **Chilkat Restaurant and Bakery** (Fifth and Main, Haines, 907/766-2920) is a smoke-free family restaurant boasting a big, tasty menu and fresh-baked pastries and bread. Out on the Haines Highway, you'll find the **33 Mile Roadhouse** (Mile 33 Haines Highway, 907/767-5510), a typical full-service roadhouse with food, gas, propane, dining, all-day breakfast, big burgers, and steaks.

LODGING

A Skagway landmark, the **Golden North Hotel** (Third and Broadway, Skagway, 907/983-2451, 907/983-2294) is the town's oldest operating hotel. Built in 1898, it preserves the feel of the era yet provides modern comforts in the rooms. Rates range from a winter low of $45 to a summer high of $75 (some private bath, some shared). The **Portland House** (Fifth and State Street, Skagway, 907/983-2493), a nine-room inn built in 1897, features a restaurant specializing broadly in American, Mexican, Italian, and Greek food. All rooms have shared baths, $30 to $45.

If you're looking for a decent budget sleep, try the 15-bed **Skagway Home Hostel** (Third between State and Main, Skagway, 907/983-2131). This hostel observes a curfew and features shuttle service, a laundry, a kitchen, and a common room. The **Westmark Inn** (Third and Spring Street, Skagway, 800/544-0970, 907/983-6000) is another installment of Alaska's nicest chain. This large, modern hotel features the Chilkoot Room restaurant, serving breakfast and dinner daily. A free shuttle will take you to or from transport links. Rates range from $80 to $140.

The **Wind Valley Lodge** (Klondike Highway, a half-mile north of historic district, Skagway, 907/983-2236) is a pleasant, AAA-approved, modern establishment within walking distance of the downtown sights. A courtesy shuttle is available to airport, docks, or town. The Siding 21 Family Restaurant completes the package. Rooms run $65 to $95; kids under 12 sleep free. **Sgt. Preston's Lodge** (Sixth and State Street, Skagway, 907/983-2521) has 30 street-level rooms with private baths, cable TV, and a courtesy shuttle. It's close to the town center. If a brothel of yesteryear appeals, try the **Skagway Inn** (Seventh and Broadway, Skagway, 907/983-2289). Rooms go for $125 (shared bath).

The **Hotel Halsingland** (Fort Seward, Haines, 800/542-6363, 907/766-2000) is a fine hotel in an original Fort Seward Victorian. Rooms with private bath start at $90, those with shared bath at $50. Nearby is the **Fort Seward Lodge** (Fort Seward, Haines, 800/478-7772, 907/766-2009). Located in the old Post Exchange, this family-owned lodge features a restaurant and saloon. Room options include shared bath, private bath, and kitchenette; rates range from $45 to $85. **A Sheltered Harbor Bed & Breakfast** (57 Beach Rd., below Fort Seward at Port Chilkoot dock, Haines, 907/766-2741) features a waterfront location, full breakfast, private baths, and views. Whether it's a cabin, bunk, or tentsite you want, you'll find it at **Bear Creek Camp & International Hostel** (Small Tracts Road, Haines, 907/766-2259). Amenities include showers, kitchen facilities, free ferry shuttle, tours, bike rental, laundry, and store. Rustic family cabins run $40 and up, dorm beds $15, and tentsites $8.

CAMPING

In Skagway, the **Backtrack Camper & RV Park** (12th and Broadway, Skagway, 907/983-3333) features hookups, some tent spaces, showers, laundry, and dump station, all within walking distance of the historic district. The **Klondike Gold Rush National Historic Park** has a campground at the site of Dyea, about five miles from Skagway on the Dyea Road.

Several Alaska State Park campgrounds are found in the Haines vicinity, all usually open from mid-May to mid-October with sites from $6 to $10. **Portage Cove State Recreation Site** is on Beach Road just south of Fort Seward (no vehicles). **Mosquito Lake State Recreation Site** is located at Mile 27 of the Haines Highway. Ten miles north of town, past the ferry dock on Lutak Road, you'll find **Chilkoot Lake State Recreation Site**. Off Mud Bay Road seven miles south of town is **Chilkat State Park**.

6
TANANA VALLEY AND THE ALASKA HIGHWAY

The Tanana River drains a vast area of eastern Alaska before it flows into the mighty Yukon at the remote town of Tanana, in the center of the state. The Alaska Highway parallels the river for almost 300 miles, from close to the Canadian border all the way to Fairbanks. If you tour the heart of the state by vehicle, you'll have to pass through the Tanana Valley and the gateway town of Tok. There is no other route (except via the once-a-month ferry that connects the Southeast and Prince William Sound).

Shortly after entering the state, Alaska Highway drivers are treated to a hundred-mile view of the Wrangell Mountains across the sprawling flats of the Tetlin National Wildlife Refuge. The highway stays above the lowlands, hugging the northern hills and affording unobstructed observation from the many turnouts. The road soon meets up with the Tanana River, continues on to Tok through a narrow stretch with bluffs and canyons, then heads into the broad farm country around Delta Junction.

Few visitors spend much time in the region; most prefer to zip through on their way to more famous sights. Some of the more intrepid take a side trip to Eagle on the Yukon River, perhaps continuing on to Dawson City, Yukon Territory, home of the Klondike Gold Rush. Whatever your ultimate destination, this wide, scenic region region is worth exploring. You'll find plenty of outstanding recreational opportunities to satisfy your personal call of the wild.

A PERFECT DAY IN THE TANANA VALLEY

For most, it's a day to drive. Whether entering or leaving the state, let the miles fly by; spend no more than an easy hour or two at selected points of interest. With a day to spare, consider a side trip to historic Eagle, enjoying the gold mining sites and "Beautiful Downtown Chicken" on the way. Or opt for one of the excellent raft, kayak, or canoe runs on the Fortymile, Tanana, or Delta Rivers. As usual, superb fishing opportunities abound.

ORIENTATION

Only three roads of consequence branch off from the Alaska Highway: the mainly gravel Taylor Highway north to Eagle, the Tok Cutoff heading southwest toward Anchorage, and the southbound Richardson Highway from Delta Junction to Valdez. You can't get lost along this vital highway corridor. Services are located at regular intervals. The few towns are small or tiny, and all are easy to navigate.

As is true along most Alaskan roads, locations are often identified by highway mile marker. For example, you'll find the Walker Fork Bureau of Land Management (BLM) Campground at Mile 82.1 of the Taylor Highway, while the Dot Lake Lodge brochure might direct you to Mile 1361.3 of the Alaska Highway. The system is wonderfully convenient for travelers trying to keep a schedule. Plan to average 45 to 55 miles per hour on this and most paved Alaskan roads.

THE U.S.–CANADA BORDER

U.S.–Canada border crossings are taken quite seriously by officials on both sides of the line. Although most travelers are waved through after answering a couple of simple questions, it pays to know the rules:

1. Carry identification. A driver's license should suffice, but it doesn't hurt to have your passport or a copy of your birth certificate—especially if you think border officials might question your citizenship.
2. Carry birth certificates for any children in your party. Heightened attention to the problem of missing children has given rise to this policy.
3. Call Canadian customs before trying to cross the border if you have a criminal record, including a DWI conviction.
4. If you're traveling with a pet, carry its current certificate of rabies vaccination, signed by a licensed veterinarian.
5. Check current Canadian firearms restrictions. Handguns are not transportable through Canada.

TANANA VALLEY & THE ALASKA HIGHWAY

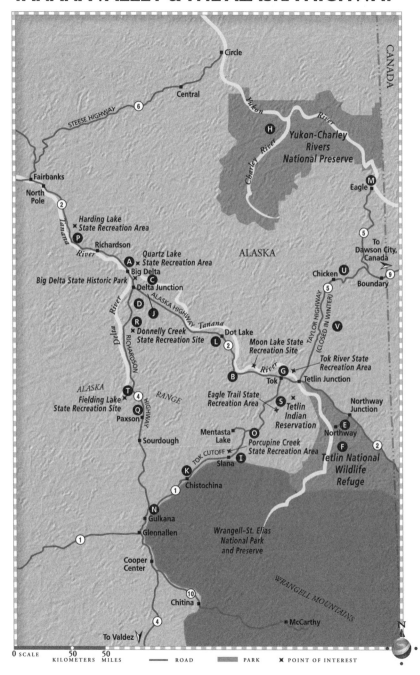

6. Carry proof that your car is insured in both nations. A letter from your insurance agent should suffice.

SIGHTSEEING HIGHLIGHTS

★★★ BIG DELTA STATE HISTORICAL PARK/TRANS-ALASKA PIPELINE CROSSING
Mile 274.5 Richardson Highway, 907/895-4201
These two sights are found near each other on the Tanana, about nine miles north of Delta Junction. The historical park features Rika's Roadhouse & Landing, built in 1910 to serve the main trade route to

---

SIGHTS

- Ⓐ Big Delta State Historical Park/ Trans-Alaska Pipeline Crossing
- Ⓑ Cathedral Bluffs
- Ⓒ Delta Junction
- Ⓓ Delta Junction Bison Range
- Ⓔ Northway
- Ⓕ Tetlin National Wildlife Refuge
- Ⓖ Tok
- Ⓗ Yukon-Charley Rivers National Preserve

FOOD

- Ⓕ Duffy's Roadhouse
- Ⓖ Fast Eddy's
- Ⓖ Golden Bear Restaurant
- Ⓖ Loose Moose Espresso Cafe
- Ⓒ Pizza Bella

LODGING

- Ⓖ Alaska 7 Motel
- Ⓓ Cherokee Lodge & RV Park
- Ⓚ Chistochina Trading Post
- Ⓛ Dot Lake Lodge
- Ⓜ Eagle Trading Company
- Ⓜ Falcon Inn Bed & Breakfast
- Ⓝ Gakona Lodge & Trading Post
- Ⓖ Golden Bear Motel
- Ⓒ Kelly's Country Inn Motel
- Ⓞ Mentasta Lodge
- Ⓟ Midway Lodge
- Ⓠ Paxson Lodge
- Ⓝ Riverview Bed and Breakfast
- Ⓟ Salcha River Lodge
- Ⓒ Victorian Inn Bed & Breakfast
- Ⓖ Young's Motel

CAMPING

- Ⓐ Big Delta State Historical Park

CAMPING (continued)

- Ⓐ Delta State Recreation Site
- Ⓡ Donnelly Creek State Recreation Site
- Ⓜ Eagle BLM Campground
- Ⓢ Eagle Trail State Recreation Area
- Ⓣ Fielding Lake State Recreation Site
- Ⓟ Harding Lake State Recreation Area
- Ⓑ Moon Lake State Recreation Site
- Ⓠ Paxson Lake BLM Campground
- Ⓘ Porcupine Creek State Recreation Area
- Ⓐ Quartz Lake State Recreation Area
- Ⓟ Salcha River State Recreation Site
- Ⓖ Tok River State Recreation Site
- Ⓤ Walker Fork BLM Campground
- Ⓥ West Fork BLM Campground

Note: Items with the same letter are located in the same area.

BORDER STATION HOURS

The U.S. and Canadian border stations are open on the schedule below:

Alaska Highway	year-round 24 hours a day
Dalton Cache	year-round 7 a.m.–11 p.m.
(Haines Highway)	
Skagway	year-round 8 a.m.–midnight
Top of the World Highway	May 15–Sept 15 9–8

the Interior gold mines. Historical exhibits (indoors and out), a self-guided walking tour, a restaurant and gift shop, and a campground round out the offerings. Just south of the park, stop for a look at the Trans-Alaska Pipeline where it bridges the river on its course from the port of Valdez to the Prudhoe Bay oilfields.

Details: *Rika's Roadhouse open 9–5. Free. (1 hour)*

★★★ **DELTA JUNCTION BISON RANGE**
Information, 907/895-4484,
www.state.ak.us/local/akpages/FISH.GAME/wildlife/
region3/refuge3/bison.htm
Once common in what is now Alaska, bison disappeared from the region at the end of the last ice age. A few were reintroduced in 1927, and the herd grew to its current count of about 500. A 90,000-acre refuge just east of Delta Junction secures grazing land for the bison while keeping them out of the barley fields across the road.

You might see bison along the Alaska Highway from about Mile 1392 to Mile 1422. Better viewing points lie between Delta Junction and about Mile 240 of the Richardson Highway, 25 miles south of town. Pull out the binoculars and see if the beasts are around.

Details: *Public access. (30 minutes)*

★★★ **TOK**
Chamber of Commerce, 907/883-5887,
www.tokalaskainfo.com
This highway junction town, the gateway to Alaska for vehicle travel-

ers, offers all travel services. Famous as a center of dog mushing, Tok hosts the annual Race of Champions Sled Dog Race in March. The town earns three stars because of two excellent visitors centers, which are listed below: The **Mainstreet Visitor Center** (Mile 1314.2 Alaska Highway, 907/883-5887, www.akpub.com/akttt/tokcc.html) is a must-stop for those wanting up-to-the-minute information on food, lodging, campgrounds, roads, and recreation. Reservation assistance is also available. The new log building features heritage and dogsledding displays.

Next door you'll find the **Public Lands Information Center** (Mile 1314 Alaska Highway, 907/883-5667, www.nps.gov/aplic), one of four strategically placed around the state. Stop here for complete information on federal and state public lands in Alaska, including parks, preserves, monuments, forests, wildlife refuges, Bureau of Land Management lands, rivers, and wilderness areas. The center keeps current listings of tour providers and takes reservations for wilderness cabins.

Details: (1 hour)

★★★ **YUKON-CHARLEY RIVERS NATIONAL PRESERVE**
Headquarters in Fairbanks, 907/456-0593; field office, near the airstrip in Eagle, 907/547-2234, www.nps.gov/yuch
The entire Charley River watershed and its 115-mile segment of the Yukon are protected in this large preserve, along with a 115-mile segment of the Yukon River. Long-distance river running is the activity of choice. Guides in Eagle offer shorter powerboat trips on the Yukon.

All of the routes in the Charley watershed require an air drop-off. One option is a nine-day route that ends in Circle City (six days for the Charley, three for the Yukon). Consult the preserve rangers or outfitters (see Fitness and Recreation, below).

Details: Water access from Eagle; air access from Eagle, Circle, Central, Tok, Delta Junction. (several days)

★★ **CATHEDRAL BLUFFS**
From about Mile 1335 and Mile 1338 of the Alaska Highway, the Tanana River passes through a steep-walled valley between the Alaska Range and the hills of the Interior. Use the turnouts and enjoy the views.
Details: Roadside stops. (30 minutes)

★★ DELTA JUNCTION
Visitor Information Center, 907/895-9941,
www.ptialaska.net/~akttt/delta.html
At the confluence of the Delta and Tanana Rivers, Delta Junction began as a station site along the WAMCATS telegraph line that ran from the Copper Valley and on to Fairbanks and the Bering Sea. It grew in importance in 1919 as a construction camp for the Richardson Highway. When a bison herd was introduced into the region in 1927, the town became known as "Buffalo Center." The Alaska Highway officially ends here, with the Richardson continuing to Fairbanks. Complete highway services are available.

Consider a stop at the **Alaska Homestead and Historical Museum** (Mile 1415.4 Alaska Highway, 907/895-4431), which features a homesteader's cabin, an operating sawmill barn, corrals, and salmon-drying racks. Sled dogs and other animals are on view.

Details: Museum open May 30 to Sept 15, 9–7. Information center open daily. (1 hour)

★★ TETLIN NATIONAL WILDLIFE REFUGE
Refuge Manager, 907/883-5312,
www.r7.fws.gov/nwr/tetlin/tetnwr.html
This sprawling lowland—one-thousand-plus square miles in area—is bounded by the Alaska Highway, the Canadian border, and the Wrangell Mountains. Along with healthy populations of bear, moose, and other common Alaskan wildlife, nearly 150 species of birds reside here. Sandhill cranes pass through in great numbers in spring and fall. Stop at the good visitors center at Mile 1229 of the Alaska Highway and enjoy the views at roadside turnouts.

Details: Visitors center open daily. (30 minutes, roadside views)

★ NORTHWAY
A short road heads a few miles south from Northway Junction (at Mile 1264 Alaska Highway) to the regional airport town of Northway, then another 1.5 miles to the traditional Athabascan village of Northway Village. The total population of the three centers is under 400. Many residents subsist in part on fish and game from the Tetlin National Wildlife Refuge. You'll find food and lodging in Northway Junction. A brief side trip to the village offers a glimpse at the real Alaska.

Details: (30 minutes)

FITNESS AND RECREATION

The Tanana Valley and the hilly region to the north are a river-runner's heaven, hosting hundreds of miles of designated National Wild and Scenic Rivers. Popular runs for raft, kayak, or canoe include the **Delta River** from Paxson to Delta Junction, the **Fortymile River** system near the Taylor Highway, the **Charley River** in Yukon-Charley Rivers National Preserve, and the **Tanana and Yukon Rivers** themselves. Check with **Circle City Charters** (Fairbanks, 907/773-8439), **Eagle Canoe Rentals** (Eagle, 907/547-2203), or **Yukon Raft Adventures** (Eagle, 907/547-2355) for options that match your interests.

FOOD

Tok and Delta Junction, the two main towns east of Fairbanks, offer a range of eating options. Many lodges and roadhouses include restaurants, which are noted in the Lodging section below.

In Tok, try **Fast Eddy's** (Mile 1313.2 Alaska Highway, 907/883-4411) for a quick and tasty meal. The lineup includes pizza, sandwiches, burgers, steaks, and seafood; open daily 6 a.m. to midnight. Nearby, the **Loose Moose Espresso Cafe** (Mile 1313.8 Alaska Highway, 907/883-5282) is a friendly place to grab a latte. Around the corner on the Tok Cutoff, the **Golden Bear Restaurant** (Mile 124.2 Tok Cutoff, 907/883-2561) shares its name with a motel, RV park, and souvenir shop.

In Delta Junction, **Pizza Bella** (downtown Delta Junction, 907/895-4841) is open daily 10 a.m. to midnight for pizza, pasta, and more.

On the Tok Cutoff between Tok and Gakona Junction, **Duffy's Roadhouse** (Mile 62.7 Tok Cutoff, 907/822-3888) offers food and services and very rustic rooms.

LODGING

Tok has a variety of lodging options. **Young's Motel** (Mile 1313 Alaska Highway, 907/883-4411) fits the bill for a clean, basic motel with satellite TV and phones. Rooms run $70 and up in summer, $50 and up in winter. On the Tok Cutoff just south of the junction, the **Golden Bear Motel** (Mile 124.2 Tok Cutoff, 907/883-2561) offers basic rooms for $50 to $95, campsites for $15 to $25.

Accommodations dot the highway between Tok and Delta Junction. About 50 miles west of Tok, you'll come to **Dot Lake Lodge** (Mile 1361.3

Alaska Highway, 907/882-2691). This full-service, roadhouse-style establishment also has camping, gas, and a restaurant. Camp and RV sites range from $6 to $14. It's open year-round. Another 50 miles brings you to **Cherokee Lodge & RV Park** (Mile 1412.5 Alaska Highway, 907/895-4814). You'll find rooms and RV camping, as well as a restaurant that's open 6 to 10 every day of the year.

For a very basic motel bed in Delta Junction, try the **Alaska 7 Motel** (Mile 270.3 Richardson Highway, 907/895-4848). Rooms are $60 to $75, less in winter. A bit nicer though still basic is **Kelly's Country Inn Motel** (Mile 270.3 Richardson Highway, 907/895-4667), where rooms go for $89 to $90 in summer. For a more personal experience with some character, book a stay at the **Victorian Inn Bed & Breakfast** (Mile 1414.5 Alaska Highway, 907/895-4636). A night in this Victorian home runs about $65, with full breakfast.

Between Delta Junction and Fairbanks, look for the **Midway Lodge** (Mile 314.8 Richardson Highway, 907/488-2939). You can grab a snooze in a $40 to $55 room or a bite at the restaurant, open daily 7 a.m. to 10 p.m. Just down the road is the **Salcha River Lodge** (Mile 322.2 Richardson Highway, 907/488-2233). Rooms are $50; the café is open from 7 a.m. to 9 p.m.

Several roadhouses lie along the Tok Cutoff between Tok and Gakona Junction. **Mentasta Lodge** (Mile 78.1 Tok Cutoff, 907/291-2324) offers a café, a laundry, gas, showers, and overnight parking. Further west, the **Chistochina Trading Post** (Mile 32 Tok Cutoff, 907/822-3366) has $65 rooms, $60 to $80 cabins, a campground, gas, gifts, restaurant, and airstrip. At Gakona Junction, you'll find the **Riverview Bed and Breakfast** (Mile 3 Tok Cutoff, 907/822-3321), a nice, smoke-free log house overlooking the Copper River and offering rooms for $65 and up and a full breakfast. Nearby is the historic **Gakona Lodge & Trading Post** (Mile 2 Tok Cutoff, 907/822-3482), dating to 1905. Attractions include the appealing Carriage House Restaurant and Trappers Den bar.

Along the central Richardson Highway between Delta Junction and Gakona Junction, **Paxson Lodge** (Mile 185 Richardson Highway, 907/822-8330) features rooms for $60 to $80, a café, bar, store, post office, airstrip, gift shop, gas, fishing licenses, and RV hookups.

Eagle has a few lodging choices, including the **Eagle Trading Company** (Front Street on the river, 907/547-2220), which also offers a café, gas, groceries, repair, store, laundry, and RV hookups. Rooms run $50 to $80. A pleasant, rustic choice is the **Falcon Inn Bed and Breakfast** (220 Front St., 907/547-2254), with rooms for $65 to $85 and up.

CAMPING

Several State Recreation Site and BLM campgrounds are found along the Alaska, Richardson, Glenn, and Taylor Highways. They usually cost from $6 to $10 and have fresh water, pit or flush toilets, tables, and grills, and they often feature river or lake access. Self-contained campers are rarely troubled when parking overnight in large turnouts or road maintenance clearings. The following options are arranged by milepost.

Alaska/Richardson Highway campgrounds include **Tok River State Recreation Site** (Mile 1309.2 Alaska Highway), **Moon Lake State Recreation Site** (Mile 1331.9 Alaska Highway), **Delta State Recreation Site** (Mile 267.1 Richardson Highway), **Big Delta State Historical Park** (Mile 274.5 Richardson Highway), **Quartz Lake State Recreation Area** (Mile 277.7 Richardson Highway), **Harding Lake State Recreation Area** (Mile 321.5 Richardson Highway), and **Salcha River State Recreation Site** (Mile 323.1 Richardson Highway).

On the Taylor Highway to Eagle, you'll find **West Fork BLM Campground** (Mile 49 Taylor Highway) and **Walker Fork BLM Campground** (Mile 82.1 Taylor Highway). To reach the very nice **Eagle BLM Campground** (Mile 160.4 Taylor Highway), head out Fourth Street, one mile west of town. The campground is adjacent to the historic cemetery; sites are free.

Options south of Tok along the Tok Cutoff Highway include **Eagle Trail State Recreation Area** (Mile 109.3 Tok Cutoff) and **Porcupine Creek State Recreation Area** (Mile 64.2 Tok Cutoff).

Three of the campgrounds along the Richardson Highway south of Delta Junction are **Donnelly Creek State Recreation Site** (Mile 237.9 Richardson Highway), **Fielding Lake State Recreation Site** (Mile 200.4 Richardson Highway), and **Paxson Lake BLM Campground** (Mile 175 Richardson Highway).

The best excursion available to drivers in eastern Alaska is a 631-mile alternative to the Alaska Highway that features a crossing of the 1,800-mile Yukon River, and visits to the historic towns of Eagle and Dawson City. The route follows the gravel Taylor Highway from Tetlin Junction (near Tok) to Eagle, the Top of the World Highway from the Taylor to Dawson City, and Yukon Highway 2 on to Whitehorse. Plan on two full days to do it justice. Maintenance on the Taylor and Top of the World Highways ends in mid-October, and the first big snow closes the road until April.

Head north on the Taylor from Mile 1301.7 of the Alaska Highway, enjoying the views as you slowly climb. Take a look at the not-quite-town of **Chicken** (Mile 66 Taylor Highway). Rumor has it early miners wanted to name their town "Ptarmigan" but couldn't spell it, so they went with the simpler name. Several old structures are visible on private land near the road. Today, "Beautiful Downtown Chicken" offers a café, a bar, a store, and gas.

Twenty miles past Chicken you can see the **Jack Wade Number 1 Dredge** (Mile 86.1 Taylor Highway), east of the road. It's one of scores of old dredges that now litter Alaska's mining regions, all once used to dig and sluice gold-bearing gravel. At the **Top of the World Highway** (Mile 95.7 Taylor Highway), turn left for the 65-

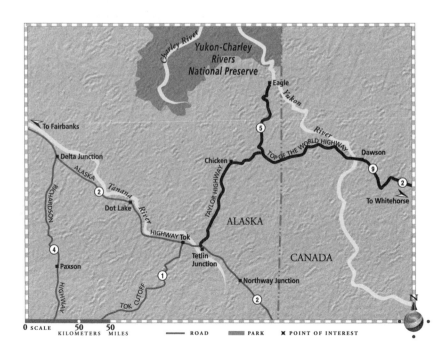

mile spur to Eagle. Remember to leave Eagle by 5 p.m. or so if you intend to cross into Canada; the border stations close at 8.

Continuing north on the Taylor, you'll descend from the ridges to finally reach the end of the road, the Yukon River, and historic **Eagle** (Mile 160.3). Turn left at Fourth Avenue for Fort Egbert, campground, airstrip, and BLM field office, or continue to the Yukon River for waterfront businesses. Han Athabascan Indians lived here when the town was established as a trading post in 1898. Eagle faded in importance with the decline of the Klondike gold fields; it survives in part because of renewed mining.

Consider taking the **Eagle Historical Society Walking Tour** (907/547-2325, www.alaska.net/~eagleak), offered daily at 10 a.m. for $5. Departing from the **1901 Courthouse** (B Street and First Avenue), the tour hits all the historic sites in the town, including the 1899 Custom House and old Fort Egbert (where Fourth Avenue meets the airstrip). Just upriver from the main town (officially known as Eagle City) is the native settlement of **Eagle Village**, home to about 30 people. Follow First Avenue upstream 2.5 miles for a look. Drop in at the field office of the Yukon-Charley National Preserve for information on float trips (located at the lower end of the airstrip).

To reach **Dawson City**, return to the junction and follow the Top of the World Highway to the border, then another 68 miles to the free ferry across the Yukon. Dawson City grew to 40,000 people almost overnight when hopeful miners flooded the region in 1897 and 1898. The population plunged when the rush ended and by 1902 only 1,000 residents were left. Many historic buildings remain and evidence of mining is everywhere.

Stop at the **Dawson City Museum and Historical Society** (Fifth Avenue and Mission, 403/993-5291) to see gold-rush photos and artifacts, open 10 a.m. to 6 p.m. through Labor Day. Admission is $3.50. Check out the Gaslight Follies at the **Palace Grand Theater** (King Street at Second Avenue); shows take place Wednesday through Monday at 8 p.m. Tickets are "family priced." Drop in at **Diamond Tooth Gerties Gambling Hall** (Queen Street and Fourth Avenue, Dawson City, 403/993-5575, www.casinocity.com/ca/yt/gerties.html), open mid-May to mid-September daily, 7 p.m. to 2 a.m., with cancan shows nightly. Admission is $4.75.

As you drive out of town on Highway 2, you'll follow the Klondike River for several miles. Signs of gold mining, past and present, are everywhere. Keep your eyes open for **Dredge #4 National Historic Site**. The 327-mile journey on through Carmacks to Whitehorse is on a fast, well-paved road.

For information on the Yukon, contact **Tourism Yukon**, P.O. Box 2703, Whitehorse, Yukon Y1A 2C6, 403/667-5340, www.touryukon.com.

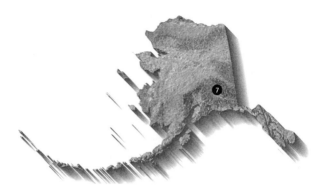

7
COPPER RIVER VALLEY

Surrounded by mountains, the Copper River gathers waters from about 30,000 square miles of drainage and carries them out through a deep valley to the sea. The lake-dotted Copper River Basin spreads west of the river, its lonely wilds popular with hunters and fishers. To the east, the high peaks of the Wrangell Mountains dominate the scenery. Mount Drum (elevation 12,010 feet) rises closest to Glenallen; behind it loom the clearly visible Mount Wrangell (14,163 feet), the largest active volcano in the United States, and lofty Mount Sanford (16,237 feet).

The Ahtna Athabascans lived in the basin for hundreds of years before explorers and trappers arrived in the 1800s. Prospectors followed, seeking gold, but it was copper that had the greatest impact on the region, leading to the establishment of the Kennecott Mine north of McCarthy. An early trade route to the Interior followed the path of what is today the Richardson Highway, while several communities began as roadhouses to service both the mine and the overland route. Today, the Trans-Alaska Pipeline parallels the Richardson, contributing service jobs and industry to the corridor.

Located at the convergence of the region's five roads, Glenallen is the only sizable settlement. It's those five roads and where they lead that are of interest to travelers. Four fan out toward Tok, Fairbanks, Valdez, and Anchorage, climbing along or away from the river through beautiful mountains. The fifth follows the Copper downstream to Chitina, then heads up the

Chitina River valley to the historic settlements of McCarthy and Kennicott in the heart of Wrangell–St. Elias National Park. Interesting diversions are found along all the routes.

A PERFECT DAY IN THE COPPER RIVER VALLEY

Head to McCarthy in Wrangell-St. Elias National Park and Preserve. Poke about the few shops and galleries and grab a bite at one of the homey eateries. Take a shuttle to Kennicott for a walk through the fascinating ruins of the Kennecott Mine. Go for a hike up the old mine road along the margins of Root Glacier, heading out onto the ice if you wish. Relax on the porch of the marvelous Kennicott Glacier Lodge, enjoying stellar views. If you're lucky, you'll be spending a night in this magnificent corner of Alaska.

ORIENTATION

This broad, wild region is best thought of as a squarish basin, about 100 miles a side, each walled off by a formidable mountain range: the Alaska Range to the north, the Wrangell Mountains to the east, the Chugach Mountains to the south, and the Talkeetna Mountains to the west. The Copper River arcs around the Wrangell Range in a broad valley before cutting through the Chugach Range to the ocean near Cordova. A good highway map is all you need to manage the roads and tiny towns.

SIGHTSEEING HIGHLIGHTS

★★★★ MCCARTHY AND KENNICOTT
Information, 907/822-5238

Kennicott started as a mining camp in 1908, growing rapidly into a small company town where drinking and gambling were forbidden. Five miles to the south, McCarthy popped up to fill the void with saloons and a red-light district, as well as stores, hotels, restaurants, and a newspaper. Mining's demise in 1938 led to the abandonment of both towns. The remaining structures have been identified by the National Trust for Historic Places as among the most endangered in the nation. Preservation efforts are underway.

Today, McCarthy is a great place to stroll, shop, eat, and stay, while the area around the Kennecott Mine ruins offers great views, glacier access, and good hiking. Though most services are back in

COPPER RIVER VALLEY

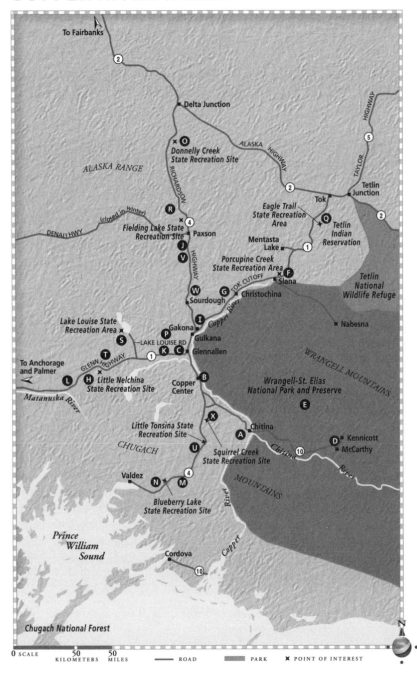

To Fairbanks

Delta Junction

ALASKA RANGE

Donnelly Creek
State Recreation Site

ALASKA HIGHWAY

RICHARDSON

TAYLOR HIGHWAY

Tok

Tetlin
Junction

Eagle Trail
State Recreation
Area

Tetlin
Indian
Reservation

DENALI HWY

(closed in winter)

Fielding Lake State
Recreation Site

Paxson

Mentasta
Lake

Porcupine Creek
State Recreation Area

Slana

Tetlin
National
Wildlife Refuge

HIGHWAY

TOK CUTOFF

Sourdough

Christochina

Copper River

Lake Louise State
Recreation Area

Gakona

Gulkana

Nabesna

LAKE LOUISE RD

Glennallen

GLENN HIGHWAY

To Anchorage
and Palmer

Little Nelchina
State Recreation Site

Matanuska River

Copper
Center

Wrangell-St. Elias
National Park and Preserve

WRANGELL MOUNTAINS

Little Tonsina State
Recreation Site

CHUGACH

Squirrel Creek
State Recreation Site

Chitina

Kennicott
McCarthy

Chitina River

MOUNTAINS

Valdez

Blueberry Lake
State Recreation Site

Copper River

Prince
William
Sound

Cordova

Chugach National Forest

N

0 SCALE		
50 KILOMETERS	50 MILES	

ROAD   PARK   ✕ POINT OF INTEREST

McCarthy, the wonderful Kennicott Glacier Lodge serves travelers at the mine. Shuttle vans link the two sites.

Although it's possible to fly in to McCarthy, most visitors come via the McCarthy Road from Chitina. The road follows the original railroad bed that carried ore trains to Cordova and can be exceedingly rough. It should be driven at modest speeds; allow at least two hours for this 61-mile stretch. Historic rail bridges are found along the route, including the narrow Kuskulana River Bridge (Mile 16), which passes 390 feet over the water. At Mile 58.2, the road ends at a parking area on the west bank of the Kennicott River. A footbridge leads into McCarthy.

Details: *For more information, contact the Copper Basin Visitor Center and Wrangell-St. Elias National Park and Preserve headquarters (see below). Scheduled air shuttle linking Anchorage, Gulkana (near Glenallen), and McCarthy is offered by Ellis Air Taxi (800/478-3368,*

SIGHTS

Ⓐ Chitina
Ⓑ Copper Center
Ⓒ Glenallen
Ⓓ McCarthy and Kenicott
Ⓔ Wrangell-St. Elias National Park and Preserve

FOOD

Ⓕ Duffy's Roadhouse
Ⓐ It'll Do Cafe
Ⓓ Roadside Potatohead
Ⓓ Tailor-Made Pizza

LODGING

Ⓒ Caribou Hotel
Ⓖ Chistochina Trading Post
Ⓐ Chitina Motel
Ⓑ Copper Center Lodge
Ⓗ Eureka Lodge
Ⓘ Gakona Junction Village
Ⓘ Gakona Lodge & Trading Post
Ⓓ Historic Kennicott Bed and Breakfast
Ⓓ Kennicott Glacier Lodge
Ⓓ McCarthy Lodge: Ma Johnson Hotel & Restaurant/Saloon

LODGING (continued)

Ⓙ Paxson Lodge
Ⓚ Ranch House Lodge
Ⓔ Riverview Bed and Breakfast
Ⓛ Sheep Mountain Lodge
Ⓜ Tsaina Lodge

CAMPING

Ⓝ Blueberry Lake State Recreation Site
Ⓞ Donnelly Creek State Recreation Site
Ⓟ Dry Creek State Recreation Site
Ⓠ Eagle Trail State Recreation Area
Ⓡ Fielding Lake State Recreation Site
Ⓢ Lake Louise State Recreation Area Campground
Ⓣ Little Nelchina State Recreation Site
Ⓤ Little Tonsina State Recreation Site
Ⓥ Paxson Lake BLM Campground
Ⓕ Porcupine Creek State Recreation Area
Ⓦ Sourdough Creek BLM Campground
Ⓧ Squirrel Creek State Recreation Site
Ⓚ Ranch House Lodge

Note: Items with the same letter are located in the same area.

907/822-3368). McCarthy–Kennicott shuttle costs $5 each way. (1 day minimum)

★★★★ WRANGELL–ST. ELIAS NATIONAL PARK AND PRESERVE

Headquarters and information, Mile 105.5 Richardson Highway, Copper Center, 907/822-5238, www.nps.gov/wrst
America's largest national park and one of its wildest, Wrangell–St. Elias encompasses more glaciers than any other, as well as the greatest collection of peaks above 16,000 feet. At 18,008 feet, Mount St. Elias is the nation's second-tallest after Denali. Entering the park by road is possible via the Nabesna Road from Slana, but McCarthy and Kennicott (see above) offer nearly the only visitor accommodations. Those exploring further should be fully equipped and competent in outdoor skills. Few official trails exist. McCarthy is also a good base for flightseeing or a drop-off for a remote cabin stay (see Fitness and Recreation, below).

The Kennecott Mine is spelled with an "e." The town of Kennicott and same-named glacier and river are spelled with an "i."

Details: *Headquarters open June–Aug daily 8–6, Sept–May Mon–Fri 8–5. Other ranger stations include: Nabesna Ranger Station, Mile 0.2 Nabesna Road (Slana, 907/822-5238); Chitina Ranger Station (Chitina, 907/823-2205, open daily 9:30–6); and Yakutat Ranger Station (Yakutat, 907/784-3295). (1 day minimum)*

★★ COPPER CENTER

Copper Center Loop Road from Mile 101 Old Richardson Highway
Long the site of an important Ahtna Athabascan fish camp, Copper Center emerged as a trade and supply center in 1896 when a roadhouse was built. The roadhouse was replaced in 1932 by Copper Center Lodge, still in operation today (see Lodging, below). Heritage exhibits are displayed at the Ashby Museum, located within the lodge (Mon–Sat 1–5, Fri 7–9; donations accepted). The Chapel on the Hill, built by Army volunteers in 1942, is found close by. Inquire at the lodge about slide presentations at the chapel. Scattered throughout the area are other historic buildings, most on private land and closed to the public.

Details: Take the Old Richardson Highway loop from Mile 100.2 or 106 of the new Richardson Highway bypass. Services are found here, as are the headquarters for Wrangell-St. Elias National Park and Preserve. For more information, contact the park headquarters (907/822-5235, www.nps.gov/wrst) or the Copper Basin Visitor Center, 907/822-5555. (1 ½ hours)

★ CHITINA

Located at the confluence of the Copper and Chitina Rivers, Chitina grew from an Ahtna Athabascan settlement into a vital railroad center. Early travelers to Alaska often arrived in Cordova by steamship, then proceeded by train to Chitina before continuing to Interior mining areas and towns by stagecoach, dogsled, or horse. Though it declined with the end of rail service, Chitina now serves as a modest gateway to Wrangell-St. Elias National Park and offers recreational opportunities.

Visit the Chitina Ranger Station (Chitina, 907/823-2205), located in the original Ed S. Orr Stage Co., which served travelers after the turn of the century. Information is available on trails, park activities, and the town of Chitina. Before traveling on to McCarthy, gas up and check your spare.

Details: Ranger station open daily 9:30–6. All services available in town. (30 minutes)

★ GLENALLEN

Located in the heart of the Copper River Basin at the crossroads of the Richardson and Glenn Highways, Glenallen is an important center of travel services. Although little here will engage the visitor, a stop at the **Copper Basin Visitor Center** (junction of Glenn and Richardson Highways, Glenallen, 907/822-5555) is worthwhile. The center features information on the entire region, helpful staff, and some minor displays.

Details: Visitors center open daily in summer 8–7. (30 minutes)

COPPER VALLEY HIGHLIGHTS

★★★ GLENN HIGHWAY AND TOK CUTOFF/ PALMER TO TOK (327 MILES)

From Palmer, the Glenn climbs past Sutton and Chickaloon along the

© Paul Otteson

Matanuska River, which separates the Talkeetna Mountains to the north from the Chugach Mountains to the south. (Note: Glenn Highway sites between Anchorage and Palmer are covered in Chapters 8 and 9.) Excellent viewpoints for the **Matanuska Glacier** (Mile 91 to 114; see Chapter 9) invite long stops. Dall sheep are commonly seen from viewpoints near **Sheep Mountain** (Mile 108 to 118). After crossing Eureka Summit (elevation 3,222 feet), the road descends gradually into the Copper River Valley, affording sweeping views of the basin and Wrangell Mountains. Fishing and boating are popular in the Lake Louise area (information 907/822-5555), reached via a 20-mile gravel road from the junction with the Glenn (Mile 159.8).

After jogging northward from Glenallen on the Richardson Highway to the services center of Gakona Junction, the Tok Cutoff segment of the Glenn Highway cuts off to the northeast. You'll pass through the Athabascan settlement of Chistochina (Mile 32.9) before reaching the Nabesna Road junction (Mile 59.8). The fairly rugged 46-mile Nabesna Road heads southeast into the northern section of Wrangell-St. Elias National Park and Preserve (no services). For area, road, and park information, visit the ranger station in Slana, just 0.2 mile down Nabesna Road. From the junction, the Tok Cutoff climbs through beautiful country, crosses over Mentasta Summit (Mile 79.4, elevation 2,434 feet), and winds down to the Tanana River Valley and Tok (Mile 125, see Chapter 1).

Details: Good, paved road. (all day)

★★★ **RICHARDSON HIGHWAY / VALDEZ TO DELTA JUNCTION (266 MILES)**

The mile markers of the Richardson officially start at the pre–1964 earthquake site of Valdez. Following a historic trade and telegraph route, it now shares the right-of-way with the often visible Trans-Alaska Pipeline. The road climbs quickly northward into the Chugach Mountains, through beautiful **Keystone Canyon** (about Mile 13 to 16, popular with rafters), and up into Thompson Pass. Just over the pass you'll come to the parking area for easily accessible **Worthington Glacier** (Mile 26.8). Stop and take the short hike up to the ice. From here, the road gradually winds down into the Copper River Valley and Glenallen (Mile 115). Consider detouring to visit Copper Center or continuing down the Edgerton Highway to Chitina and McCarthy (see above).

North of Glenallen the road climbs again, past the junction with the Tok Cutoff (Mile 128.6) and up into the Alaska Range. The junction with the wild and wonderful Denali Highway (see Chapter 15) is in the "town" of Paxson (Mile 185.5). Slow down and enjoy the views along the shores of lovely **Summit Lake** (about Mile 192 to 197). It's all downhill after crossing Isabel Pass (Mile 197.6, 3,000 feet). Stop to read the story of the **Black Rapids Glacier** (Mile 225.4), famous for "galloping" forward three miles from its present terminus in 1936–1937. Consider pulling over at viewpoints lower down (Miles 241.3 and 262.6) to scan for bison that roam the **Delta Junction Bison Range** (see Chapter 1).

After reaching Delta Junction (Mile 266), the Richardson continues on to Fairbanks (see Chapter 16).

Details: *Good, paved road. (6–8 hours)*

FITNESS AND RECREATION

Hike up along the edge of **Root Glacier** from the Kennecott Mine ruins. Explore the terminus of **Worthington Glacier** on the road to Valdez. Walk the open country around **Summit Lake** and Isabel Pass on the Richardson Highway. Turn off anywhere a view catches your eye and stroll.

Some great float trips are possible in the basin. **Keystone Raft & Kayak Adventures, Inc.** (Valdez, 907/835-2606), hosts a variety of raft and kayak trips from one to 10 days long on the Chitina, Copper, Tana, Tonsina, and Talkeetna Rivers, as well as through Keystone Canyon. **Copper Oar Rafting** (McCarthy, 800/523-4453, 907/554-4453, www.alaskan.com/vendors/copper_oar.html) offers a full slate of great Wrangell-St. Elias raft trips from a few hours to several days, as well as raft/hike and raft/flight combinations. **Osprey Expeditions** (Copper Center, 907/882-5422) hosts guided wilderness raft trips throughout the Copper River Basin.

If you're looking for a relaxing day or two of fishing, consider a stay at one of the **Lake Louise** lodges (information at Copper Basin Visitor Center, Glenallen, 907/822-5555). Flightseeing, shuttle flights, drop-offs, and pickups are offered by **Wrangell Mountain Air** (McCarthy, 800/478-1160, 907/554-4411) and **McCarthy Air** (McCarthy, 888/989-9891, 907/554-4440, www.alaskan.com/mccarthyair/).

FOOD

Most eateries in the region are connected to full-service roadhouses, lodges, and hotels. Several of these are listed in the Lodging section, below.

On the Tok Cutoff, **Duffy's Roadhouse** (Mile 62.7 Tok Cutoff, 907/822-3888, 907/822-3133) offers vehicle services and a decent café, but no lodging. Chitina features the aptly named **It'll Do Cafe** (Chitina, 907/823-2244). It'll do nicely. Open daily.

McCarthy is ready for visitors with several small eating spots, including **Roadside Potatohead** (McCarthy). Burgers, burritos, fries, and more are on the menu. How could you go wrong? Nearby (everything is "nearby") is **Tailor-Made Pizza** (McCarthy), where pizza shares the menu with ice cream, salad, soda, beer, and wine—all in a very pleasant setting.

LODGING

In Glenallen, the **Caribou Hotel** (Mile 187 Glenn Highway, Glenallen, 800/478-3302, 907/822-3302) features modern rooms from $130 and up, some with hot tubs.

East of Glenallen, several options lie along the Tok Cutoff between the Richardson Highway Junction and Tok. Cabins at the **Gakona Junction Village** (Mile 0 Tok Cutoff, Gakona, 888/462-3221, 907/822-3664) are $100 in summer. The historic **Gakona Lodge & Trading Post** (Mile 2 Tok Cutoff, Gakona, 907/822-3482), a Valdez Trail roadhouse dating to 1905, is home to the well-known Carriage House Restaurant. Rooms are $50 to $70. The smoke-free **Riverview Bed and Breakfast** (Mile 3 Tok Cutoff, Gakona, 907/822-3321) features rooms for $65 and up in a nice log home overlooking the Copper River; a full breakfast is served. The rustic **Chistochina Trading Post** (Mile 32 Tok Cutoff, 907/822-3366) offers rooms, cabins, a sauna and hot tub, restaurant, campground, airstrip, gas, and gifts.

North of Glenallen, between Gakona Junction and Delta Junction on the Richardson Highway, is the **Paxson Lodge** (Mile 185.5 Richardson Highway, Paxson, 907/822-3330). Rooms run $60 to $80, and the lodge has a café, bar, store, post office, gift shop, airstrip, RV hookups, and gas. Sells fishing licenses, too.

Between Glenallen and the Matanuska area, the Glenn Highway has a few options. **Sheep Mountain Lodge** (Mile 113.5 Glenn Highway, 907/745-5121), a lovely, rustic log lodge and cabins, has a dining room and bar and offers rafting, hiking trails, and wildlife-viewing excursions. Rates run $50 (for a four-person "dorm" room with shared bath) to $125 (cabin). Opened in 1937, **Eureka Lodge** (Mile 128 Glenn Highway, 907/822-3808) was the first roadhouse on the Glenn. All services are available. Rooms are $55 and up. The **Ranch House Lodge** (Mile 173 Glenn Highway, 907/822-3882) features a rustic log lodge, bar, restaurant, and $50 cabins.

Copper Center boasts the wonderful **Copper Center Lodge** (Mile 101 Richardson Highway, Copper Center, 907/822-3245), a classic, historic Alaska roadhouse inn. Rates run $85 single/double (private bath), $75 single/double (shared bath). The excellent restaurant is open from 7 a.m. to 9 p.m.

Between Copper Center and Valdez on the Richardson Highway is the **Tsaina Lodge** (Mile 35 Richardson Highway, Valdez, 907/835-3500), featuring nice accommodations ($95 and up in summer, $160 and up in winter), and the fantastic Tsaina Lodge Restaurant. Enjoy the glacier views at this home of the World Extreme Skiing Championships.

In Chitina, the **Chitina Motel** (Chitina, 907/823-2211) offers basic accommodations. Rooms are $60; inquire at the grocery.

McCarthy and Kennicott feature some fine options. In McCarthy, try the **Ma Johnson Hotel & Restaurant/Saloon** (McCarthy, 907/554-4402). The hotel offers historic rooms with modern shared baths, while "Beer, Bull & Grub" are served up at the restaurant/saloon. Five miles up the road in Kennicott, in a renovated historic building among the ruins, you'll find one of my favorites, the **Kennicott Glacier Lodge** (Kennicott, 800/582-5128, 907/258-2350). Rates are $120 single, $170 double (with McCarthy shuttle, tour), plus $40 for meals. The only lodge/restaurant at the old Kennecott Mine site, it features a great view and fine restaurant. The **Historic Kennicott Bed and Breakfast** (#14 Silk Stocking Row, Kennicott, 907/554-4469) is another great choice. This small B&B is located in an old mine house, $120 for two people, $240 for the whole house (sleeps four).

CAMPING

Several State Recreation Site and BLM campgrounds are found along area highways. They usually cost from $6 to $10 and have fresh water, pit or flush toilets, tables, and grills, and they often feature river or lake access. The following options are arranged by milepost.

Options along the Tok Cutoff include **Porcupine Creek State Recreation Area** (Mile 64.2 Tok Cutoff) and **Eagle Trail State Recreation Area** (Mile 109.3 Tok Cutoff).

Several campgrounds are found along the Richardson Highway between Delta Junction and Glenallen: **Donnelly Creek State Recreation Site** (Mile 237.9 Richardson Highway), **Fielding Lake State Recreation Site** (Mile 200.4 Richardson Highway), **Paxson Lake BLM Campground** (Mile 175 Richardson Highway), **Sourdough Creek BLM Campground** (Mile 147.6 Richardson Highway), and **Dry Creek State Recreation Site** (Mile 118 Richardson Highway, Glenallen).

The Glenn Highway between Glenallen and the Matanuska Glacier Region features the following campgrounds. **Little Nelchina State Recreation Site** (Mile 137.6 Glenn Highway) has free campsites but no treated water source. From the Lake Louise Road Junction (Mile 159.8 Glenn Highway), a 20-mile good gravel road leads to the fishing, hunting, and boating area around Lake Louise. The area hosts four lodges and the **Lake Louise State Recreation Area** campground. Fifteen miles from Glenallen is **Tolsona Creek State Recreation Area** (Mile 173 Glenn Highway).

Campgrounds found south of Glenallen along the Richardson Highway include **Squirrel Creek State Recreation Site** (Mile 79.6 Richardson Highway), **Little Tonsina State Recreation Site** (Mile 65.1), and **Blueberry Lake State Recreation Site** (Mile 24.1).

In addition to the areas listed above, a number of roadhouses have camping and RV areas. Free camping in pullouts is not uncommon.

8
PRINCE WILLIAM SOUND/VALDEZ, CORDOVA, & WHITTIER

Prince William Sound is famous for its mountain-rimmed beauty, its abundance of fish and wildlife, and its devastation in 1989 by a leaking oil tanker. It was here that the *Exxon Valdez* spilled 258,000 barrels of oil into the water, about 20 percent of its cargo. Though the area's overall recovery has been strong, certain animal populations still suffer from toxic contamination and food-chain disruption.

The oil spill was not the region's first cataclysm. In 1964, Valdez and Cordova both were rocked by a great earthquake and ensuing tsunamis. Cordova had to move and rebuild its harbor, while the entire town of Valdez was relocated. The region has seen it all, but it remains one of Alaska's most beautiful areas and is all the more remarkable a travel destination for having suffered.

Several cruise companies offer packages that include a day in the sound, usually on their way to Seward and rail connections to Denali. Bus tours and independent travelers are best served by the A.M.H.S. ferries that link Valdez, Cordova, and Whittier. If driving, consider putting your car on the ferry in Valdez for the trip to Whittier, then taking the new road from Whittier to Portage to access Kenai, Anchorage, and beyond (Portage to Valdez works just as well).

Other routing can incorporate Cordova, my favorite Prince William Sound town. Consider flying to Cordova from Anchorage, then returning via Valdez and Whittier by ferry and train.

ORIENTATION

Valdez, Cordova, and Whittier each nestle deep in an inlet projecting from this ragged, island-peppered sound: Whittier in the west, Valdez in the north, Cordova in the east. It's about 100 miles by air from Whittier to Cordova, and within that range dozens of glaciers flow down from the Chugach Mountains into the many tortuous bays. The towns themselves are small and easily navigated. Town maps are available at visitors centers and kiosks, and in the pamphlet racks of hotels, motels, airports, ferry docks, and restaurants.

THE *EXXON VALDEZ* OIL SPILL

When 12 million gallons began draining from the *Exxon Valdez* into Prince William Sound on March 23, 1989, events followed that continue to serve as a lasting lesson to all. After much delay caused by corporate attempts to minimize the disaster, a huge clean-up effort was mounted, involving some 11,000 people, 1,400 vessels, and 80 aircraft.

The leaking tanker contaminated 1,500 miles of coastline with oil. The spill killed about 5,000 sea otters, 300 bald eagles, 350 harbor seals, 13 killer whales, and perhaps a third of a million seabirds. Countless more animals were injured and suffered habitat degradation and disruption of feeding and reproductive cycles. The spill damaged salmon and herring fisheries, as well as many species living in shallows below the low-tide level. Many animal populations in heavily oiled intertidal zone areas were devastated.

Exxon spent more than $1 billion on the cleanup, much of it, perhaps, wasted. The painstaking cleaning of oiled birds and mammals saved just a few. The disposal of materials used to absorb spilled oil represented a huge environmental problem in itself. Some experts estimate more oil was burned by the ships, planes, and vehicles involved in the cleanup than was spilled by the tanker. Miles of shoreline scrubbed by pressure hoses were left in worse shape biologically than stretches that were never touched.

Today, about a decade later, visitors are unlikely to see any signs of the spill. The only remaining oil is that which was driven deep into the beaches by pressure hoses. Chemical analyses of air, water, plants, and animal tissue show limited and diminishing effects. Many local animal populations have enjoyed strong recoveries. Regionally, however, harbor seals, sea otters, certain salmon runs, Pacific herring, and several bird populations still lag behind their pre-spill numbers.

Primarily, it is because Alaska is vast and wild that Prince William Sound is on a solid road to a full, if scarred, recovery. Alaska is not a fragile museum of

CORDOVA

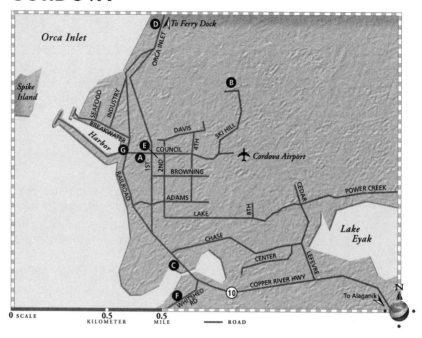

SIGHTS

A Cordova Historical
   Museum
B Mount Eyak

FOOD

C Baja Taco
D Cookhouse Cafe
E Killer Whale

LODGING

F Cordova Rose Lodge
G Reluctant Fisherman

A PERFECT DAY IN PRINCE WILLIAM SOUND

It's a great day to be on the water, nudging up to the massive face of Columbia Glacier or winding past the many academic namesake glaciers of College Fiord. Even if you're just riding the A.M.H.S. ferry from port to port, the beauty of the sound will dazzle you.

If you prefer a land-based day, a tour out to the Copper River Delta, Million Dollar Bridge, and Childs Glacier can't be beat. At the end of the day, you'll have a chance to stroll about the easy town of Cordova to soak in the ambiance of genuine Alaska. Valdez-based visitors can raft Keystone Canyon, while those in Whittier can hike into Portage Pass.

---

yesteryear like so many of the world's wildlands; the land and seas here are still powerful on their own behalf. But while time works to restore the wilderness, human development continues to threaten it. With luck, our species eventually will be cured of its seemingly insatiable hunger to humanize all the Earth.

WHITTIER TRAIN AND FERRY CONNECTIONS/THE NEW ROAD

Traveling between Prince William Sound and Anchorage or the Kenai Peninsula once involved taking one of six daily train shuttles (four on Wednesday and Thursday) between Portage and Whittier. Motorists drove their vehicles up onto flatbed railcars and stayed inside them during the 45-minute trip.

For current information about the new road being built to connect Portage and Whittier, call the Alaska Railroad (800/544-0552, 907/265-2494).

At the time of publication, the construction of a short road between Portage and the tunnel was nearing completion. The new route allows visitors to drive directly between the ferry dock in Whittier and the Seward Highway junction in Portage, making the rail shuttle obsolete. Since the tunnel—wide enough for only one vehicle—accommodates both train and auto traffic, users must observe a strict schedule.

SIGHTSEEING HIGHLIGHTS

★★★★ COLUMBIA GLACIER EXCURSION

Boat tours from Valdez to Columbia Glacier are an excellent option. The massive face of the glacier rises up to 300 feet above the waterline. A wall of ice that separated from the glacier face several years ago may prevent boats from getting close to the glacier, but the setting is impressive, encompassing bay, bergs, glacier, and Chugach Mountains. Allow six hours for a basic tour. Longer trips take in more area highlights. The A.M.H.S. Valdez–Whittier ferry once took an hour-long detour to enter Columbia Bay for viewing but now simply slows at the bay mouth.

Boat tours and kayak adventures are offered by several providers. **Alaskan Wilderness Sailing and Kayaking** (Valdez,

907/835-5175) lists skippered sailing, guided kayaking, and outdoor education on their menu. **Raven Sailing Charters & Berth and Breakfast** (Valdez, 907/835-5863) will host you for a night or take you out on a sailing charter or kayak drop-off. **Prince William Sound Cruises and Tours** (Valdez, 800/992-1297, 907/835-4731, www.kenaifjords.com/princewilliamsound) offers tour-boat, sailing, hiking, wildlife, kayaking, and lodge packages from Whittier and Valdez.

Details: (half day minimum)

★★★★ COPPER RIVER DELTA TOUR
Copper River Northwest Tours, Cordova, 907/424-5356
From Cordova, van tours take visitors on the 48-mile Copper Highway through the bountiful waterfowl and fish-spawning habitat of the Copper River delta. The highway follows an old railroad grade that carried ore trains from the Kennecott Mine to Cordova from 1908 to 1936. At the end of the road is the Million Dollar Bridge, built so the railroad could sidestep Childs and Miles Glaciers, which meet the river on opposite sides. Twenty years after the last train rolled, the bridge was opened as a highway bridge but was closed after a section collapsed in the 1964 earthquake. A temporary connector reopened the bridge in the mid-1970s, but in 1995 flood damage closed it again.

In Cordova, obtain a list of area hiking trails from the Chugach National Forest office (Cordova Ranger District, 612 Second St., 907/424-7661).

Tours also include stops for wildlife viewing. A short side road leads from Million Dollar Bridge to the viewing area for Childs Glacier, which sometimes calves bergs into the river, sending waves across the water to dampen riverside observers.

Details: Call for current schedule, information, and custom tour options. Cost is $35, lunch optional. (6 hours)

★★★ CORDOVA
Chamber of Commerce, 907/424-7260,
www.ptialaska.net/~cchamber
One of my favorite Alaska destinations, this genuine working town is off the beaten path, inaccessible by road, unvisited by cruise ships,

and located at the end of the ferry line. The area boasts scenic beauty, good trails, and interesting history—all easily accessible. Arriving planes and ferries are met by a van that shuttles visitors to town (though the 0.75-mile walk from ferry pier to town center is easy). North of the ferry, the coast road winds along Orca Inlet and past "Hippie Cove," so named because several low-budget residents live there in vans, trailers, and tents. In town, stop at the **Cordova Historical Museum** (Centennial Building, 622 First St., 907/424-6665), located with the visitors center at First and Browning. The museum features cultural artifacts of Chugach, Eyak, and Tlingit peoples (open in summer Mon–Sat 10–6; winter Tue–Fri 1–5, Sat 2–4).

You might be able to book a chairlift ride to the summit of **Mount Eyak** (walk up Browning Street, left on Fourth, right on Council, left on Sixth to Mount Eyak Ski Basin, 907/424-7766). In summers past, the lift has operated Monday, Friday, and Sunday by appointment (six-person minimum; fee $7, $5 students, under 12 free). Of course, the lift also runs during ski season.

Details: Accessible by air or ferry. (half day)

★★★ **VALDEZ**
Visitor Information Center, 800/770-5954, 907/835-4636, www.alaska.net/~valdezak
The northernmost ice-free port on the continent, Valdez was established in the winter of 1897–1898 at the head of the All-American Route to the Interior gold fields. Virtually destroyed in the 1964 earthquake, the town was rebuilt from scratch four miles west of its original location. Valdez is set in one of the state's most spectacular locations, with high, ice-crested peaks rising steeply almost from

CARS IN CORDOVA

In the Cordova area, car rental is available at the **Reluctant Fisherman** hotel (800/770-3272, 907/424-3272) and **Blue Heron Inn** (907/424-3554), and by **Cordova Auto Rentals** (907/424-5982).

VALDEZ

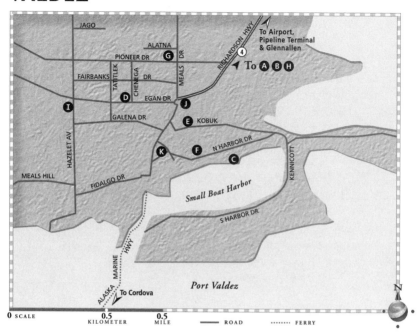

SIGHTS

Ⓐ Alyeska Marine Terminal
Ⓑ Crooked Creek Salmon Viewpoint
Ⓒ Harbor Plaza
Ⓐ Trans-Alaska Pipeline
Ⓓ Valdez Museum and Historic Archive

FOOD

Ⓔ Fu Kung
Ⓕ Mike's Palace
Ⓖ Chinooks Books and Coffee

LODGING

Ⓗ Brookside Inn
Ⓘ Keystone Hotel
Ⓙ Totem Inn

CAMPING

Ⓚ Valdez Bear Paw Camper Park

Note: Items with the same letter are located in the same area.

---

water's edge. Next to the small boat harbor, you'll find the pleasant shops and restaurants of **Harbor Plaza**.

Across the harbor from town, the "tank farm" and tanker port mark the south end of the **Trans-Alaska Pipeline**. For a look at the facility that receives up to 75,000 barrels per hour through the pipeline, stores it in huge tanks, then loads it onto 70 tankers per month, tour the **Alyeska Marine Terminal** (across Port Valdez from Valdez, 907/835-2686). Tours are offered May through September daily at 10, 1, 4, and 7:30. Call for reservations and directions. Admission is $15, $7.50 for ages 6 to 11, under 6 free.

Local heritage exhibits are on display at the **Valdez Museum and Historic Archive**, three blocks from the harbor (217 Egan, Valdez, 907/835-2764, www.alaska.net/~vldzmuse). Displays include a restored steam fire engine, log cabin, lighthouse, photographs, and audiovisual programs (open in summer Mon–Sat 9–6, Sun 8–5; winter Mon–Fri 10–5, Sat 12–4). Admission is $3, $2.50 over age 64, $2 ages 14–18, under 14 free. (1 hour)

Where Crooked Creek meets Port Valdez along the Richardson Highway just outside of town, you'll find the **Crooked Creek Salmon Viewpoint** (Richardson Highway, Valdez). An observation platform facilitates viewing of salmon on their annual spawning run. **Details**: *Accessible by air, ferry, and Richardson Highway. (half day)*

★★ **WHITTIER**
Visitor Information, 907/472-2379
Alaska's main military port until 1960, Whittier has since earned a mild reputation as a home to those who don't wish to be found. The population has dropped from its one-time high of 1,200 to just 300, giving the town a ghostly aura.

The empty Buckner Building contributes heavily to the abandoned look. Once known as a "city under one roof," it housed a thousand apartments, a bowling alley, hospital, theater, library, shops, gymnasium, and pool. Nearby is the thoroughly un-Alaskan, 14-story Begich Towers, a condominimium complex. Although Whittier's military ghost-town ambiance may not fit most tourists' expectations, the townspeople are friendly and the surroundings spectacular.

Most of the few shops cluster around the boat harbor. Cruise ships won't use the port until taxation and docking facility issues are resolved, but ferry passengers regulary use Whittier as a transfer point for the Kenai Peninsula, Anchorage, or the Interior. A daily passenger train links Whittier and Anchorage.
Details: *(2 hours)*

FITNESS AND RECREATION

In Valdez, consider a rafting excursion down Keystone Canyon with **Keystone Raft and Kayak Adventures** (Valdez, 907/835-2606). The company also

PRINCE WILLIAM SOUND REGION

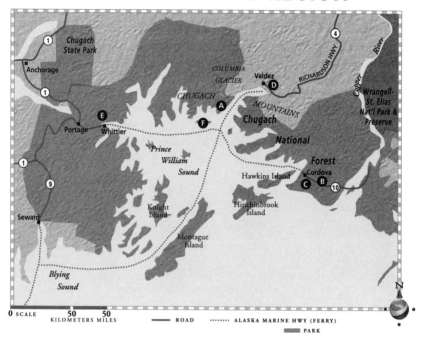

SIGHTS

Ⓐ Columbia Glacier Excursion
Ⓑ Copper River Delta Tour
Ⓒ Cordova
Ⓓ Valdez
Ⓔ Whittier

FOOD

Ⓔ Irma's Outpost

LODGING

Ⓔ Anchor Inn
Ⓔ Captain Ron's Berth and Biscuit
  Hotel
Ⓕ Growler Island Wilderness Camp

CAMPING

Ⓔ Whittier Public Campground

Note: Items with the same letter are located in the same area.

offers a variety of raft, kayak, hiking, and wilderness adventures throughout the state. Day trips in Keystone Canyon, ranging from $35 to $60, include an hour or so on the river.

In Cordova, the **Crater Lake Trail** (2.4 miles, 1,500-foot gain) is a great choice for hikers. From town, follow Power Creek Road 1.5 miles along the north shore of Eyak Lake to just past the airstrip. Head north at the trailhead up a steep contour, with Mount Eyak on your left. Enjoy the lake at trail's end or try for a summit for that extra view.

In Whittier, you can check out **Portage Glacier** from the back side. Take West Camp Road (the only road) west from town, past Army Bunker Road, to the **Portage Pass Trail** (two miles, 700-foot gain). The trail crosses the stream, then climbs easily to a small lake and pass with splendid views of Portage Glacier. Another great Whittier option is to rent a kayak, or sign on for a guided kayak tour, and explore **Passage Canal**. Either choice can be arranged through **Prince William Sound Kayak Center** (Whittier, 907/472-2452, 907/276-7235 in Anchorage).

FOOD

Restaurants in hotels and motels are listed in the Lodgings section, below.

Browse the area near the small boat harbor to find good eateries in Valdez. **Fu Kung** (207 Kobuk St., Valdez, 907/835-5255) boasts a big Chinese menu, tasty and a bit pricey. If you're hungry, try the famous "lasagna and halibut" plate at **Mike's Palace** (201 N. Harbor Dr., Valdez, 907/835-2365), open 11 to 11. Try **Chinooks Books and Coffee** (126 Pioneer Dr., 907/835-4222) for breakfast, lunch, or a cup o' joe, followed by a look at their books and gifts.

A snack shack I really like in Cordova is **Baja Taco** (New Harbor, in the lot below Railroad Street at Nicholoff, Cordova, 907/424-5599). Enjoy delicious Mexican food and outdoor seating—when the weather is good! Another favorite, the **Cookhouse Cafe** (Cannery Row, a half-mile walk from town center, Cordova, 907/424-5926) caters mainly to the fishers and fish-processing workers, serving local seafood, burgers, and "sourdough breakfasts." It's open May through September 5:30 a.m. to close; Sunday brunch is served. The **Killer Whale** (First Street, Cordova, 907/424-7733) is a great little deli café teamed with a bookshop. Omelets, sandwiches, soups, salads, and coffee round out the menu.

In Whittier, the few options at the docks include **Irma's Outpost** (Harbor Triangle, Whittier, 907/472-2461), a delicatessen offering pastries and to-go items.

LODGING

The **Brookside Inn** (1465 Richardson Highway, 2.2 miles east of town, 907/835-9130) is an appealing B&B with a wooded setting and access to a salmon stream right on the property. Rooms range from $90 to $150. The

Keystone Hotel (Hazelet Street at Egan, near the ferry, Valdez, 907/835-3851), open May to October, has been nicely remodeled and features full amenities. Rooms go for $85 to $115. **Totem Inn** (100 Egan Dr, Valdez, 907/835-4443) is a high-grade establishment with rooms for $104 in summer, 30 percent less in winter. The inn features a good family-style restaurant of the same name.

My favorite place in Cordova is the **Cordova Rose Lodge** (1315 Whitshed Rd., a half-mile from town past the camper park, Cordova, 907/424-7673)—a restored barge (on land) and cottage. Rooms are $50 and up. Cordova's answer to a luxury hotel, the **Reluctant Fisherman** (407 Railroad Ave., on the water at a small boat harbor, Cordova, 800/770-3272907/424-3272) features the Reluctant Fisherman Restaurant and bar with a view. Rates range from $85 to $135 in season, $95 to $135 off season. Car rentals are $60 to $75 per day, unlimited mileage.

In Whittier, **Captain Ron's Berth & Biscuit Hostel** (Whittier, 907/235-4368 winter, 907/472-2393 summer) is a good budget lodging choice. **Anchor Inn** (Whittier Street at Depot, Whittier, 907/472-2354) is a dive—though it features a bar, grocery, and coin laundry. Stay here as a last resort.

For a great wilderness lodge experience, try **Growler Island Wilderness Camp** (in Valdez, 800/992-1297, 907/835-4731, or www.kenaifjords.com/princewilliamsound), which is associated with Prince William Sound Cruises and Tours. You can take a boat out from either Valdez or Whittier, and return to either town to continue a journey across the sound. Kayaking, hiking, and glacier touring are among the options offered. A night at the lodge goes for $100, including meals, $75 for ages 4 to 12, under 3 free. Round-trip or continuing boat passage costs $120, $70 for children, guided boat tour included.

CAMPING

At **Valdez Bear Paw Camper Park** (North Harbor Drive at Meals Avenue, Seward, 907/835-2530), tentsites cost $15 to $17, hookups $20 to $22. Located at the small boat harbor in town, this is a good place to stay if you need to catch an early morning ferry.

Decent, convenient, and cheap, **Whittier Public Campground** (Glacier Street on Whittier Creek, above town, Whittier) offers sites for $5.

9
MATSU

Northeast of Anchorage is the region known as "MatSu," named for the two rivers that dominate the area. The Matanuska River begins at the foot of the famous Matanuska Glacier, then runs east past Sutton and Palmer before draining into Knik Arm. The Susitna River flows south from the Alaska Range through a wide basin and into Cook inlet. The lowlands east of the Susitna encompass scores of lakes, hundreds of scattered homes, and the towns of Wasilla and Palmer.

Palmer, the long-established center of the state's primary agricultural region, was settled by homesteaders in the early 1900s. In 1935, a New Deal program brought 200 families north to attempt to farm the basin as part of the Matanuska Valley Colony. Descendants of those who succeeded still live in the area. Much of the famous giant Alaskan produce is grown here, thanks to the months of unending daylight. Today, Palmer is a bustling town worth a visit.

Wasilla began as a railroad town serving miners in the Talkeetna Mountains; it is named after a Dena'ina chief. As you drive through, you'll keep waiting to arrive—only to find after a few miles that the businesses are thinning out and you're out of town. Recently, the town has grown rapidly, an extension of greater Anchorage. The original, tight-knit settlement has all but disappeared, replaced by the stretch of new homes and businesses that comprise a burgeoning bedroom community of Anchorage.

MATSU REGION

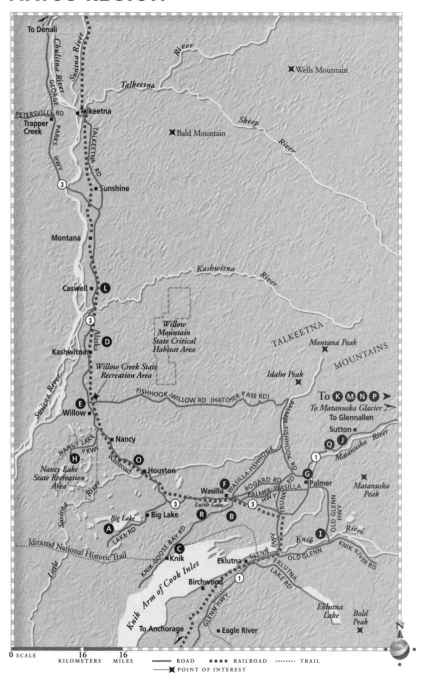

To Denali

Chulitna River

Susitna River

GEORGE

Talkeetna River

River

× Wells Mountain

PETERSVILLE RD Talkeetna

Trapper
Creek

PARKS HWY

TALKEETNA RD

Sheep

River

× Bald Mountain

③

Sunshine

Montana

Kashwitna River

Caswell **L**

③

Alaska

Kashwitna **D**

Willow
Mountain
State Critical
Habitat Area

TALKEETNA

Montana Peak ×

MOUNTAINS

Willow Creek State
Recreation Area

Idaho Peak ×

FISHHOOK-WILLOW RD (HATCHER PASS RD)

To **K M N P**

Susitna River

E
Willow

To Matanuska Glacier
To Glennallen

PALMER-FISHHOOK RD

Sutton

NANCY LAKE PKWY

Nancy

Q **J**

Matanuska River

H

Railroad

O

Houston

①

Nancy Lake
State Recreation
Area

River

WASILLA-FISHHOOK

BOGARD RD

G

Palmer

Matanuska
Peak ×

F

Wasilla

PALMER-WASILLA
HWY

OLD GLENN HWY

③

TRUNK RD

Lucile Lake

③

Iditarod National Historic Trail

Big Lake ■ Big Lake

LAKE RD

R

B

Knik

I

River

KNIK RIVER RD

Little

River

KNIK GOOSE BAY RD

A

C

Knik

Eklutna

GLENN HWY

OLD GLENN

EKLUTNA LAKE RD

Knik Arm of Cook Inlet

Birchwood ■

①

Eklutna
Lake

Bold
Peak ×

GLENN HWY

To Anchorage

■ Eagle River

N

0 SCALE
KILOMETERS
16

16
MILES

—— ROAD   ▪▪▪▪ RAILROAD   ·········· TRAIL

——✖ POINT OF INTEREST

A PERFECT DAY IN MATSU

Head out to the edges of MatSu to explore the wildlands. Take your time on the Glenn Highway; check out the roadside Alpine Historical Park in Sutton, poke around the fiercely independent community of Chickaloon, and drop down to the Glacier Park Resort for a close-up look at the Matanuska Glacier. Perhaps you're up for a long day winding through Hatcher Pass— enjoy a picnic by the Little Susitna River, tour the ruins of Independence Mine State Historic Park, and pause often to amble and take photos. Or maybe you'd prefer to head up the Parks Highway, visiting Nancy Lake Recreation Area for a two-hour paddle, or trying your luck fishing in Willow Creek.

For information on the entire MatSu region, contact the MatSu Visitor Center (Mile 35.5 Parks Highway, 907/746-5000, www.alaskavisit.com).

SIGHTS

- **A** Big Lake
- **B** Iditarod Trail Sled Dog Race Headquarters
- **C** Knik Museum & Mushers Hall of Fame
- **D** Lucky Husky Racing Kennel
- **E** Miners Last Stand Museum
- **F** Museum of Alaska Transportation & Industry
- **G** Musk Ox Farm
- **H** Nancy Lake State Recreation Area
- **F** Old Wasilla
- **G** Palmer
- **I** Williams' Reindeer Farm

FOOD

- **F** Cheppo's Fiesta Restaurant
- **F** Deli Restaurant & Bakery
- **G** Frontier Coffee Shop
- **G** Mary's Fish & Burgers
- **G** Pioneer's Pizza

LODGING

- **J** Chickaloon Bed & Breakfast
- **G** Colony Inn
- **G** Fairview Motel & Restaurant
- **K** Glacier Park Resort
- **G** Hatcher Pass Bed & Breakfast
- **F** Lake Lucille Inn/Best Western
- **F** Roadside Inn
- **G** Rose Ridge Bed & Breakfast
- **L** Sheep Creek Lodge
- **M** Tundra Rose Bed & Breakfast
- **B** Willow Trading Post Lodge
- **F** Windbreak

CAMPING

- **A** Big Lake North State Recreation Site
- **A** Big Lake South State Recreation Site
- **N** Bonnie Lake State Recreation Site
- **J** King Mountain State Recreation Site
- **O** Little Susitna River Campground
- **P** Long Lake State Recreation Site
- **K** Matanuska Glacier State Recreation Site
- **Q** Moose Creek State Recreation Area
- **R** Rocky Lake State Recreation Site
- **B** Willow Creek State Recreation Area

Note: Items with the same letter are located in the same area.

ORIENTATION

The populated area of MatSu spills out of the Matanuska valley, then swings northward between the Talkeetna Mountains and Susitna River. The Glenn Highway and Parks Highway combine as the major artery through it all.

Central Palmer is laid out in a grid a few blocks wide, framed by the Matanuska River to the east and Glenn Highway to the west. The Palmer Visitor Center (723 South Valley Way, downtown by the tracks, 907/745-2880) is open daily, May to September, from 8 to 7.

The businesses of Wasilla are stretched out along the Parks Highway, surrounded by scattered pockets of homes. For information and area history, visit the Dorothy G. Page Museum & Visitor Center (323 Main Street, Wasilla, 907/373-9071).

PALMER AND WASILLA SIGHTSEEING HIGHLIGHTS

★★★ MUSK OX FARM
Mile 50.1 Glenn Highway, Palmer, 907/745-4151, www.muskoxfarm.org

This private, nonprofit farm maintains a captive herd of musk ox, once hunted nearly to extinction in the state. Qiviut (KEE-vee-uht)—the soft fur from the animal's underside—is harvested from the herd and used in the creation of traditional textile products by subsistence thread makers and craftspeople. The herd also serves as breeding stock for the reintroduction of musk ox to the wild, creating new herds and adding to those now established on Nunivak Island, the Arctic Coast, and the North Slope. Enjoy a close look at these magnificent beasts.

Details: Mother's Day–Sept daily 10–6; tours begin every 30 minutes. $8 adults, less for seniors and children. (1 hour)

★★★ WILLIAMS' REINDEER FARM
Mile 11.5 Old Glenn Highway, seven miles south of Palmer, 907/745-4000, www.corecom.net/~reindeer

More than 300 reindeer (essentially domesticated caribou) roam across this farm south of Palmer. You can also view moose, elk, and Sitka blacktail deer. It's a great stop for families. Visitors can feed and pet the reindeer and take horseback rides. Guided tours are offered on the farm.

Details: May–Sept daily 10–6. $5 adults, less for seniors and children. (1 hour)

★★ **IDITAROD TRAIL SLED DOG RACE HEADQUARTERS**
Mile 2.2 Knik Road, south of Wasilla, 800/478-5155, 907/376-5155, www.iditarod.com
At the official headquarters of "the last great race on Earth," you can get a look at a team of sled dogs and enjoy a conversation with a musher and race veteran. Displays on race history are featured; a gift shop peddles souvenirs.
Details: Open year-round, in summer daily 8–7. Free. (1 hour)

★★ **KNIK MUSEUM & MUSHERS HALL OF FAME**
Mile 13.9 Knik Road, south of Wasilla, 907/376-7755
Musher portraits, old racing gear, and race history exhibits are housed in a restored turn-of-the-century building. The museum also features artifacts and archives of the old gold-rush town of Knik, which thrived here from about 1898 to 1916.
Details: June–Aug Wed–Sun 12–6. $2 adults, $1.50 seniors, free for small children. (30 minutes)

★★ **MUSEUM OF ALASKA TRANSPORTATION & INDUSTRY**
3800 W. Neuser Dr., from Mile 47 Parks Highway, Wasilla, 907/376-1211, www.alaska.net/~rmorris/mati4.htm
Building and grounds are dotted with wonderful transport gems, including trains, planes, automobiles, and various memorabilia. True buffs could spend hours exploring.
Details: May–Sept daily 9–6 (closed Sun and Mon in winter). $5 adults, $4 students and seniors, $12 family, under 8 free. (1½ hours)

★★ **PALMER**
A fine town for a look about. Get a walking-tour pamphlet at the visitors center—or even a free loaner bike! After perusing the shops and perhaps grabbing a bite to eat, drop by the **Alaska State Fairgrounds** (2075 Glenn Highway, Palmer, 800/850-3247, 907/745-4827, www.akstatefair.org). If your timing is right, you can enjoy the fair (last week in August through Labor Day), or take a walk through the collected historic structures of Colony Village.
Details: Visitors center, Elmwood Avenue at South Valley Way, downtown by tracks. (1 hour)

★ OLD WASILLA
323 Main St., Wasilla, 907/373-9071
Right behind the Dorothy G. Page Museum & Visitors Center on Main Street, **Town Site Park** features seven preserved historic buildings from Wasilla's past. If you're in Wasilla on a summer Wednesday between 4 and 7 p.m., stop by the park for the weekly farmer's market. The Page Museum itself displays heritage exhibits. Tourist information and literature are available.
Details: *Open daily in summer.* (1 hour)

PARKS HIGHWAY SIGHTSEEING HIGHLIGHTS/WASILLA TO TALKEETNA

The Parks Highway grows progressively wilder as it leaves the sprawl of Wasilla heading north. In the lowlands, you can access fishing and recreation areas, vacation cabins, and scattered highway services. Beyond Willow, human habitation thins, traffic spreads out, the land rises, and you gradually ease into "wild Alaska" mode—unless, of course, you're headed south, in which case you'll experience the opposite reality. The route's interesting attractions include the following.

★★★ NANCY LAKE STATE RECREATION AREA
Ranger station, Mile 1.3 Nancy Lake Parkway, from Mile 67.2 Parks Highway, 907/495-6273
This large recreation area encompasses a region of low, forest-covered hills interspersed with numerous lakes. Hiking trailheads, canoe put-ins, and a 98-site campground are reached via the 6.5-mile park road. Of special note is the Lynx Lake Loop, an eight-mile canoe route that links a chain of lakes. Several reservable cabins are found on islands and lakeshores, offering accommodations to overnight canoeists and hikers.
Details: *Public access. Canoe rentals available from Tippecanoe (Willow, 907/495-6688). (2 hour picnic or a multi-day trip)*

★★ BIG LAKE
Many locals choose Big Lake—the region's largest and most developed recreational lake—to enjoy vacation cabins, fishing, and boating. Take the Big Lake Road turnoff from the Parks Highway about seven miles west of Wasilla. Services are available in the small business district on Big Lake Road. The area supports three campgrounds (see

Camping, below), and a few lodges operate along the lakeshore. The **Alaska State Fish Hatchery** beyond Rocky Lake offers free tours. Along some backroads, you'll see the scars of a conflagration that consumed thousands of acres of spruce forest and destroyed several structures in 1996.

Details: *Public access. Information from Big Lake Chamber of Commerce, Big Lake, 907/892-6109. (half day minimum)*

★★ **LUCKY HUSKY RACING KENNEL**
Mile 80 Parks Highway, Willow, 907/495-6470,
www.luckyhusky.com
This convenient facility offers a glimpse into the world of sled-dog racing. Touristy but educational, visitors can even take a ride in a sled—a wheeled sled in summer.

Details: *May–Sept Wed–Mon 10–6, by reservation otherwise. $24 sled ride and tour, $6 tour alone, $60 30-minute fall ride with training demonstration. (1 hour)*

★ **MINERS LAST STAND MUSEUM**
Mile 68.7 Parks Highway, Willow, 907/495-6479
As you drive along the Parks Highway, you'll easily spot this thoroughly Alaskan creation that blends gift shop, museum, and theme attraction. The memory of prospector-turned-notorious-gangster Soapy Smith is preserved in displays. At least pull over for a long look.

Details: *Open daily in summer. $3. (30 minutes)*

FITNESS AND RECREATION

Opportunities abound for outdoor adventure in and around MatSu.

Castle Mountain Outfitters (Chickaloon, 907/745-6427) offers short trail rides and extended horsepack trips up into the Talkeetna Mountains. Nearby in Sutton, **North Star Treks** (Sutton, 907/745-3144) sponsors guided hikes, cross-country ski trips, all-women trips, and custom adventures in the Talkeetna and Chugach Mountains.

Several companies offer trips up the Knik River, which drains from Knik Glacier into Knik Arm. **Hunter Creek Outfitters** (Palmer, 907/745-1577) offers day and overnight guided float trips and kayak rentals. **Knik Glacier Adventures** (Palmer, 907/746-5133) features airboat tours, cabin rentals, and llama treks.

Planning to visit during the winter? How about a dogsled trip with the mushers of **Lucky Husky Racing Kennel** (Willow, 907/495-6470)? **Rafter**

T Ranch Trail Rides (Palmer, 907/745-8768) features winter dog mushing and sleigh rides and summer horseback riding in the Hatcher Pass area.

In the Nancy Lake and the Susitna basin, kayak rentals and tours are offered by **Susitna Expeditions** (Big Lake, 800/891-6916), while canoe and raft rentals are available from **Tippecanoe** (Willow, 907/495-6688).

Near Wasilla, the **Crevasse Moraine Trail System** (seven total miles, much shorter hikes possible, no significant gain) is popular with runners, hikers, and cross-country skiers. Several interconnecting trails wind through glacial moraine deposits. From Mile 1.98 of Palmer-Wasilla Highway, take Loma Prieta Drive to the end.

FOOD

Many of the Lodging listings below also identify cafés and restaurants. Keep them in mind, too.

In downtown Palmer, the friendly **Frontier Coffee Shop** (West Evergreen, Palmer) is open daily 6 a.m. to 10 p.m. At **Mary's Fish & Burgers** (535 W. Evergreen, Palmer, 907/745-0190) you'll find—surprise, surprise—fish and burgers along with other American favorites. Tasty **Pioneer Pizza** (Palmer Wasilla Highway near Trunk Road, Palmer, 907/745-5400) is open 11 to 10 weekdays, until 11 on weekends.

The usual fast-food chains and highway-style eateries punctuate the Parks Highway in Wasilla. The **Deli Restaurant & Bakery** (185 E. Parks Highway, Wasilla, 907/376-2914) serves breakfast and lunch fare such as deli sandwiches and Italian dishes. It's open Monday through Saturday year-round. Right on the highway, **Cheppo's Fiesta Restaurant** (731 W. Parks Highway, Wasilla, 907/373,5656) serves Mexican dishes.

LODGING

Palmer features several lodging possibilities, including the **Colony Inn** (325 Elmwood St., Palmer, 800/478-7666 in Alaska, 907/745-3330). Once the Matanuska Valley Colony teachers dorm, it is now more comfortable. Rooms are $80 to $100. If you're looking for a little nightlife, the **Fairview Motel & Restaurant** (Mile 40.5 Glenn Highway, Palmer, 907/745-1505) hosts live local bands in the hotel bar. Rates range from $50 to $65 summer, $45 to $60 winter.

In Wasilla, a nice choice is the **Lake Lucille Inn/Best Western** (1300 W. Lake Lucille Dr., Wasilla, 800/528-1234, 907/373-1776), with 54 rooms (suites and smoke-free available), a restaurant and lounge, fitness center, Jacuzzi, and even a lighted ice rink ($95 to $125). Decent, basic rooms for $45 and up are offered at the **Roadside Inn** (Mile 45.9 Parks Highway, Wasilla, 907/373-4646), which also has a restaurant. Rooms at the **Windbreak** (Mile 49.5 Parks Highway, Wasilla, 907/376-4109) go for $65. The motel has an on-site café. West of Wasilla on the Parks Highway is the **Willow Trading Post Lodge** (Willow Station Road, turn at Mile 69.5 Parks Highway, left at post office after tracks, Willow, 907/495-6457). This country lodge has a good location, lots of character, a cozy restaurant and bar, and friendly hosts. Rooms and cabins range from $50 to $80. Even if you don't spend the night at the **Sheep Creek Lodge** (Mile 88.2 Parks Highway, Willow, 907/495-6227), stop for a meal or even just a look inside this impressive log structure. Primitive cabins are $30 and up. Camping is available.

The B&B Association of Alaska, MatSu Chapter (Wasilla, 800/401-7444), represents more than 30 area bed-and-breakfasts, plus cabins, host homes, suites, and apartments.

Along the Glenn Highway east of Palmer, the **Chickaloon Bed & Breakfast** (Mile 76.5 Glenn Highway, four miles from General Store, Chickaloon, 907/745-1155, 907/355-6573) features a large, private cottage with a sundeck and mountain view. Rates are $85 to $105. You can stay near the terminus of the Matanuska Glacier at the **Glacier Park Resort** (Glenn Highway East, Palmer, 907-745-2534), where rooms are $50. Explore Matanuska Glacier on non-guided walk-in trips or on guided tours ($6.50) by appointment. A campground and gift shop are located here as well. The closest B&B to Matanuska Glacier is the **Tundra Rose Bed & Breakfast** (Mile 109.5 Glenn Highway, base of Sheep Mountain, 800/315-5865 in Alaska, 907/745-5865), offering good access to Dall sheep viewing. Rates are $90 for a double, $10 for each additional guest.

If you're heading to or through Hatcher Pass, two B&Bs are on the way. The cabins of **Rose Ridge Bed & Breakfast** (Palmer, 907/745-8604) include private entrance, private bath, and continental or full breakfast on a quiet, wooded five acres. The brand new **Hatcher Pass B&B** (Palmer, 907/745-6788, www.AlaskaOutdoors.com/HPBB) features cozy log cabins with private baths and kitchenettes. Breakfast is served to you in the cabin. Cabins run $65 single, $75 double, $10 for each additional person.

CAMPING

Near Wasilla are the campgrounds around Big Lake. The **Big Lake North State Recreation Site** and **Big Lake South State Recreation Site** (Big

Lake Road, from Parks Highway, seven miles west of Wasilla) both offer campgrounds and lake access. Nearby **Rocky Lake State Recreation Site** also has camping.

A couple of public camping options lie along the Parks Highway west and north of Wasilla. **Little Susitna River Campground** (Mile 57.3 Parks Highway) is an 86-site developed campground operated by the City of Houston. **Willow Creek State Recreation Area** (follow the road at Mile 70.8 Parks Highway four miles) offers $10 sites and creek access.

Between Palmer and the Matanuska Glacier on the Glenn Highway, five State Recreation Areas feature campsites. **Moose Creek State Recreation Area** (Mile 54.6 Glenn Highway) has 12 campsites ($10 fee). There's a nice campground on the banks of the Matanuska River with 22 sites ($10) at **King Mountain State Recreation Site** (Mile 76.1 Glenn Highway). Turn up a short gravel road to reach the eight free campsites of **Bonnie Lake State Recreation Site** (Mile 83.2 Glenn Highway). One of my favorites on the route because of the great canyon scenery is **Long Lake State Recreation Site** (Mile 85.3 Glenn Highway), featuring nine free campsites near the lake. Another fine option is **Matanuska Glacier State Recreation Site** (Mile 101 Glenn Highway), with 12 campsites ($10), short trails, and excellent glacier views.

Scenic Route: Hatcher Pass and Independence Mine

Most Alaska roads seem to cross over mountain passes reluctantly. The Hatcher Pass Road seems to do it just for fun. Originally an access road built to serve the mines in the Talkeetna Mountains, the road now offers travelers an avenue through high peaks and history. If you're driving the Parks Highway between Cook Inlet and Denali and have an extra four hours to burn, opt for this wonderful alternative route. The crisp air and views at the top of the 3,886-foot pass are splendid.

A highlight of the route is **Independence Mine State Historic Park** (information: Anchorage 907/269-8400, Wasilla 907/745-3975; park visitors center, park entrance, open summer 11 to 7, 907/745-2827). Robert Lee Hatcher staked the first gold claim along Willow Creek in 1906. It wasn't long before companies were mining the source lodes around Hatcher Pass. In the peak year of 1941, the Alaska-Pacific Consolidated Mining Company (largest of those working the pass) had 83 claims and produced almost 35,000 ounces of gold. The last of the mines closed in 1951. Independence Mine, one of the original sites before consolidation, was secured as a State Historic Park in 1980. Visitors can wander among the buildings, machinery,

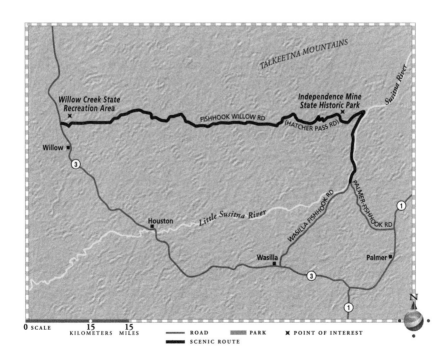

shafts, tailings, and ruins—all in a magnificent mountain setting above treeline. Tours are offered at 1:30 and 3:30, with a 4:30 tour added on weekends and holidays.

Recreational opportunities abound around Hatcher Pass in the Talkeetna Mountains. Experienced river runners can match their kayaking skills to the white water of the Little Susitna. Downhill and cross-country skiing are winter options. Excellent trails and ridge routes allow access to the backcountry and high peaks. For complete information, contact the Alaska Department of Natural Resources (MatSu Headquarters, Division of Parks and Outdoor Recreation, Wasilla, 907/745-3975).

10
ANCHORAGE AND VICINITY

Arrive in Anchorage after days in the backcountry and it will seem familiar. The strip malls, chain stores, office towers, tract homes, and fast-food joints of "Everycity" are knit together with good old all-American traffic! Anchorage serves as a major international transportation hub. The busy airport handles flights from around the north Pacific. Merrill Field and Lake Hood Seaplane Base are bustling centers of the small-plane activity that is such a big part of intrastate transport. Even so, 250,000 people are only 250,000 people. Twenty minutes and a little luck will take you from one end of town to the other, and all you have to do to see the edge of the city center is to peer a couple of blocks down a side street.

Downtown Anchorage hosts arts facilities, hotels and restaurants, nightspots, parks, coffeeshops, and bookstores. One of Alaska's finest museums is located here, as is the Alaska Experience Center, which shows IMAX films of state wonders. The city is also home to a decent botanical garden and a good zoo exhibiting native Alaskan and other wildlife.

Recreational opportunities for Anchorage residents are plentiful and outstanding. More than 120 miles of bike trails weave throughout the city. City parks, greenbelts, and the 11-mile Tony Knowles Coastal Path offer places to walk, jog, canoe, cross-country ski, and just take it easy, right in town. Several excellent trails lace the foothills of Chugach State Park. Birding opportunities exist along protected coastal flats. The Alaska

ANCHORAGE

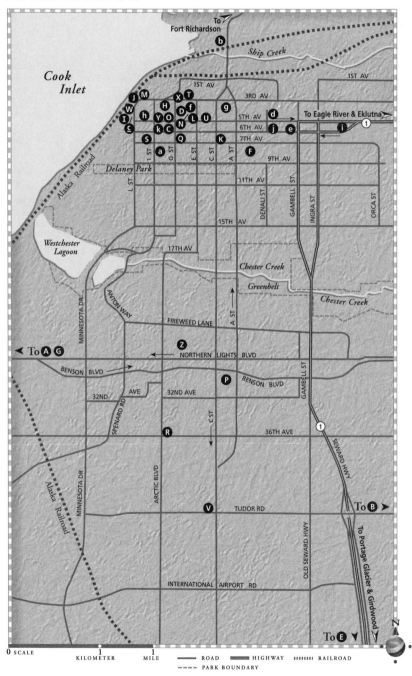

classics of fishing and flightseeing are easily available, while winter brings skiing, skating, snowmobiling, and dog mushing. You'll even find some very good golf courses.

A PERFECT DAY IN ANCHORAGE

In the morning, pick an outdoor activity that suits you, such as an easy stroll through the Alaska Zoo, Potter Marsh, or the Botanical Garden, or an off-trail walk along the high ridges of Chugach State Park. In the afternoon, explore downtown Anchorage, saving an hour for an IMAX show at the Alaska Experience Center. Duck into shops, visit the Public Lands Information Center, look out over Cook Inlet from Resolution Park, and visit the excellent Anchorage Museum. In the evening, enjoy your best—and perhaps only—chance for fine dining in Alaska. Choose from the list of great restaurants below, then, after dinner, ascend to one of the hotel-top lounges for a drink and a long view in the lingering twilight. If you'd like to go late, Anchorage nightlife can satisfy many preferences. Enjoy.

SIGHTS

- **A** Alaska Aviation Heritage Museum
- **B** Alaska Botanical Gardens
- **C** Alaska Experience Center
- **D** Alaska Public Lands Information Center
- **E** Alaska Zoo
- **F** Anchorage Museum of History and Art
- **G** Earthquake Park
- **H** Imaginarium
- **I** Oscar Anderson House
- **J** Resolution Park and Captain Cook Monument
- **K** Wolf Song of Alaska

FOOD

- **L** Downtown Deli & Cafe
- **M** Elevation 92
- **N** F Street Station
- **O** Glacier Brew House
- **P** Harry's
- **Q** Humpys Great Alaskan Alehouse

FOOD (continued)

- **R** Jen's
- **S** La Mex
- **T** Marx Brothers' Cafe
- **U** Phyllis's Cafe and Salmon Bake
- **V** Sea Galley & Pepper Mill Restaurant
- **W** Simon and Seafort's
- **X** Snow Goose
- **Y** Thai Cuisine
- **Z** V.I.P. Restaurant

LODGING

- **a** Anchorage Youth Hostel
- **b** Comfort Inn
- **c** Copper Whale Inn
- **d** Days Inn
- **e** Econo Lodge
- **f** Hilton Anchorage Hotel
- **g** Holiday Inn
- **h** Hotel Captain Cook
- **i** Rodeway Inn
- **j** Sheraton
- **k** Westmark

ORIENTATION

Anchorage occupies the tip of a peninsula set between two branches of Cook Inlet–Knik Arm to the north and Turnagain Arm to the south. The Turnagain shore is steep, largely uninhabitable land, much of it part of Chugach State Park and Chugach National Forest. Knik Arm has gentler shores that host the bedroom communities of Eagle River, Peters Creek, and Birchwood. The Alaska and Aleutian Ranges are visible across Cook Inlet to the west, while on a clear day Denali can be seen, small but presidential on the horizon, 140 miles away.

Downtown is roughly laid out in a grid pattern. The Glenn Highway ends in the heart of town, splitting into two one-ways: Fifth Avenue (westbound) and Sixth Avenue (eastbound). The cross streets (north-south) running through much of downtown are assigned letters, with Fourth and F roughly at the center of it all. Anchorage's main north-south route is Seward Highway, a freeway in the south part of town that splits into two one-ways downtown: Ingra Street (northbound) and Gambell Street (southbound). Use a map to navigate the rest of the city. The People Mover is a fair bus system you can use to get around town (907/343-6543).

ANCHORAGE SIGHTSEEING HIGHLIGHTS

★★★★ ALASKA EXPERIENCE CENTER
705 W. Sixth Ave., Anchorage, 907/276-3730,
www.alaska.net/~alaskaxp/
Perhaps my favorite Anchorage attraction, Alaska Experience is an IMAX theater with a three-story, curved screen that puts you right into the action. Alaska the Greatland is one of the 40-minute films

---

AMBLING ANCHORAGE
If you want to get a feel for the streets of Anchorage, take a walking tour. You can get a walking-tour map at the Log Cabin Visitor Information Center (downtown, Fourth Avenue and F Street, 907/274-3531). The center is open 7:30 to 7 in the summer, 8 to 6 in May and September, and 9 to 4 during the rest of the year.

---

that might be showing when you visit. IMAX fools your brain into believing you're on a swooping flight through tight canyons and over high passes. Just close your eyes if you get a little queasy.

Also at the center, the Alaska Earthquake Exhibit features exhibits, murals, a movie, and a floor that shakes you in your seat. *Details: Open in summer daily 9–9, spring and fall 11–7, winter 12–6. $7 adult IMAX, $5 adult earthquake exhibit, $4 children IMAX or exhibit, $10 and $7 for both. (1 hour)*

★★★★ ANCHORAGE MUSEUM OF HISTORY AND ART
121 W. Seventh Ave., Anchorage, 907/343-4326, www.ci .anchorage.ak.us/Services/Departments/Culture/Museum/
This excellent museum offers a fine permanent art collection and 20 touring exhibits annually. On the second floor, the 15,000-square-foot Alaska Gallery displays artifacts and dioramas related to the state's native and settlement history. A Children's Gallery has hands-on opportunities for young ones. Daily native dance performances are presented in the theater. A pleasant café and museum shop round out the scene. *Details: Mid-May–mid-Sept daily 9–6; winter Tue–Sat 10–6, Sun 1–5. $5 adults, under 18 free. (1½ hours)*

★★★ ALASKA PUBLIC LANDS INFORMATION CENTER
Old Federal Building, Fourth Avenue and F Street, Anchorage, 907/271-2737, www.nps.gov/aplic
Complete information is available here for all of Alaska's state and federal parks, preserves, refuges, and other public lands. Similar centers are located in Tok and Fairbanks. Exhibits, videos, a theater, and a bookstore are found here as well. It's a must-stop for the wise explorer. Call for a schedule of special programs. *Details: Open summer daily 9–5:30, Mon–Fri 10–5:30 rest of the year. (30 minutes)*

★★★ ALASKA ZOO
4731 O'Malley Rd., east from Seward Highway, Anchorage, 907/346-2133, www.goworldnet.com/akzoo.htm
Elephants in Alaska? Although this zoo specializes in native species, it houses several exotic animals as well. Many of the native animals were originally injured or orphaned and placed here after being rescued and deemed unsuitable for reintroduction to the wild. Two hours is all it takes to see this compact but well-endowed facility.

Details: *Open summer daily 9–6, Oct–Apr Wed–Mon 10–5. $7 adults, $6 seniors, $5 ages 12–17, $4 under 12, under 3 free. (2 hours)*

★★ ALASKA AVIATION HERITAGE MUSEUM
South shore of Lake Hood Seaplane Base, 907/248-5325, www.alaska.net/~aahm/index.htm
Military and pioneer exhibits supplement the 21 rare and historical bush planes preserved here. A 60-seat theater offers a short film. Visitors can observe the traffic at the Lake Hood Seaplane Base adjacent to the museum.
Details: *Take International Airport Road west to Aircraft Drive. Open May 15–Sept 15 daily 9–6, in winter Tue–Sat 10–4. (1 hour)*

★★ IMAGINARIUM
737 W. Fifth Ave., Anchorage, 907/276-3179, www.imaginarium.org
Hands-on exhibits and activities make this a good, educational choice for kids of all ages. Exhibits include Bubbles, the Marine Life Touch Tank, Polar Bear Lair, Physics of Toys, and more.
Details: *Open daily 10–6. $5 adults, $4 ages 65 and up, $4 ages 2–12, under 2 free. (1¹/₂ hours)*

★★ POTTER MARSH
Mile 117.4 Seward Highway, Anchorage, www.dnr.state.ak.us/parks/asp/relasite.htm
Potter Marsh is part of the Anchorage Coastal Wildlife Refuge that protects coastal wetlands and tide flats along the shores of Cook Inlet. Boardwalks allow visitors to access bird habitat and to observe the spawning run in a salmon stream. The marsh, parking lot, and walks border the Seward Highway to the east where the road meets Turnagain Arm, just south of Anchorage. A new nature center is planned for the bluffs above the marsh.
Details: *Public access. (45 minutes)*

★★ WOLF SONG OF ALASKA
Sixth Avenue and C Street, Anchorage, 907/346-3073, www.wolfsongalaska.org
This combination wolf exhibit/education center and gift shop is operated by Wolf Song, a nonprofit organization "dedicated to promoting an understanding of the wolf through educational pro-

grams, research, and increased public awareness." Stop in to increase your appreciation of the wolf and what it means to the northlands.
Details: *Open daily 9–5. Free. (30 minutes)*

★ **ALASKA BOTANICAL GARDENS**
Campbell Airstrip Road and Tudor Road,
Anchorage, 907/770-3692
Plants from a variety of Alaska eco-regions are cultivated here. Although still under development, the two completed gardens feature paths with interpretive signs. Call regarding guided tours.
Details: *Open daily 9–9. Take Tudor Road east, turn right on Campbell Airstrip Road, park in the Benny Benson School lot. Donation. (1 hour)*

★ **BELUGA POINT**
Mile 110.3 Seward Highway
Pull out the binoculars and scan the waters for the white beluga whales sometimes in the vicinity. You also might see one of the periodic "bore tides" that race up Turnagain Arm under certain conditions. An interpretive display offers information on both.
Details: *(15 minutes)*

★ **EARTHQUAKE PARK**
Northern Lights Boulevard, west of Wisconsin Street
When the great earthquake struck on Good Friday in 1964, a huge section of land on the coast southwest of downtown subsided dramatically, destroying 75 homes. The park preserves the area, now a tree-covered landscape of broken ridges and troughs barely above sea level. Though an interpretive display tells the story and short trails offer access to coastal views, the thick vegetation that has grown since the disaster almost completely obscures the destruction.
Details: *Take Northern Lights Boulevard west, past Wisconsin Street. Public access. (15 minutes–1 hour)*

★ **OSCAR ANDERSON HOUSE**
420 M St., Anchorage, 907/274-2336,
www.alaskan.com/akencinfo/oscar.html
Swedish immigrant Oscar Anderson—the self-proclaimed "18th person to set foot in Anchorage"—built this home in 1915. The first

wood-frame house in Anchorage, it is the only historic home in the city that serves as a museum. Admission includes a guided tour.

Details: *Mid-May–Sept daily 12– 4. $2 adults, $1 seniors and ages 5–12. (1 hour)*

★ POTTER SECTION HOUSE STATE HISTORIC SITE
Mile 115.3 Seward Highway, 907/345-5014

Potter was the "camptown" that hosted the workers who laid the tracks for the Alaska Railroad routes south of Anchorage. Located just south of Anchorage along the Seward Highway, the site features railcars, historical items, a trailhead, and the headquarters of the vast Chugach State Park that encompasses much of the land east of the city.

Details: *Open summer daily 8–4:30, winter Mon–Fri 8–4:30. (30 minutes)*

★ RESOLUTION PARK AND CAPTAIN COOK MONUMENT
Third Avenue and L Street, Anchorage

Make sure to visit this small waterfront park on your walk through downtown Anchorage. Enjoy the views under the watchful eye of Captain James Cook's statue. Cook sailed up the inlet that bears his name in May of 1778.

Details: *Public access. (15 minutes)*

GREATER ANCHORAGE SIGHTSEEING HIGHLIGHTS

★★★★ CHUGACH STATE PARK
Headquarters, Mile 115 Seward Highway, 907/345-5014; Visitors Center, Mile 12 Eagle River Road, exit Mile 13.4 Glenn Highway, 907/694-2108; Eklutna Ranger Station, Mile 10 Eklutna Lake Road, 907/688-0908, www.highalaska.com/Guide/Southcentral/csp-info.html

As the nation's third-largest state park, this stunning park preserves a sizable portion of the Chugach Mountains and serves as Anchorage's eastern boundary. Glaciers crown peaks in the east, while long valleys drain generally northwestward into Cook Inlet. With 30 designated hiking trails, several mountain-bike routes, and popular watersports locations, recreational opportunities abound.

To the north along Knik Arm, the Eagle River Road follows the Eagle River a dozen miles into the mountains, providing access to trails and a popular river run. Further east, another access road runs from Eklutna to beautiful Eklutna Lake, which features a campground, easy trails, and picnic spots. Ship Creek and other streams provide similar access from Anchorage, while city streets lead to the heights for popular climbs and ridge walks.

A couple of trails are mentioned under Fitness and Recreation, below, but you might want to stop for information at a park office for a complete list.

Details: *Visitors center open daily in summer 10–5; headquarters open Mon–Fri 8–4:30; call for Eklutna Ranger Station hours. Lifetime Adventures (Anchorage, 800/952-8624, 907/746-4644) offers kayak trips on Eklutna Lake. Half-day raft or kayak trips on the Eagle River and other trips are offered by Midnight Sun River Runners (Anchorage, 800/825-7238, www.sinbad.net/~msrr); "the physically challenged are welcome." (half to full day)*

★★★★ **ALYESKA TRAMWAY/GIRDWOOD**
1000 Arlberg Ave., from Mile 90 Seward Highway, Girdwood, 800/880-3880, 907/754-1111, www.alyeskaresort.com; Girdwood information at 907/222-7669, www.girdwoodalaska.com
Girdwood is a classic ski town, home both summer and winter to people who spend a lot of time outdoors. Mount Alyeska and the popular Alyeska Ski Resort are the primary attractions for the vacationers who stay in the chalets, cabins, and condos scattered throughout the valley. Dominating the scene is the huge Alyeska Prince Hotel, perhaps the premier resort in the state (see Lodging, below). Stop in the Girdwood Townsquare for a walkabout and snack. For area information and trail maps, visit the Chugach National Forest Office (Monarch Mine Road, just north of railroad crossing, Girdwood, 907/783-3242).

A gondola ride to the 2,300-foot level of Mount Alyeska is great fun any time of year. Depending on when you visit, you can enjoy the ski runs or hiking trails, or simply take in the views. Dine at the lovely Seven Glaciers Restaurant or munch more casually at the Glacier Express snack shop (call 907/754-3500 for all Alyeska restaurants). The tram station and ticket windows are located behind the Alyeska Prince Hotel.

ANCHORAGE REGION

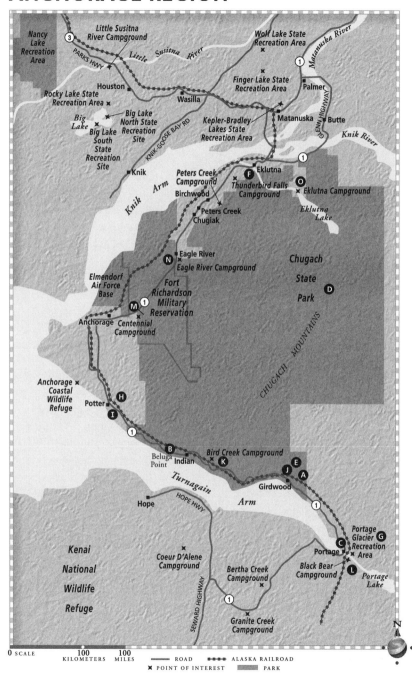

Nancy Lake Recreation Area

❸ Little Susitna River Campground

PARKS HWY

Little Susitna River

Wolf Lake State Recreation Area ✘

Matanuska River

❶

Houston

Rocky Lake State Recreation Area ✘

Wasilla

Finger Lake State Recreation Area ✘

Palmer

GLENN HIGHWAY

Big Lake ✘

Big Lake South State Recreation Site

Big Lake North State Recreation Site

KNIK-GOOSE BAY RD

Kepler-Bradley Lakes State Recreation Area

Matanuska ✘

Butte

Knik River

❶

✘ Knik

Knik Arm

Peters Creek Campground

Birchwood

Eklutna ■

❻ F

Thunderbird Falls Campground

❶

O ✘ Eklutna Campground

Eklutna Lake

Peters Creek ✘

Chugiak

✘ Eagle River

N

Eagle River Campground

Chugach State Park

D

Elmendorf Air Force Base

M ❶

Fort Richardson Military Reservation

CHUGACH MOUNTAINS

Anchorage ■

Centennial Campground

Anchorage ✘ Coastal Wildlife Refuge

Potter ■

H

I

❶

B

Beluga Point

Indian

Bird Creek Campground

K

E

J A

Turnagain

Girdwood

❶

Hope

HOPE HWY

Arm

Portage Glacier Recreation Area

G

Kenai National Wildlife Refuge

✘ Coeur D'Alene Campground

Bertha Creek Campground ✘

C

Portage ■ ✘

Black Bear Campground

L

Portage Lake

SEWARD HIGHWAY

❶

Granite Creek Campground ✘

N

Details: Call for summer tramway hours. Rides cost $16, $12 Alaskans, $10 ages 8–17, $7 under 8. (2 hours)

★★★ EKLUTNA VILLAGE HISTORICAL PARK
Exit Mile 25.3 (northbound) or Mile 26.3 (southbound)
Glenn Highway, Eklutna Village, 907/688-6026,
www.alaskaone.com/Eklutna

Located at the junction of several traditional trails, Eklutna has been continuously occupied by the Dena'ina (or Tanaina) Athabascan natives since 1650. The Eklutna Village Historical Park hosts the oldest standing structure in the region, the small St. Nicholas Russian Orthodox Church. Nearby are several colorful Spirit Houses, placed by the Dena'ina over the graves of relatives. Access to both is through the Heritage House, which features Dena'ina displays and offers local arts and craft items for sale.

Details: Summer daily 8–6, guided tours every half-hour. $3.50 admission includes tour. (1 hour)

★★★ PORTAGE GLACIER RECREATION AREA
Chugach National Forest, Mile 78.9 Seward Highway,
Begich Boggs Visitor Center, 907/783-2326

Due primarily to its accessibility from the busy Seward Highway, Portage Glacier in Portage valley is Alaska's most popular single vis-

SIGHTS
- **Ⓐ** Alyeska Tramway/Girdwood
- **Ⓑ** Beluga Point
- **Ⓒ** Big Game Alaska
- **Ⓓ** Chugach State Park
- **Ⓔ** Crow Creek Mine National Historic Site
- **Ⓕ** Eklutna Village Historical Park
- **Ⓖ** Portage Glacier Recreation Area
- **Ⓗ** Potter Marsh
- **Ⓘ** Potter Section House State Historic Site

FOOD
- **Ⓙ** Alpine Diner and Bakery
- **Ⓙ** The Bake Shop
- **Ⓙ** Chair Five Restaurant

LODGING
- **Ⓙ** Westin Alyeska Prince Hotel
- **Ⓙ** Winner Creek Bed and Breakfast

CAMPING
- **Ⓚ** Bird Creek Campground
- **Ⓛ** Black Bear Campground
- **Ⓜ** Centennial Park Campground
- **Ⓝ** Eagle River Campground
- **Ⓞ** Eklutna Lake Campground
- **Ⓟ** Williwam Campground

Note: Items with the same letter are located in the same area.

itor attraction. The park road winds a few miles to the visitors center at the east end of Portage Lake. The rocks here were deposited by the glacier in 1893, but since that time, the ice has receded three miles up the valley and is only partially visible from the center. Two miles beyond the visitors center on the lake's south shore, boat tours offer people the chance for a closer look. While the setting is lovely, Portage Glacier is not nearly as spectacular as the tidewater glaciers of Kenai Fjords, Prince William Sound, or the Southeast.

Enjoy the easy nature paths, perhaps on a ranger-guided hike from the excellent Begich, Boggs Visitor Center. Portage valley has two good campgrounds. Short trails lead to views and small glaciers.

Details: *Public access. Day tours from Anchorage offered by Gray Line of Alaska (907/277-5581), $21. (2–4 hours)*

★★ **BIG GAME ALASKA**
Mile 79 Seward Highway, Portage, 907/783-2025, www.alaska.net/~jrrealty/biggame/
For a guaranteed close-up view of some of Alaska's native species, you can't do much better than this. Though not exactly an animal rescue center, Big Game Alaska is home to several animals who were injured or orphaned and could not be returned to the wild. Animals include musk ox, caribou, sitka black-tailed deer, elk, moose, bison, and bald eagles. There's a nice gift shop and an informative staff.

Details: *June–Aug daily 9:30–7:30, Sept–May daily 11:30–dusk. $5 adults, $3 ages 4–15, under 4 free. (1 hour)*

★★ **CROW CREEK MINE NATIONAL HISTORIC SITE**
Crow Creek Road, North of Girdwood, 907/278-8060
Following the path of the original Iditarod Trail, Crow Creek Road follows Crow Creek into the Chugach Mountains. Three miles up Crow from its junction with Alyeska Access Road, this century-old mine site features eight original buildings, a gift shop, and a campground. You can wander and explore.

Details: *May 15–Sept 15 daily 9–6. Admission fee. (1 hour)*

FITNESS AND RECREATION

Superb recreational opportunities abound in and around Anchorage. The 11-mile **Tony Knowles Coastal Path**, a designated National Recreation Trail, is a great paved and gravel route for walking, jogging, skiing, and cycling. The route begins downtown and ends in Kincaid Park at the end of Raspberry Road.

Urban greenbelts offer more opportunity for walks. The **Chester Creek Greenbelt** boasts 13 miles of paved trail, stretching east to west from the Alaska Pacific University campus to lovely Westchester Lagoon, where you can hook up with the coastal path. It's easy to devise a pleasant walking loop that takes in town, park, lake, and ocean.

Popular day-hike trails are found in the foothills of the **Chugach Mountains** in Chugach State Park, with two quite different options starting at the Glen Alps Trailhead. From New Seward Highway, take O'Malley Road east about four miles to Hillside Drive, turn south one mile to Upper Huffman Road, then east again about 0.75 mile to Toilsome Hill Drive. Follow Toilsome Hill Drive as it winds up to the trailhead. You'll find the wheelchair-accessible **Anchorage Overlook Trail** (0.25 mile, 50-foot gain), an easy paved and gravel stroll to an overlook deck with stunning Anchorage and sunset views. The most popular climb in Alaska is the **Flattop Mountain Trail** (1.5 miles, 1,300-foot gain). Watch for rocks dislodged by hikers above you as you climb up to stellar views.

Some 120 miles of designated bike routes wind through the city. There are great birding opportunities along protected coastal flats and tidelands. Rafts can be rented, bicycles booked, canoes confirmed, and flights and fishing figured out. Get information at the Public Lands Information Center, Log Cabin Visitor Center, and Chugach State Park Headquarters—all described above.

FOOD

Downtown Anchorage is loaded with great places to eat, including the hotel restaurants listed in the Lodging section, below.

You'll find several spots that team good ales with decent food. **F Street Station** (325 F St., Anchorage, 907/272-5196) is a pleasant, upscale pub that serves upscale pub grub. **Humpys Great Alaskan Alehouse** (610 W. Sixth Ave., Anchorage, 907/276-2337), another ale and food place popular with the energetic set, has 40-plus microbrews on tap. The **Glacier Brew House** (735 W. Fifth Ave., Anchorage, 907/274-2739) is a new and happening place to enjoy site-brewed beers and good food.

Phyllis's Cafe and Salmon Bake (436 D St., Anchorage, 907/273-6656), a good choice for visitors, features indoor/outdoor seating, a big menu, and fun decor. It's open daily 8 to midnight. The choice for tasty south-of-the-border cuisine in Anchorage is **La Mex** (900 W. Sixth Ave., 907/274-7678). Alaska governor Tony Knowles owns the popular **Downtown Deli & Cafe** (525 W. Fourth Ave., Anchorage, 907/276-7116). Perhaps you'll see him enjoying a sandwich. **Thai Cuisine** (444 H St., Anchorage, 907/277-8424) is a favorite for outstanding—what else?—Thai cuisine.

If you're ready for some fine cuisine after a week or two of roadhouse fare, try the following establishments. The **Snow Goose** (Third Avenue and G Street, 907/277-7727) is a new restaurant with a marvelous mixed menu. Enjoy the fine views of Cook Inlet as you dine on excellent seafood at the **Elevation 92** (Third Avenue and L Street, 907/279-1578), situated 92 feet above sea level by Resolution Park, where downtown meets the water. **Simon and Seafort's** (420 L St., Anchorage, 907/274-3502) is a top choice with Cook Inlet views and a menu that features great seafood, prime rib, fine desserts, and much more. **Marx Brothers' Cafe** (627 W. Third Ave., Anchorage, 907/278-2133) is in a refurbished, bluff-top frame house built in 1916. How about a fine vintage with your seafood mousse or baked halibut with macadamia nut crust? Reservations are necessary.

Other great spots are scattered throughout this increasingly sprawling city. The huge and popular **Sea Galley & Pepper Mill Restaurant** (4101 Credit Union Dr., Anchorage, 907/563-3520 Sea Galley, 907/561-0800 Pepper Mill) features big and tasty meals of seafood, steaks, prime rib, and pasta. My aunt swears that the **V.I.P. Restaurant** (555 W. Northern Lights Blvd., Anchorage, 907/279-8514) has the best Korean food in town (and she should know). Chinese cuisine is served here as well. **Jen's** (701 W. Sixth Ave., 907/561-5367) is famous for its great wine selection and the short but amazing menu that changes with the chef's vision of the day. **Harry's** (101 W. Benson Blvd., Anchorage, 907/562-5994) is named after Harry Truman, who died at Spirit Lake in the eruption of Mount St. Helens. Not too pricey, it serves a good Sunday brunch.

In Girdwood, try the **Alpine Diner and Bakery** (Girdwood Station Mall, Mile 90 Seward Highway, Girdwood, 907/783-2550), open daily 7 to 10. It serves burgers, sandwiches, Italian dishes, baked goods, and espresso drinks. The **Bake Shop** (Alyeska Boardwalk, Alyeska Ski Resort, Girdwood, 907/783-2831), open daily 7 to 7 (until 8 on Saturday), plies breakfast, soup, pizza, sandwiches, and baked goods. The **Chair Five Restaurant** (Linblad Street, Girdwood Townsquare, 907/783-2500) features fresh halibut, pasta dishes, burgers, and pizza, as well as more than 65 microbrews, six on tap.

LODGING

Downtown Anchorage hosts several major U.S. hotel and motel chains offering the quality and rates you'd expect from that particular chain. These accommodations are also found near the airport and along the Glenn and Seward Highways.

Some chain accommodations located downtown include **Comfort Inn** (111 W. Ship Creek Ave., 907/277-6887), **Days Inn** (321 E. Fifth St., 800/329-7466), **Econo Lodge** (642 E. Fifth Ave., 907/274-1515), **Holiday Inn** (239 W. Fourth Ave., 907/279-8671), **Rodeway Inn** (1104 E. Fifth Ave., 907/274-1650), **Sheraton** (401 E. Sixth St., 907/276-8700), and **Westmark** (720 W. Fifth Ave., 907/258-2040).

Downtown Anchorage offers some excellent lodging options. A top choice is the **Hilton Anchorage Hotel** (500 W. Third Ave., Anchorage, 800/445-8667, 907/272-7411). Rates range from $150 to $170 in winter, $195 to $215 mid-May through September. Even if you're not spending the night at the Hilton, take in the view from the Top of the World Restaurant and bar on the summit floor. The other large downtown hotel is the excellent **Hotel Captain Cook** (Fourth and K Street, Anchorage, 800/843-1950, 907/276-6000). Rates range from $230 to $240 in summer, $130 to $140 winter. Here, too, you'll find a great rooftop restaurant and bar with a splendid view. The pleasant **Copper Whale Inn** (440 L St., Anchorage, 907/258-7999) overlooks Cook Inlet. Rooms go for $100 and up in summer, $55 and up in winter.

Budget travelers can opt for a hostel bunk. Located conveniently downtown, **Anchorage Youth Hostel** (700 H St., Anchorage, 907/276-3635) has 95 beds; rates are $16 for members, $19 non-members. The hostel is closed noon to 5 and enforces a midnight curfew; reservations are advised.

Girdwood hosts many B&Bs, cabins, and vacation condos. **Winner Creek B&B** (Mile 2.9 Alyeska Highway, Girdwood, 907/783-5501, www.alaskan.com/winnercreek) is a lovely log home with three rooms, river-rock fireplace, private guest entrance and hot tub, all just a five-minute walk from the slopes. At the foot of the Alyeska Tram and ski slopes, the **Westin**

Alyeska Prince Hotel (1000 Arlberg Ave., Girdwood, 800/880-3880, 907/754-2111, www.alyeskaresort.com) is Alaska's top resort hotel, pampering guests with full amenities. Rates range widely, from $125 to $1,500.

CAMPING

The best campground in Anchorage proper is the **Centennial Park Campground**, 907/333-9711, with $13 sites; RVs are okay. Take Boundary Road east from Muldoon Road, just south of Glenn Highway. Free showers, too!

Along Knik Arm northeast of Anchorage, Chugach State Park campgrounds are a good choice. At Mile 25.3 of the Glenn Highway, take the Eklutna Lake Road to reach **Eklutna Lake Campground** (Mile 10 Eklutna Lake Road, 907/688-0908). The **Eagle River Campground** can be reached by taking Hiland Road toward the mountains from Mile 12 of Glenn Highway.

Along the Seward Highway and Turnagain Arm is Chugach State Park's **Bird Creek Campground** (Mile 101 Seward Highway).

Portage Glacier Recreation Area features two nice National Forest campgrounds. The **Williwam Campground** and **Black Bear Campground** are both about 1.5 miles west of the visitors center.

NIGHTLIFE

Several of the alehouses listed in the Food section, above, are fine places to spend an evening. To raise the price, class, views, and elevation a notch, head up the elevators in the **Hotel Captain Cook** or **Hilton Anchorage Hotel** for a nightcap in their rooftop clubs (see Lodging, above). If you're up for a youthful, rough-edged, rock-and-roll scene, check out the legendary and infamous **Chilkoot Charlie's** (2435 Spenard Rd., Anchorage, 907/272-1010).

For information about Anchorage performing arts, contact the splendid Anchorage Center for the Performing Arts (621 W. Sixth Ave., 907/263-2787), a popular venue for theater, dance, and music.

Dinner theater Alaska-style, the **JoAnn & Monte Show** (Sheraton Hotel, 401 E. Sixth St., downtown Anchorage, reservations 907/278-8318) spoofs life in the 49th state through music and comedy. The show runs mid-May through August, Tuesday through Saturday. Dinner and show cost $35, show alone $12.50. The **Whale Fat Follies** (Fly by Night

Club, 3300 Spenard Rd., Anchorage, 907/279-7726), hosted by the renowned "Mr. Whitekeys," puts on an all-Alaskan musical comedy multimedia floor show. Performances, which begin at 8 p.m., run Tuesday through Saturday; tickets cost $12 to $17.

The performing arts are well represented in Alaska's only metropolis. Call to check the current schedule for any of the following. **Alaska Chamber Singers** (907/333-3500) is a group of 40 area professionals and teachers. **Alaska Junior Theater** (907/333-3500) stages professional theater for young audiences. **Anchorage Concert Association** (907/272-1471) offers top touring performers and shows. **Anchorage Opera** (907/279-2557) is the only professional opera in the state. **Anchorage Symphony Orchestra** (907/274-8668), an 80-piece orchestra, offers several series.

11
SEWARD AND THE EASTERN KENAI PENINSULA

The eastern Kenai Peninsula is dominated by the rugged Kenai Mountains and the great icefields that cap their higher reaches. Glaciers flow down valleys from these heights, some meeting the inlets of Prince William Sound and Kenai Fjords with cliff-like faces that calve ice into the sea. Further inland, long-distance and fishing trails lace the valleys and passes. There are many points where you can park and hike in to a hidden lake or up onto a ridge above treeline.

The chief town of the eastern Kenai and the only significant settlement on the south Kenai coast is Seward. Named for William Henry Seward, the secretary of state who secured Alaska for the United States in 1867, the town was founded in 1902 by surveyors for the Alaska Railroad. Seward is situated at the head of wildlife-rich Resurrection Bay, named by Alexander Baranof in 1791 when he sheltered here on the Russian Sunday of the Resurrection. The strategically located bay served as a vital supply port during World War II. Otters, whales, and seals are frequently seen in the foreground as fishing vessels, tour boats, cargo ships, or ferries pass behind.

Seward plays many roles. As a port, it serves commercial, recreational, and fishing boats, as well as ferry and cruise ships. The main base for boat tours to Kenai Fjords National Park, it is also a travel destination in its own right. Visitors can enjoy shops, accommodations, waterfront and beach strolling, parks, and restaurants. There is great fishing from the shore and in area lakes and streams. Easily accessible Exit Glacier is nearby, and outfitters for kayak trips and backcountry drop-offs are plentiful. More than 20 fishing charter companies operate from the boat harbor.

A PERFECT DAY IN SEWARD

Join the many who opt for a boat tour of Kenai Fjords National Park. If you don't mind being on the water for much of the day, take one of the longer cruises. Shorter trips typically explore only Resurrection Bay, while longer tours round the point and head for tidewater glaciers in the heart of the park.

If you have an extra chunk of time before or after your cruise, head up to Exit Glacier to get close to a river of ice. If you feel ambitious, try hiking up a bit of the trail that follows the margin of the gla-cier's right side. The path climbs steeply and somewhat precariously to great views and eventually allows access to the vast Harding Icefield.

ORIENTATION

The Seward Highway and Alaska Railroad run north-south through the mountains, linking Seward and Portage. From Mile 37 of the Seward, the Sterling Highway provides access to the lowlands of the west.

Almost everything of interest in Seward is on or near the waterfront, within a block or two of the Seward Highway. The cruise docks are at the north end of town, the fishing and tour boat harbor toward the middle, and the town center and ferry dock a half-mile south of that. The visitors center, museum, ferry terminal, and many businesses are found on or near the south end of Third Avenue (Seward Highway), Seward's main street. Consider a leisurely tour on "Seward's Trolley," which runs May through September daily 10 to 7. Fares are $1.50 one way or $3 all day, youth half price.

SEWARD AREA SIGHTSEEING HIGHLIGHTS

★★★★ **ALASKA SEALIFE CENTER**
301 Railway Ave., Seward, 800/224-2525, 907/224-6300,
www.alaskasealife.org
Most of the $50 million spent to build this outstanding new marine research and exhibit facility came from the *Exxon Valdez* oil-spill settlement. The center is "dedicated to understanding and maintaining the integrity of the marine ecosystem of Alaska through research,

SEWARD

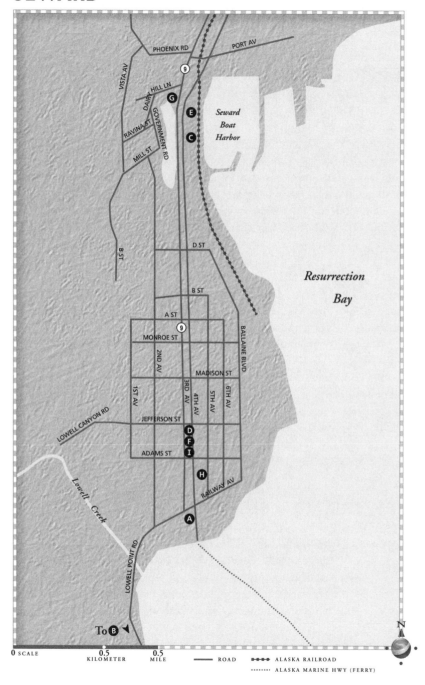

PHOENIX RD

PORT AV

VISTA AV

DAIRY HILL LN

⑨

Ⓖ

Ⓔ

RAVINA ST

GOVERNMENT RD

Ⓒ

*Seward
Boat
Harbor*

MILL ST

B ST

D ST

*Resurrection
Bay*

B ST

A ST

MONROE ST

⑨

2ND AV

MADISON ST

1ST AV

3RD AV

4TH AV

5TH AV

6TH AV

BALLAINE BLVD

LOWELL CANYON RD

JEFFERSON ST

Ⓓ

Ⓕ

Ⓘ

ADAMS ST

Ⓗ

RAILWAY AV

Ⓐ

Lowell Creek

LOWELL POINT RD

To Ⓑ ◂

N

0 SCALE

0.5
KILOMETER

0.5
MILE

ROAD

ALASKA RAILROAD

ALASKA MARINE HWY (FERRY)

rehabilitation, and public education." You can view Steller's sea lions, harbor seals, marine birds, and fish in naturalistic habitats.
Details: *Open summer daily 8–8, winter 10–5. $12.50 adults, $10 ages 7–12, under 7 free. (1½ hours)*

★★★★ **EXIT GLACIER**
Kenai Fjords National Park, Visitors Center, 1212 Fourth Ave., Seward, 907/224-3375, www.nps.gov/kefj
The easily accessible Exit Glacier is one of many born in the vast Harding Icefield that drapes the central Kenai Mountains west of Seward. Take the nine-mile Exit Glacier Road from Seward to reach the parking lot. A visitors center offers information, and a short walk on an easy path brings you right up to the ice.

For tourist information and maps, stop by the Railcar Seward Visitor Information Cache (at Third and Jefferson, 907/224-3094, 907/224-8051, www.seward.net/chamber).

Those ready for a challenge can attempt the difficult trail on the glacier's northern side. The route follows the glacier for about 3.5 miles, ascending more than 2,500 feet to reach the pass and access to the icefield. Consult the ranger before setting out.
Details: *Public access. User fee of $5 per vehicle, $3 for hikers and bikers. (1 hour)*

★★★★ **KENAI FJORDS NATIONAL PARK/BOAT TOURS**
Visitors Center, 1212 Fourth Ave., Seward, 907/224-3375, www.nps.gov/kefj
This splendid park preserves much of the ragged south coast of the Kenai Peninsula, from the vast Harding Icefield down to marvelous, glacier-carved fjords. Every morning and afternoon, tour boats head

SIGHTS
- Ⓐ Alaska Sealife Center
- Ⓑ Coastal Trail
- Ⓒ Kenai Fjords National Park/Boat Tours
- Ⓓ Seward Museum

FOOD
- Ⓔ Ray's
- Ⓕ Resurrect Art Coffee House Gallery

LODGING
- Ⓖ Breeze Inn
- Ⓗ Hotel Seward/Best Western
- Ⓘ Van Gilder Hotel

CALVING GLACIER, KENAI PENINSULA

© Paul Otteson

out to explore Resurrection Bay; longer tours continue on to watch Holgate Glacier calve cascades of ice into the sea and to circle islands dotted with basking seals and bird rookeries. If your time on the Kenai Peninsula is limited, this option should top your list. Several companies offer boat tours. Kenai Fjords Tours (boat harbor, Seward, 800/478-8068, 907/224-8934, www.alaskan.com/kenaifjords) offers tours of varying lengths—3, 4, 5, 6, 7.5, 9.5, and 10.5 hours—to various parts of the park; some include land-based visits. Departure times vary. Prices range from $60 to $140, half price for kids; meals are served on longer tours. Major Marine Tours (boat harbor, Seward, 800/764-7300, www.majormarine.com) offers a full-day trip, departing at 11:45 and returning at 7:30, that costs $100 ($50 for kids under 12) and includes meal. The half-day trip departs at 1 p.m. and costs $64 ($32 under 12). The evening trip departs at 6 p.m. and costs $50 ($24 under 12). Renown Charters (boat harbor, Seward, 800/655-3806, 907/272-2151, www.renowncharters.com) offers cruises lasting 2.5, 4, and 6 hours on smaller boats; one takes only 42 passengers. Rates range from $50 to $100, $2 per year of age for children up to 12. Allen Marine Tours (small boat harbor, Seward, 888/305-2515, 907/276-5800, www.alaskaone.com/wildlifequest/) operates a stable, catamaran-style tour boat for six-hour cruises that take in Holgate Glacier for $100, $36 for kids under 13, under 3 free. Lunch, snacks, and drinks are provided.

Flightseeing over the Harding Icefield and Kenai Fjords is offered by Scenic Mountain Air, Inc. (Moose Pass, 800/478-1449, 907/288-3646). Flights are based in Moose Pass, 30 miles north of Seward on the Seward Highway.

Details: Public access to park. Visitors center open Memorial Day–Labor Day daily 8–7, weekdays 8–5 in winter. (half to full day)

★★★ COASTAL TRAIL
4.5 miles, from coast road, Seward
If you're looking for a good, sea-level hike with interesting highlights, follow the coast road from the south end of town to Lowell Point and the trailhead. The trail sticks to the shore, past a good campsite and on to Caines Head State Park and some World War II bunkers. To avoid wet stretches, plan to start the hike about 2 to 2.5 hours before the scheduled low tide. Watch for otters, seals, and eagles.

Details: Public access. (half day)

★★ SEWARD MUSEUM
Jefferson at Third, Seward, 907/224-3902
Operated by the Resurrection Bay Historical Society, the museum features local heritage displays, including exhibits on the 1964 earthquake, Seward history, and native culture.
Details: May–mid-October daily 9–5, call for winter hours. Admission $2. (1 hour)

EASTERN KENAI PENINSULA SIGHTSEEING HIGHLIGHTS

★★★ HOPE
Gold prospectors were busy in Hope as early as 1889, and miners are still working area claims today. The town was named on a whim when early residents chose to honor the youngest passenger on the next arriving boat, who turned out to be none other than Fred Hope. Today, about 200 people live in the area, a fraction of the gold-boom high of 3,000 a century ago.

Hope is a great place to escape the traffic and crowds of the Kenai Peninsula and enjoy a bit of quiet historical charm. The little general store has been serving customers since 1896, and several other vintage buildings still stand. You can walk to the old townsite or grab a bite at the local café. Stop at a local gold and jewelry shop to talk with folks who still live the mining life.
Details: End of Hope Highway, 20 miles from Mile 56.7 Seward Highway (2 hours)

★★ SEWARD HIGHWAY/PORTAGE GLACIER TO SEWARD (78.9 MILES)
From Portage, the Seward Highway crosses south onto the Kenai Peninsula and climbs to Turnagain Pass (Mile 68.5, elevation 988 feet), a favorite winter sports area. Snowmobilers head out west of the road, while cross-country skiers own the east. Winding down to the Hope Highway Junction (Mile 56.7), the road climbs again up to an open pass and beautiful Summit Lakes (Mile 47.2 and Mile 45.5), which encourage a long driving break or at least a stop for a photograph.

Descending gradually again, you'll pass the double junction with the Sterling Highway (Mile 37.7 and Mile 37), which leads to the Kenai River, Kenai, and Homer. The settlement of Moose Pass

(Mile 29.4) began as a camp for the builders of the Alaska Railroad, which parallels the road from here to Seward. North of Moose Pass, the rail line follows the lonely route of the original Iditarod Trail to Portage.

South of Moose Pass, the highway reaches the upper end of Kenai Lake, source of the Kenai River, hugging its shores for several miles. Just before reaching Seward, you'll find the junction for the Exit Glacier Road (Mile 3.7), where visitors can turn for the eight-mile trip to the foot of Exit Glacier (see above). In short minutes, you reach Seward and the head of wildlife-rich Resurrection Bay.

Details: (2–3 hours)

FITNESS AND RECREATION

Enjoy a short hike on one of the great trails in the area. The easy **Two Lakes Trail** (0.5 mile, no gain), located right in town, makes a nice loop starting a block north of A Street from First Avenue and returning to Second Avenue north of Van Buren. Both tough and rewarding is the **Mount Marathon Trail** (two miles, 3,000-foot gain). This is the route of the annual July 4th Mount Marathon Race in which kamikaze racers struggle to a high spur on the mountain's flank, then hurtle pell-mell down the gravely slope to the finish—bruised and battered, but conscious. The trailhead is found at the end of Lowell Street (Jefferson Street) near the water tanks.

Along the Seward Highway, consider the **Carter Lake Trail** (3.3 miles, 1,000-foot gain). From Mile

For a complete list of hiking trails and information on cabin rentals, contact the Public Lands Information Office (Anchorage, 907/271-2737, 800/271-2599 for cabin info, www .nps.gov/aplic).

33.1 of the Seward Highway, this route climbs above treeline to the east end of lovely Crescent Lake. For a longer trip, you can continue another 16 miles along the lake and back down to the Sterling Highway via Crescent Creek. The easy, sometimes brushy **Ptarmigan Creek Trail** (four miles, 200-foot gain) starts near Ptarmigan Creek Campground at Mile 23.1 Seward Highway, reaching Ptarmigan Lake in four miles with little elevation gain. There's good fishing, or you can continue along the narrow lake's northern shore.

Sea kayaking in Resurrection Bay and Kenai Fjords is a great option. **Sunny Cove Sea Kayaking Co.** (907/345-5339, www.sunnycove.com) hosts day trips that include a cruise to Fox Island, kayak instruction, 2.5- to 4-hour

EASTERN KENAI PENINSULA

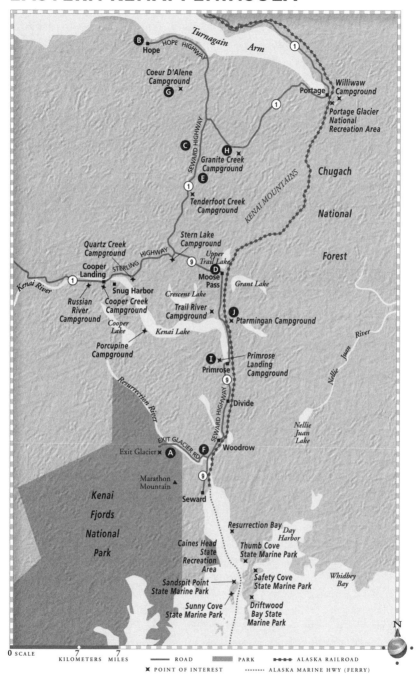

Turnagain
Arm

B Hope
HOPE HIGHWAY

Coeur D'Alene
Campground
G ✗

Portage
Williwaw
Campground ✗

Portage Glacier
National
Recreation Area

SEWARD HIGHWAY

C
Granite Creek
Campground

H ✗

E
① ✗
Tenderfoot Creek
Campground

Stern Lake
Campground

Quartz Creek
Campground ✗

Cooper
Landing

STERLING HIGHWAY

Kenai River

Russian
River
Campground

Snug Harbor ■

Cooper Creek
Campground

Cooper
Lake

Porcupine
Campground

Upper
Trail Lake
⑨ ✗

Moose
Pass

Crescent Lake

Trail River
Campground ✗

Kenai Lake

D

Grant Lake

J
✗ ✗ Ptarmigan Campground

KENAI MOUNTAINS

Chugach

National

Forest

Nellie Juan River

I ✗
Primrose

⑨

Primrose
Landing
Campground

Divide

Nellie
Juan
Lake

SEWARD HIGHWAY

Resurrection River

EXIT GLACIER RD

Exit Glacier ✗ **A**

Marathon
Mountain ▲

Seward

F
Woodrow

⑨

Kenai

Fjords

National

Park

Resurrection Bay
Day
Harbor

Caines Head
State
Recreation
Area

Thumb Cove
State Marine Park ✗

Sandspit Point
State Marine Park ✗

Safety Cove
State Marine Park ✗

Whidbey
Bay

Sunny Cove
State Marine Park

Driftwood
Bay State
Marine Park

N

0 SCALE   7   7
KILOMETERS MILES   ━━━ ROAD   ▦ PARK   ▪▪▪▪ ALASKA RAILROAD
                        ✗ POINT OF INTEREST   ·········· ALASKA MARINE HWY (FERRY)

wilderness paddle, meal(s), and return cruise for $140 to $160. **Alaska Kayak Camping Co.** (Lowell Point, Seward, 907/224-6056, 907/224-2323, www.seward.net/kayakcamp) rents kayaks and all gear for $100 per day per person, with discounts for longer periods or larger groups.

FOOD

As usual, a number of great eating choices are found in area hotels and motels; check the listings in the Lodging section, below.

In Seward, **Ray's** (boat harbor, Seward, 907/224-5606), right on the water, serves lunch and dinner daily. Tasty entreés include such specialties as Cedar Planked Salmon and Macadamia Nut Crusted Halibut. There's a lively bar and a harbor view. For a dose of art with your coffee and snack, visit the **Resurrect Art Coffee House Gallery** (320 Third Ave., in an old church, Seward, 907/224-7161).

In Hope, the **Discovery Cafe** (Hope Highway, Hope, 907/782-3282) is "where the gold miners meet," and it's possible, too, since there are several active claims in the area and some people who've been working them for a long, long time.

LODGING

Perhaps the nicest hotel right in town is the **Hotel Seward/Best Western** (221 Fifth Ave., Seward, 800/528-1234, Alaska only 800/478-4050, 907/224-

---

SIGHTS
- **A** Exit Glacier
- **B** Hope
- **C** Seward Highway/Portage Glacier to Seward

FOOD
- **B** Discovery Cafe

LODGING
- **B** Bear Creek Lodge
- **B** Henry's One Stop
- **B** Seaview Cafe and Motel
- **D** Spruce Moose Bed and Breakfast
- **E** Summit Lake Lodge
- **D** Trail Lake Lodge
- **F** Windsong Lodge

CAMPING
- **G** Coeur D'Alene Campground
- **H** Granite Creek National Forest Campground
- **B** Porcupine Campground
- **I** Primrose Creek Campground
- **J** Ptarmigan Creek Campground
- **J** Trail River Campground

Note: Items with the same letter are located in the same area.

2378), near the Alaska Sealife Center. Rooms start at $150 and feature queen beds, HBO, shuttle service, voicemail, hair dryers, and other amenities. A National Historic Site, the **Van Gilder Hotel** (308 Adams St., Seward, 800/204-6835, 907/224-3079) brings you close to Seward's history, comfortably. Rooms range from $95 to $120 with private bath, $75 with shared bath. It's open only May 15 to October 1. The **Breeze Inn** (1306 Seward Highway, Seward, 907/224-5238) is a nice, modern motel right in town. Rooms and Jacuzzi-equipped suites, most with nice views, range from $110 to $170. The Breeze Inn restaurant is next door.

For a comfortable night in a more secluded setting, try the pleasant **Windsong Lodge** (Exit Glacier Road, two miles north of Seward, 800/208-0200, 907/224-7116). For $160 a night you enjoy queen beds, full bath, satellite TV, VCR, and in-room coffee. The Resurrection River borders the property. The fine Resurrection Bay Roadhouse is adjacent to the lodge, serving seafood and more.

Several lodging options are found along the Seward Highway between Seward and Portage Glacier. In Moose Pass, the **Trail Lake Lodge** (Mile 29.5 Seward Highway, Moose Pass, 907/288-3101) has the works, including restaurant, bar, motel, showers, laundry, and salmon bake. Rooms range from $90 to $100. A stone's throw up the road, the **Spruce Moose Bed and Breakfast** (Mile 30.1 Seward Highway, Moose Pass, 907/288-3667) features two appealing chalet homes, great for families or groups. **Summit Lake Lodge** (Mile 45.5 Seward Highway, Cooper Landing, 907/595-1520) sits right between the two lovely lakes in a wonderful high-pass area above treeline. The rustic rooms are nice. There's a good restaurant and bar.

Henry's One Stop (Mile 16 Hope Highway, Hope, 907/782-3222) offers $50 doubles and $16.50 RV sites along with laundry, showers, groceries, and propane (no credit cards). **Bear Creek Lodge** (Hope Highway, Hope, 907/782-3141) rents rooms for $80 in summer, $50 in winter. **Seaview Cafe and Motel** (Main and B Streets, Hope, 907/782-3364), located in a turn-of-the-last-century building, features a bar, gift shop, and café.

CAMPING

Along the Seward Highway between Portage Glacier and Seward are four National Forest campgrounds. Turn west one mile through a residential area to reach **Primrose Creek Campground** (Mile 17 Seward Highway) with $6 sites overlooking Kenai Lake. The **Ptarmigan Creek Campground** (Mile 23.1 Seward Highway), east of the road, has 16 sites for $6 each. **Trail River Campground** (Mile 24.2 Seward Highway) has $6 campsites and access to the shores of Kenai Lake. **Granite Creek National Forest Campground** (Mile 63 Seward Highway) features good creekside sites for $6, with fishing and trail access.

Two nice National Forest campgrounds are found near Hope. **Coeur D'Alene Campground** (Palmer Creek Road, 12 miles from Hope Highway) is in a pleasant valley, near mine sites. **Porcupine Campground** (end of Hope Highway, Hope) has good sites near the Gull Rock trailhead.

12
WESTERN KENAI PENINSULA

The Kenai Peninsula is Alaska's "vacationland." Every weekend in summer, thousands of Anchorage residents stream south to favorite fishing spots, campgrounds, cabins, and lodges in the western Kenai lowlands. The roads can be bumper-to-bumper with traffic, the shores of the Kenai River elbow-to-elbow with folks fishing. Travel to and through the Kenai Peninsula is much more relaxed during the week.

Western Kenai slopes gradually westward from the Kenai Mountains to Cook Inlet. The Kenai River drains the heart of the region, passing through the huge Kenai National Wildlife Refuge with its maze of lakes, forest, and wetlands. In the west near the Cook Inlet coast is one of Alaska's fastest-growing regions. In this buildable area around Kenai and Soldotna, small roads meander to homes, cabins, campsites, fishing access, and scores of small lodges and B&Bs.

Options for hiking, camping, boating, and relaxing in the area are excellent, but sightseeing attractions are few. The towns of Kenai and Ninilchik have important points of historic interest, while Soldotna supports two good visitors centers. Good beach access is possible via North Kenai Road, Kalifonsky Beach Road, Cohoe Loop Road, and parts of the Sterling Highway. Rafting the Kenai River Canyon, enjoying a wilderness lodge stay, digging clams along Cook Inlet, or canoeing the wonderful routes of the Kenai Wilderness are other possibilities.

A PERFECT DAY ON THE WESTERN KENAI PENINSULA

For many travelers, the perfect day involves driving through the region to reach the attractions of Homer and Kachemak Bay. But if it's recreation you want, the western Kenai Peninsula has many perfect days in store for you. How about digging a couple dozen razor clams for dinner? You can enjoy the beach and history of Ninilchik Village after your dig, then retire to your campsite for a splendid meal. Perhaps a long day paddling the Swan Lake Canoe Trail appeals to you. You'll discover raptor nests, explore coves and channels, and observe moose munching willow leaves.

Or maybe Alaska's favorite pastime is on the agenda. License and gear in hand, you can find your spot along the banks of the Kenai or near the mouth of one of several spawning streams and go after that 50-pound king. Nothing can match the thrill of that big strike—except, perhaps, the first delicious bite of a salmon steak grilled at your riverside campsite in bright Alaska summer twilight.

ORIENTATION

A map and the highway guide below are your best friends in this wide region, but it's hard to get lost. The Sterling Highway and Kenai Spur Highway are the only roads of consequence. Important secondary roads are often loops that lead back to the highway. Smaller, meandering backroads, however, can cause some confusion. Road junctions are your best landmarks in spread-out towns such as Sterling, Soldotna, and even Kenai.

KENAI PENINSULA SIGHTSEEING HIGHLIGHTS

★★★ HISTORIC KENAI
Around Mission and Overland Avenues, Kenai, information at 907/283-1991, www.visitkenai.com
The Dena'ina Indian village of Skitok (shki-TUK) had existed for years at the site where the Kenai River meets the sea before Russian fur traders established Kenai in 1791. The town grew into a regional trade center. Fishing and fish processing are now the main industries, along with oil-related commerce.

Start your Kenai visit at the excellent **Kenai Visitors and Cultural Center** (11471 Kenai Spur Highway, Kenai, 907/283-

WESTERN KENAI PENINSULA

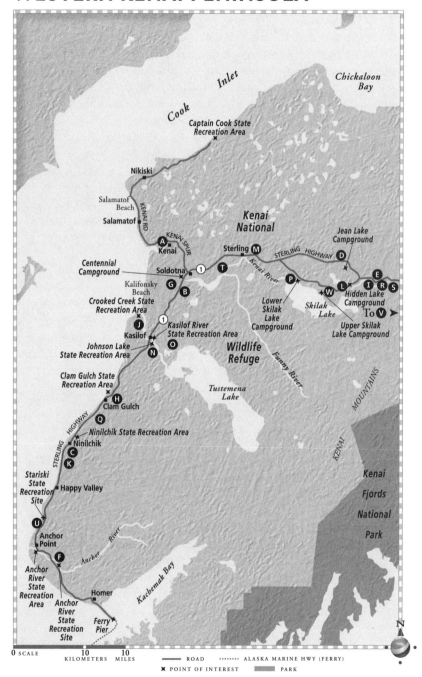

Cook Inlet

Chickaloon Bay

Captain Cook State Recreation Area

Nikiski

Salamatof Beach
Salamatof

KENAI RD

Kenai National

KENAI SPUR

A Kenai

Sterling **M**

STERLING HIGHWAY

Jean Lake Campground **D**

Centennial Campground

Soldotna

Kenai River

E

T

Kalifonsky Beach **G**

B

P

L

I **R** **S**

Crooked Creek State Recreation Area

Lower Skilak Lake Campground

W

Skilak Lake

Hidden Lake Campground

To **V**

J

1 Kasilof River State Recreation Area

Upper Skilak Lake Campground

Kasilof

O

Johnson Lake State Recreation Area

N

Funny River

Wildlife Refuge

Clam Gulch State Recreation Area

Tustemena Lake

H

Clam Gulch

MOUNTAINS

Q

Ninilchik State Recreation Area

STERLING HIGHWAY

Ninilchik

KENAI

C

K

Kenai

Stariski State Recreation Site

Happy Valley

Fjords

National

Park

U

Anchor Point

Anchor River

F

Anchor River State Recreation Area

Anchor River State Recreation Site

Homer

Kachemak Bay

Ferry Pier

N

0 SCALE
10 KILOMETERS   10 MILES — ROAD ········ ALASKA MARINE HWY (FERRY)
✖ POINT OF INTEREST   PARK

1991, www.visitkenai.com), located on Main Street south of the Kenai Spur Highway. Close to the main historical attractions, the heritage exhibits and videos offer a good introduction to area history and culture (open summer Mon–Fri 9–8, Sat–Sun 11–7; winter Mon–Fri 9–5, Sat 10–4). From the visitors center, turn right on Overland Avenue to reach old Kenai, situated near the bluffs overlooking Cook Inlet.

The most visible landmark is the **Holy Assumption of the Virgin Mary Orthodox Church**, first built in 1849, then replaced by the present structure in 1895. Across a green from the church's striking, onion-shaped domes is the more modest **St. Nicholas Chapel**, built in 1906 near the burial spots of church leaders. Just

SIGHTS

Ⓐ Historic Kenai
Ⓑ Kenai National Wildlife Refuge Visitor Center
Ⓒ Ninilchik
Ⓑ Soldotna Historical Society Museum
Ⓓ Sterling Highway/Seward Highway to Homer

FOOD

Ⓐ Blue Grouse Drive-In
Ⓑ Don Jose's
Ⓒ Happy Wok
Ⓑ Hogg Heaven Cafe
Ⓐ Little Ski-Mo Burger-N-Brew
Ⓒ Lunch Box
Ⓐ Paradiso's
Ⓑ Sal's Klondike Diner
Ⓑ Through the Seasons Restaurant

LODGING

Ⓒ Beachcomber Motel
Ⓐ Beaver Creek Cabin Rentals
Ⓑ Best Western King Salmon
Ⓒ Homestead House Bed and Breakfast
Ⓐ Katmai Hotel
Ⓐ Kenai Kings Inn
Ⓔ Kenai Princess Lodge

LODGING (continued)

Ⓑ Kenai River Lodge
Ⓔ Red Salmon Guest House
Ⓑ RiverSide House
Ⓑ Soldotna Bed & Breakfast Lodge
Ⓑ Soldotna Inn

CAMPING

Ⓕ Anchor River Campground
Ⓖ Centennial Park Campground
Ⓗ Clam Gulch Campground
Ⓘ Cooper Creek Campground
Ⓙ Crooked Creek Campground
Ⓚ Deep Creek Campground
Ⓛ Hidden Lake Campground
Ⓜ Isaak Walton Campground
Ⓝ Johnson Lake Campground
Ⓞ Kasilof River Campground
Ⓟ Lower Skilak Lake Campground
Ⓠ Ninilchik Campground
Ⓡ Quartz Lake Campground
Ⓢ Russian River Campground
Ⓣ Scout Lake and Morgan Lake Campgrounds
Ⓤ Stariski Campground
Ⓥ Stern Lake Campground
Ⓦ Upper Skilak Lake Campground

Note: Items with the same letter are located in the same area.

up the street is the site of **Fort Kenay**, built in 1869 and garrisoned for less than two years. A reconstructed barracks can be viewed. Take the short walk down Mission Road from Overland Avenue to reach **Cook Inlet overlooks**, from which beluga whales are sometimes spotted.
Details: *Consult visitors center for hours.* *(1 1/2 hours)*

★★★ **NINILCHIK**
Information, 907/567-3518, www.recworld.com/ncoc
Employees retiring from the Russian-American Trading Company established this charming oceanside village. Many were Russians who had married native Alaskan women and preferred to settle in Alaska rather than return to their homeland. Their descendants have survived here for at least 140 years.

Call or visit the Kenai Peninsula Visitor Center at Mile 96 Sterling Highway in Soldotna, 907/262-1337, www.soldotnachamber.com/data/visitors.

The historic village at the river mouth is reached via a short, marked road from Mile 135.1 of the Sterling Highway; the right fork leads to the village, the left to the beach and clamming area of **Ninilchik State Recreation Area**. Visit the classic, historic **Russian Orthodox Church** and cemetery perched on the bluff above the shore. A short path climbs to the site from the village below, or you can reach it by vehicle from Mile 134.7 of the Sterling Highway. The village hosts a couple of shops and a small B&B. More services are accessible from the highway.
Details: *West of Mile 135.1 Sterling Highway.* *(1 hour)*

★★ **SOLDOTNA HISTORICAL SOCIETY MUSEUM**
Centennial Park Road, just west of Mile 96.1 Sterling Highway, Soldotna, 907/262-1337
Enjoy regional heritage and wildlife exhibits. A historic log village of buildings gathered from around the area is found on the grounds.
Details: *Open summer Tue–Sat 10–4, Sun 12–4.* *(1 hour)*

★★ **STERLING HIGHWAY/SEWARD HIGHWAY TO HOMER (140 MILES)**
When you turn from the Seward Highway onto the Sterling, you enter fishing heaven. Note that during the summer, and especially in

June, campgrounds and accommodations along the Kenai and other streams and lakes are jammed. Visit Kenai midweek or in the shoulder seasons—unless you, too, wish to fish.

The first milepost of the Sterling is actually Mile 37, reflecting the distance from Seward to the junction. It immediately descends several miles to the west end of Kenai Lake, past the junction with Snug Harbor Road (Mile 47.9) and into the enclave of Cooper Landing (Mile 48.4). Snug Harbor Road allows recreational access to **Kenai and Cooper Lakes**, while Cooper Landing offers complete highway and recreational services.

At Mile 54.7, the highway crosses out of Chugach National Forest and into the **Kenai National Wildlife Refuge**. Refuge, fishing, and recreation information is available at the U.S. Fish & Wildlife Service Information Cabin (Mile 58). The cabin is at the east junction of Skilak Lake Loop Road (Mile 58), which provides access to large Skilak Lake and several campgrounds, linking up with the Sterling again at Mile 75.2.

You'll know it as soon as you cross out of the Kenai National Wildlife Refuge around Mile 76 and head into **Sterling** (Mile 81). Many back roads provide access to campgrounds, B&Bs, vacation cabins, fishing spots, and more. The Swanson River Road (Mile 83.4) heads north for access to several lakes and the put-ins for the outstanding **Swan Lake Canoe Trail** and **Swanson River Canoe Trail** (see Fitness and Recreation, below).

Turn north at the Kenai Spur Highway Junction (Mile 94.2) to reach Kenai, Nikiski, and the surrounding region. Otherwise, enter the heart of **Soldotna** (around Mile 95), where you'll find complete services. When you reach the Kalifonsky Beach Road/Funny River Road Junction (Mile 96.1), you have two options. You can turn west, then take the first right for the Visitor Information Center and Soldotna Historical Society Museum (see above). Or turn east, then take the first right for the Kenai National Wildlife Refuge Visitor Center (see the Sightseeing Highlight entry on the next page for details). A side trip down the Kalifonsky Beach Road can be an interesting alternate loop, rejoining the Sterling at Mile 108.8.

Another recreation and vacation area is centered around **Kasilof** (Mile 108). A number of campgrounds and fishing spots exist in the vicinity, while the Cohoe Loop Road (Miles 111 and 114.3) provides access to the coast and small settlement of Cohoe. After the tiny community of Clam Gulch, a long, undeveloped stretch ends at Ninilchik (Mile 135.1). Turn west here to reach the historic village (see above). The highway continues on to Anchor Point (Mile 156.7), largely a residential satellite of Homer. Just north of town, you'll pass the westernmost point of the North American highway grid.

The Sterling Highway heads out through Homer (Mile 172.8) to road's end at the tip of Homer Spit (Mile 179.5, see Chapter 13).

Details: *Paved road, open year-round, 140 miles from the Seward Highway to Homer. (3 hours with no stops)*

★ **KENAI NATIONAL WILDLIFE REFUGE VISITOR CENTER**
Ski Hill Road, Soldotna, 907/262-7021,
www.r7.fws.gov/nwr/kenai/kenainwr.html
Turn east at Mile 96.1 Seward Highway onto Funny River Road, then right to the top of Ski Hill Road or turn east directly onto Ski Hill Road at Mile 97.9 Sterling Highway. Information, exhibits, and presentations here are excellent.

Details: *Open Mon–Fri 8–4:30, weekends 10–6. (45 minutes)*

FITNESS AND RECREATION

An important section of Kenai Wildlife Refuge protects the **Swan Lake and Swanson River Canoe Trails**, one of only two designated federal canoe wildernesses in the United States. Take the Swanson River Road north from Sterling about 15 miles, then turn east on Swan Lake Road into a gap in the Kenai Wilderness unit of the refuge. The 80-mile, 40-lake Swanson River route is to the north, while the 60-mile, 30-lake Swan Lake route is south of the road. Roadside put-ins and parking are marked. **Morning Star Tours** (Kenai, 907/283-5621) offers guided canoe day trips in the region. **Kenai Canoe Trails** (888/655-4723) hosts day paddles and longer guided trips. In Soldotna, the **Fishin' Hole** (139 B Warehouse St., Soldotna, 907/262-2290) rents canoes. **Weigner's Backcountry Guiding** (Sterling, 907/262-7840) offers day trips and overnighters from $115 that include all gear and meals.

Alaska Rivers Co. (Cooper Landing, 907/595-1226) features guided float and fishing trips on the Kenai River.

The **Clam Gulch State Critical Habitat Area** between Homer and Cohoe is home to one of the major concentrations of razor clams in the Pacific. Diggers are allowed 60 clams per person in a day; the best results depend on lower-than-average low tides. Clamming access is found at Miles 111,

114, 135, 137.2, and 157 of the Sterling Highway. You can rent clamming gear or sign on for guided clamming with **Bob's Piscatorial Pursuits** (Soldotna, 907/260-5362, 360/374-2091 in winter, www.piscatorialpursuits.com).

FOOD

As is typical in Alaska, many if not most eating places are associated with lodging options. Check the Lodging section, below, for other dining choices.

The Sterling Highway in Soldotna is peppered with options. **Seasons Restaurant** (43960 Sterling Highway, Soldotna, 907/262-5006) is a very nice place, open from 11 to 3 for lunch and 5:30 to 10 for dinner. **Sal's Klondike Diner** (44619 Sterling Highway, Soldotna, 907/262-2220) offers just what you'd expect, and you can enjoy it 24 hours a day, year-round. For some decent Mexican food and maybe a margarita, try **Don Jose's** (44109 Sterling Highway, Soldotna, 907/262-5700). **Hogg Heaven Cafe** (44715 Sterling Highway, Soldotna, 907/262-4584) is a breakfast favorite for omelets and more.

You'll probably spot the Dairy Queen, McDonald's, and KFC as you enter Kenai, but there are other choices. One of Kenai's better restaurants, **Paradiso's** (Kenai Spur Road, one block east of the visitors center, Kenai, 907/283-2222) features a good but pricey Greek-based menu with Mexican and Italian options as well. With a name like **Little Ski-Mo Burger-N-Brew** (Spur Highway, Kenai, 907/283-4463), how can you miss? They serve every kind of burger imaginable; give it a try. How about the **Blue Grouse Drive-In** (43890 Kenai Spur Highway, Kenai, 907/283-4281) for an easy bite?

Ninilchik is home to the **Happy Wok** (15945 Sterling Highway, Ninilchik, 907/567-1060), featuring quick and tasty stir-fries and other good stuff. Also in town is the **Lunch Box** (66845 Swan Court, Ninilchik, 907/567-7304).

LODGING

Enjoy rustic luxury overlooking the Kenai River at the **Kenai Princess Lodge** (Mile 47.7 Sterling Highway, Cooper Landing, 800/426-0500, 907/595-1425). Rates at this tourist hotel range from $230 to $250 mid-June to August, $130 to $150 in shoulder season. A more pleasant place is the **Red Salmon Guest House** (Mile 48.2 Sterling Highway, Cooper Landing, 907/595-1733), featuring rooms from $80 to $100, private cabins for $130. Breakfast is served in a riverside dining room.

Perhaps the nicest choice in the area is the **Soldotna Bed & Breakfast Lodge** (399 Lovers Lane, Soldotna, toll-free 877/262-4779, 907/262-4779, www.soldotnalodge.com). Full breakfast can be served as early as 4:30 a.m. so you can pursue those kings. Tour and fishing packages are available. The **Best Western King Salmon** (35546 Kenai Spur Highway, Soldotna, 907/262-5857) offers dependable quality and a restaurant; rooms are $120 to $160. Right on the river, the **Kenai River Lodge** (Kenai River Bridge, Soldotna, 907/262-4292) affords nice views and easy fishing access. Rooms range from $60 to $110. **Soldotna Inn** (35041 Kenai Spur Highway, Soldotna, 907/262-9169) is a good motel and features Mykels Restaurant. Rooms run from $85 to $105. For the whole package, try the **RiverSide House** (44611 Sterling Highway, Soldotna, 907/262-0500). It is indeed right on the river and features a hotel, restaurant, lounge, and RV park, as well as a fishing guide service.

Contact Accommodations on the Kenai (Soldotna, 907/262-2139) for books B&Bs, lodges, cabins, charters, and more.

For a more Alaskan-style experience, book a cabin from **Beaver Creek Cabin Rentals** (Kenai, 907/283-4262). Cabins, right on the water, go for $100 to $150 per night. The **Katmai Hotel** (10800 Kenai Spur Highway at Main Street, Kenai, 907/283-6101) is a fine, basic establishment with $40 to $90 rooms and Ricky's Sourdough Café. The **Kenai Kings Inn** (10352 Kenai Spur Highway, Kenai, 907/283-6060) is another serviceable choice with basic rooms for $60 to $100. Dine at Don Again's Restaurant.

For a friendly, family B&B experience in the historic seaside community of Ninilchik, try the **Homestead House B&B** (66670 Oilwell Rd., Ninilchik, 888/697-3474, 907/567-3412) with rooms from $70. Fishing packages are offered. On the beach in Ninilchik Village is the **Beachcomber Motel** (Beach Access Road, Ninilchik, 907/567-3417), with rooms from $60 to $70 you'll want for their location, not their luxury.

CAMPING

Nowhere in Alaska is there a greater concentration of National Forest and State Recreation campgrounds than along the Kenai River and coast of Cook Inlet, all accessible from the Sterling Highway. Even so, virtually every site can be filled on the weekends from mid-June into August as Alaskans pour into the region in quest of salmon. Sites range from $6 to $10 and have fresh water, bathrooms, tables, and firepit/grills.

Campgrounds with at least 10 sites include: **Stern Lake** (Mile 37.4 Sterling Highway), **Quartz Lake** (Mile 45 Sterling Highway), **Cooper Creek** (Mile

50.5 Sterling Highway), **Russian River** (Mile 52.6 Sterling Highway, two miles in), **Isaak Walton** (from Mile 82 Sterling Highway), **Scout Lake** and **Morgan Lake** (from Mile 84.9 Sterling Highway via Scout Lake Loop), **Centennial Park** (Mile 96.1 Sterling Highway, turn west 0.1 mile), **Kasilof River** (Mile 109.4 Sterling Highway), **Johnson Lake** (Mile 110 Sterling Highway, go east, turn right at T), **Crooked Creek** (Mile 111 Sterling Highway, two miles west), **Clam Gulch** (Mile 117.4 Sterling Highway, 0.5 mile in), **Ninilchik** (Mile 134.5 Sterling Highway), **Deep Creek** (Mile 137.3 Sterling Highway), **Stariski** (Mile 151.9 Sterling Highway), and **Anchor River** (Mile 156.9 Sterling Highway, Old Seward Highway to Beach Access Road to reach six campgrounds).

Take 19-mile, gravel Skilak Loop Road from Mile 58 or 75.2 of the Sterling Highway to reach the following campgrounds (miles listed are from the east junction with the Sterling): **Hidden Lake** (0.5 mile on Skilak Road), **Upper Skilak Lake** (8.5 miles on Skilak Road, two miles on spur), and **Lower Skilak Lake** (13.8 miles on Skilak Road).

13
HOMER AND
KACHEMAK BAY

Homer anchors the southern end of the Sterling Highway and is the hub for several travel possibilities. The A.M.H.S. ferry stops here, offering access to Seldovia, Kodiak, Seward, and points beyond. Famous worldwide as a center for halibut sport fishing, the town is gaining renown as an artist colony; several galleries are found in the area. Though the scattered town lacks a true center, access to the various attractions and services is easy.

The town of Homer was named for Homer Pennock, an adventurer from New York who arrived with his shipmates on Homer Spit in 1896 seeking gold. It was a natural spot to establish a community, offering safe harbor and access to the rich fisheries of Kachemak Bay and Cook Inlet. With the completion of the Sterling Highway in the early 1950s, Homer gained a road link to the rest of the state.

The town's most distinctive feature is Homer Spit, a sandy, 4.5-mile projection into Kachemak Bay. Charter companies, gift shops, fishing spots, lodgings, and camping areas lie along Homer Spit Road, along with the famous Land's End Resort and the infamous Salty Dawg Saloon. The ferry pier and tour boat docks are also located on the spit.

The charming village of Seldovia is just across Kachemak Bay. A favorite summer boat tour crosses to the island enclave of Halibut Cove, famous for coastal beauty, art galleries, and the Saltry Restaurant. Backing both towns are the splendid Kenai Mountains, preserved in Kachemak State Park and State Wilderness Park. Across Cook Inlet, the active Augustine and Iliamna volcanoes rise like restless sentinels.

A PERFECT DAY IN HOMER

In the morning, visit the Pratt Museum, which contains an excellent exhibit on the *Exxon Valdez* spill. Then tour some of the galleries in town or drop by the Alaska Maritime National Wildlife Refuge Visitor Center. Head to Homer Spit in time for your pre-booked noon departure for Halibut Cove. Enjoy the scenery of the Kenai Mountains as you cover the five miles across Kachemak Bay to Ismailof Island aboard the historic *Danny J*. A meal at the Saltry is a must. On your return, duck into the old Salty Dawg for refreshment. Wind down with an evening stroll on Bishop's Beach.

ORIENTATION

When the Sterling Highway enters town, follow the road and you'll reach Homer Spit. Officially, the Sterling becomes Homer Bypass Road, merges into Lake Street, swings left onto Ocean Drive and then right onto Homer Spit Road. If it's downtown Homer you want, watch for Pioneer Street as you enter town and take a left. Most of Homer's eateries, the theater, library, and more are on Pioneer; the Pratt Museum is a block away on Bartlett Street.

Visitor information is available from the Homer Chamber of Commerce at 135 Sterline Highway, 907/235-7740, www.homeralaska.com, open daily 9 to 8.

Homer Tours offers—oddly enough—tours of Homer (Homer, 907/235-6200); stops include the Pratt Museum, Homer Spit, galleries, and shops. Kachemak Bay Transit (Homer, toll-free 877/235-9101, 907/235-3795) links Homer and Anchorage daily, with stops all along the Sterling and Seward Highways.

HOMER SIGHTSEEING HIGHLIGHTS

★★★ HALIBUT FISHING EXCURSION

Many charter companies based in Homer and Seldovia will take you out for a day of halibut fishing. To line up a boat and captain with

HOMER

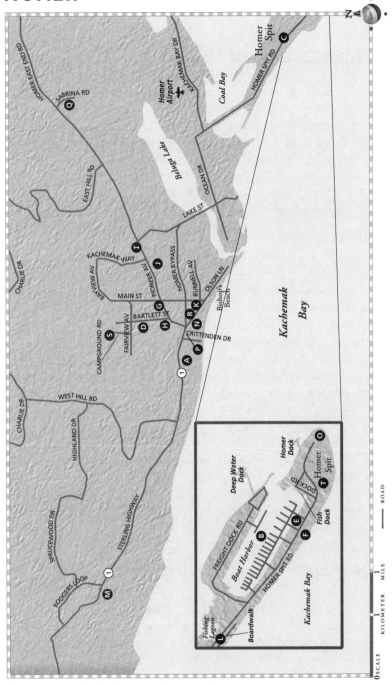

Homer Spit

Coal Bay

HOMER SPIT RD

KACHEMAK BAY DR

Homer Airport

Beluga Lake

OCEAN DR

LAKE ST

Kachemak Bay

HOMER EAST END RD

SABRINA RD

EAST HILL RD

CHARLIE DR

KACHEMAK WAY

BAYVIEW AV

PIONEER AV

HOMER BYPASS

BUNNELL AV

OLSON LN

Bishop's Beach

MAIN ST

BARTLETT ST

FAIRVIEW AV

CRITTENDEN DR

CAMPGROUND RD

CHARLIE DR

WEST HILL RD

HIGHLAND DR

SPRUCEWOOD DR

STERLING HIGHWAY

RODGERS LOOP

Deep Water Dock

Homer Dock

Homer Spit

DOCK RD

FREIGHT DOCK RD

Boat Harbor

HOMER SPIT RD

Fish Dock

Kachemak Bay

Fishing Lagoon

Boardwalk

ROAD

0 SCALE

1 KILOMETER

1 MILE

just one call, contact the **Central Charter Booking Agency** (Homer, 800/478-7847, 907/235-7847), which has access to about a dozen fishing boats and books various guides and tours, such as flightseeing and bear viewing. **Homer Alaska Referral** (Homer, 907/235-8996) will match your interests and comfort needs to the appropriate boat and trip. The service also books area flightseeing and tours, lodging statewide, Kenai River fishing, and Kenai Fjords tours.

Details: *(half to full day)*

★★★ **HOMER SPIT**
Via Homer Spit Road, Homer
This 4.5-mile strip of sand stretches nearly halfway across Kachemak Bay. The currents and tides of Cook Inlet created the spit in an age-long effort to smooth the rough edges of the coastline. The 1964 quake reduced its width in parts by as much as two-thirds. Since then, efforts have been undertaken to stabilize the spit with rocks and breakwaters.

Along the road, you'll find places to beachcomb and camp. Most of the businesses are near the spit's end, including shops and eateries, the small boat harbor, ferry dock, tour companies, fishing charters, and Land's End Resort. Other than the Salty Dawg (see below), there really aren't any specific attractions. Enjoy.

Details: *(1 1/2 hours)*

SIGHTS

Ⓐ Alaska Maritime
   National Wildlife
   Refuge Visitor Center
Ⓑ Halibut Fishing
   Excursion
Ⓒ Homer Spit
Ⓓ Pratt Museum
Ⓔ Salty Dawg Saloon

FOOD

Ⓕ Boardwalk Fish and
   Chips
Ⓖ Cafe Cups
Ⓗ Espresso Express

FOOD *(continued)*

Ⓘ Knife, Fork & Spoon
Ⓙ Neon Coyote Cafe
Ⓚ Two Sisters Espresso
   and Bakery
Ⓛ Whale's Cove

LODGING

Ⓜ Bay View Inn
Ⓝ Bidarka Inn/Best
   Western
Ⓞ Land's End Resort
Ⓟ Ocean Shores Motel
Ⓠ Road Runner Bed &
   Breakfast

CAMPING

Ⓡ Driftwood Inn and RV
   Park
Ⓢ Karen Hornaday Park
Ⓣ Land's End RV Park

SIDE TRIP: HALIBUT COVE

Take a day trip out to Halibut Cove village, located at the mouth of Halibut Cove on Ismailof Island. Once an important center for the thriving herring fishery of Kachemak Bay, it is now home to about 80 people, including several artists. Only about 10,000 guests are allowed to visit the village each summer. A few blocks of boardwalk host some galleries and the excellent Saltry Restaurant (see below). For information on the village, call 907/235-7847.

The way to get to Halibut Cove is via **"Danny J" Tours** *(reserve via Central Charters, 907/235-7847). This charming old fishing boat covers the five miles from Homer Spit to Halibut Cove on two daily round trips throughout the summer. The Danny J departs at noon for day trips with a 4 p.m. return, and at 5 p.m. for residents, Saltry diners, and overnight guests. Jakolof Ferry Service (see Seldovia Side Trip) operates a daily boat from Jakolof Dock.*

The renowned **Saltry Restaurant** *(Halibut Cove, 907/296-2223) is the only restaurant in Halibut Cove. Specializing in seafood, the menu includes fresh and international specials daily, pasta, chowders, and fresh mussels. Breads are baked in-house, and salads come from local gardens. Reservations are suggested.*

For overnights, try the **Quiet Place Lodge** *(Halibut Cove, 907/296-2212, www.quietplace.com). The name says it all. It's $185 for two in a cabin with shared bath. A complete breakfast is included in the price. Dinners are offered every other evening. The lodge offers kayak and skiff rentals.*

★★★ PRATT MUSEUM
3779 Bartlett St., Homer, 907/235-8635,
www.alaska.net/~pratt

All aspects of the *Exxon Valdez* oil spill and its aftermath are explored in perhaps the best exhibit at this fine museum. Elsewhere, visitors can enjoy aquariums and a tide-pool tank, an old homestead cabin, and an extensive display on the "Cultures of Kachemak Bay." A small botanical garden and nature trail are found on the grounds. Kids might enjoy aquarium feeding time, Tuesdays and Fridays at 4 p.m.

Inquire about the Historic Harbor Tour sponsored by the museum and the Kachemak Bay Wooden Boat Society.

Details: *Mid-May–mid-Sept daily 10–6 (Thu–Sat until 8); winter Tue–Sun 12–5, closed January. $4 adults, $3 seniors, $2 ages 13–18, $1 ages 6–12, under 6 free. (1–2 hours)*

★★★ SALTY DAWG SALOON
Homer Spit Road, Homer, 907/235-9990

This wonderful establishment, thick with character, is reputed to be a hangout for the rougher edges of the population. The Salty Dawg comprises two joined cabins, the first built in 1897, the second in 1909. Separately, the structures once served as Homer's first post office, a rail station, grocery store, mining office, schoolhouse, and residence. Joined in 1957 to serve their current purpose, the bar was moved to its present location after the 1964 quake.

Take a seat at one of the thick-topped plank tables etched with knife-carved initials from 10,000 nights of drinking. Enjoy the pure Alaskan ambiance—though, these days, you're as likely to see GoreTex jackets and camera bags as you are to spot knife scars and eye patches.

Look for the small, fake lighthouse as you drive the Homer Spit Road.

Details: *(30 minutes–full evening)*

★★ ALASKA MARITIME NATIONAL WILDLIFE REFUGE VISITOR CENTER
451 Sterling Highway, Homer, 907/235-6961,
Refuge Manager 907/235-6546,
www.r7.fws.gov/nwr/akmnwr/akmnwr.html

Whether or not you're one of the few who will visit the Aleutians and Bering Sea Islands, this center is worth a stop. The vast Alaska Maritime National Wildlife Refuge encompasses thousands of square miles of islands, shoreline and ocean and protects extensive wilderness, vital fisheries, and outstanding bird and mammal habitat. The visitor center features displays, information on the refuge, and literature about recreation options available through area wildlife tour providers.

The visitor center also offers ranger-guided morning coastal walks on Bishop's Beach and Land's End. Call or visit for walk times and more information.

Details: Memorial Day–Labor Day daily 9–6; call for off-season hours. *(30 minutes)*

FITNESS AND RECREATION

It's pleasant to hike along Bishop's Beach, perhaps as far as the low headland of Bluff Point. The beach is accessible via a picnic area from Bunnell Avenue. Trail rides along the shore of Kachemak Bay are offered by **Trails End Horse Adventure** (Mile 11.2 East End Road, 907/235-6393). Rates are $20 for a one-hour ride, $50 to $65 for half-day rides.

True North Kayak Adventures (Homer, 907/235-0708, book through Central Charters, 907/ 235-7847) offers one-day guided kayak trips on Kachemak Bay, lunch included. A water taxi shuttles out to the company's island base, where you'll learn what you need to know before setting out. No experience is necessary.

If the thought of bobbing on the swells doesn't appeal to you, consider a land-based fishing trip with the **Walking River Guide** (Fritz Creek, out East End Road, 907/235-7429). Riverbank fishing and clamming are both offered, $125 per person, less for large groups.

You can enjoy helicopter flightseeing and "heli-hiking" with **Maritime Helicopters** (Homer airstrip, 907/235-7771). Custom options are available, including a glacier landing, Halibut Cove visit, Barren Islands beachcombing, or circling Augustine volcano.

FOOD

Some eateries are found at the accommodations listed in the Lodging section, below, notably the Land's End Resort restaurant.

In the heart of town, you can't miss the interesting exterior of **Cafe Cups** (168 W. Pioneer Drive, Homer, 907/235-8330). The menu, interior, and evening guest poets complete the artistry of the place. It's open from 7:30 a.m. to 10 p.m. Enjoy great food at good prices at the **Neon Coyote Cafe** (435 Pioneer, Homer, 907/235-6226). For vegetarian dishes, soups, salads, sandwiches, sundaes, and shakes, drop in at the **Knife, Fork & Spoon** (510 E. Pioneer, Homer, 907/235-1955). **Two Sisters Espresso and**

Birders will want to take advantage of the Birdwatchers Hotline (in Homer, 907/235-7337), which provides information on birding activities, sightings, and locations.

KACHEMAK BAY REGION

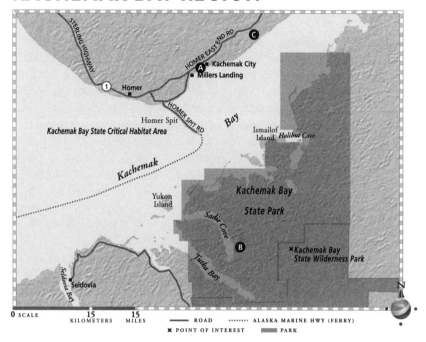

FOOD
Ⓐ Homestead Restaurant

LODGING
Ⓑ Sadie Cove Wilderness Lodge
Ⓒ Seaside Farm/Hostel & Camping

Bakery (106 W. Bunnell, Homer, 907/235-2280) features espresso, baked goods, and an art gallery. It's a great place to collect your thoughts. If the weather allows, you can enjoy your latte and panini on the pleasant deck in front of **Espresso Express** (280 W. Pioneer, Homer, 907/235-3688).

Out on the spit, hit the shops of Cannery Row to find **Boardwalk Fish & Chips** (Homer, 907/235-7749). It's fast and tasty. At the **Whale's Cove** (Thompson Boardwalk, 4025 Homer Spit Rd., Homer Spit, 907/235-4328), enjoy char-broiled halibut or salmon steaks, homemade chowder, burgers, and more. It's open daily noon to 9.

Head out East End Road to reach the **Homestead Restaurant** (Mile 8.2 East End Road, 907/235-8723), featuring local seafood and prime rib. It's open daily 5 to 10; reservations are suggested.

The charming town of Seldovia on the south side of Kachemak Bay is a wonderful choice for a day trip or overnight excursion from Homer. Long the site of a native fish camp, the modern community was established by Russian settlers in the 1870s. In 1891 they built St. Nicholas Orthodox Church, which stands today a fully restored community landmark and designated National Historic Site. Scandinavians arrived for the herring boom in the 1920s and stayed on to harvest halibut, salmon, and crab.

Residents constructed a boardwalk in 1931 to facilitate travel through town, earning Seldovia its designation as "the boardwalk town." The 1964 earthquake caused coastlands to sink and tide waters to wash over the boardwalk and into buildings. Subsequently, parts of the town were moved and reconstructed in the same theme; a portion of the original boardwalk may still be seen at the south end of Main Street.

Stroll Main Street for the shops, and walk along the boardwalk and slough. The **Seldovia Historic Museum** (Anderson Way at "Swamp Troll Strollway," Seldovia) displays heritage items. A town walking tour is marked by informative signs. Take Main Street north to Spring Street, which curves up to the trailhead of the Otterbahn Trail. The trail passes through forest and by boardwalk across a lagoon to reach the beach. Contact the Chamber of Commerce (Seldovia, 907/234-7612) for information. There's a visitors kiosk at the airstrip and an information center at Synergy Artworks.

Jakolof Ferry Service (based in Homer Spit, 907/235-2376, www.xyz.net/~jakolof) has service to Sadie Cove Lodge and Jakolof Dock ($45, tours more). From the dock, a taxi or tour bus (907/234-8000) takes you in to Seldovia. **Homer Air** (Homer airstrip, 907/235-8591) is a great choice for reaching Seldovia and enjoying some flightseeing on the way. The company offers a variety of packages, as well as Seldovia stopover fares.

LODGING

The **Land's End Resort** (4786 Homer Spit Rd., Homer, AK 99603, 800/478-0400, 907/235-0400) is Homer's most famous lodging option. Located at the very tip of Homer Spit, the resort offers pleasant rooms, a good restaurant, a big deck, and great views. Rates run from $95 to $125 in

Package boat tours are offered by **Rainbow Charters** (Cannery Row Boardwalk, Homer Spit, 907/235-7272); fares cost $55, $48 for seniors, $43 for "juniors." The A.M.H.S. ferry **M/V Tustamena** (907/235-8449 in Homer; see Chapter 14, Kodiak and the Wild Southwest) connects Homer and Seldovia about twice a week.

Seldovia boasts several appealing eateries on Main Street. Try the **Buzz Coffeehouse/Cafe** (Main Street, across from Russian church, 907/234-7479) for "gourmet food with a local flavor." Specializing in vegetarian dishes and espresso drinks, it is open 6 to 6 daily in summer. The **Mad Fish Restaurant** (Main Street at Fulmore, Seldovia, 907/234-7676) features local fresh seafood, burgers, steaks, and wine and beer; it's open daily for lunch and dinner.

My top choice for lodging in Seldovia is the wonderful **Seldovia Rowing Club Bed & Breakfast** (boardwalk, Seldovia, 907/234-7614). With sunset views of Seldovia Slough through picture windows, big decks, homey suites with all the comforts, and a charming and friendly keeper, you'll regret you aren't staying longer. Another good option is the **Swan House B&B** (Seldovia, 800/921-1900, 907/234-8888). Rooms with shared or private bath are available in this modern wood frame nestled among the trees by a lake. Seldovia's **Boardwalk Hotel** (boardwalk, Seldovia, 907/234-7816) offers a one-night package that includes water taxi from Homer for $120. The hotel features rooms with private baths and a harbor-view deck. Call to inquire about cruise–overnight-flight packages starting at $130.

Camping in Seldovia is available at **Wilderness Park** (Jakolof Bay Road, Seldovia, 907/234-7643). If you're tenting, you can camp on the beach.

winter, $110 to $160 in summer. The **Bay View Inn** (Mile 170 Sterling Highway, Homer, 800/478-8485 in Alaska, 907/235-8485) features great views and very nice rooms, including fireplace suites and a honeymoon cottage. Rates are $95, $140 for suites and cottage. The **Ocean Shores Motel** (3500 Crittendon, Homer, 907/235-7775) has rooms for $95 and up with ocean views. On the way into town, you'll find the **Bidarka**

© Paul Otteson

Inn/Best Western (575 Sterling Highway, Homer, 907/235-8148), a full-service hotel with restaurant and bar. Summer rates are $105 to $125.

Two good options out the East End Road attract adventure travelers and backpackers. A variety of accommodations awaits visitors at the wonderful **Seaside Farm/Hostel & Camping** (58335 East End Rd., Homer, 907/235-7850). Hostel bunks go for $15, tentsites $6, cabins $55. Bring your own bedding (rental $3). The **Road Runner B&B** (Sabrina Road from East End Road, Homer, 907/235-6581, 907/235-3678) is known as a meeting place for visitors from around the world. Rates range from $35 to $65.

For a nice remote stay, try **Sadie Cove Wilderness Lodge** (in Kachemak Bay State Park, 888/283-7234, 907/235-2350, www.triple1.com/usa/ak/SadieCove2.htm), right on the shore of the deep bay. Activities here include salmon fishing, guided hikes, kayaking, clamming, Halibut Cove tours, and more. Visitors stay in comfortable rustic cabins. Rates are $175 per person per night, plus $40 round-trip water taxi from Homer.

CAMPING

Land's End RV Park (4786 Homer Spit Rd., Homer, 907/235-0404) is the best option for campers or RVs on the spit. Sites run $14 to $23. **Driftwood Inn and RV Park** (135 W. Bunnell St., Homer, 800/478-8019, 907/235-

8019, www.netalaska.com/driftwood) offers 22 full-hookup RV sites, as well as 21 motel rooms. You'll find 33 campsites at **Karen Hornaday Park**, a city park perched above the ball fields near Bartlett and Fairview Avenues. Enjoy nice bay views.

For several campgrounds along the Sterling Highway north of Homer, see Chapter 12, Western Kenai Peninsula.

14
KODIAK AND THE WILD SOUTHWEST

With 8,000 residents, Kodiak is by far the largest town on Kodiak Island, known as the "Emerald Isle" for its lush vegetation. The island has been occupied by Alutiiq (Sugpiak) Eskimos and their predecessors for perhaps 9,500 years. Russians established the first non-native settlement on the island in 1784. In 1792, Alexander Baranof founded Kodiak (then called Pauloysk) at its present site.

Three events this century have shaken Kodiak. On June 6, 1912, Novarupta volcano erupted across the strait, blacking out the town for three days and blanketing the island with a layer of ash as much as two feet deep. Thirty years later, Kodiak became a major staging area for World War II operations. Most recently, the 1964 earthquake wrecked the Kodiak waterfront. All of this history is preserved in several excellent sights.

The rest of the Southwest is filled with opportunities for adventure. Remarkable Katmai National Park and McNeil River State Game Sanctuary host an amazing concentration of brown bears. The barren Alaska Peninsula and Aleutian Islands feature volcanoes, superb birding, and lonely villages. To the north of Bristol Bay, the town of Dillingham is a base for visiting Wood-Tikchik State Park or Walrus Islands State Game Reserve. Across Cook Inlet from Anchorage, Lake Clark National Park protects some of Alaska's most rugged mountains.

A Southwest adventure will take you beyond the crowds and treat you to some of the best the state has to offer.

A PERFECT DAY AROUND KODIAK

Bear viewing beats out all other options for visitors to this area. If you've planned ahead *and* won the lottery (literally; see details below), you'll see your bears at McNeil River. If you decide to splurge on a trip to Brooks Camp in Katmai National Park, you'll have more company and fewer bears, but still a remarkable experience. If time is tight, take a "guaranteed" bear-viewing flight from Kodiak, trusting the pilot to know where the wild things are. Any way you go, having 1,000-pound brown bears feast just a few short feet away from where you watch in awe is a highlight—not just of a trip, but of a lifetime.

ORIENTATION

In Kodiak, Rezanof Drive stays within a couple blocks of the waterfront as it winds from the airport, through the heart of town, and around to Fort Abercrombie State Park, encompassing the area of most interest to visitors. The heart of town and all the chief historic sites are found between the small boat harbor and the bridge to Bear Island and between Rezanof Drive and the water.

Pick up information and a town map at the Kodiak Convention & Visitors Bureau (100 Marine Way, Kodiak, 907/486-4782, www.kodiak.org). For the other Southwestern highlights listed below, contact the information sources noted.

KODIAK SIGHTSEEING HIGHLIGHTS

★★★★ GUARANTEED BEAR VIEWING

"Guaranteed?" you might ask. That's exactly what it means. Pilots know where the bears are feeding, and they will take you to see them—in some places landing a floatplane within 50 feet of the blasé bears. You'll watch as half-ton beasts catch the hapless salmon, eating their brains, skin, and roe, then discarding the rest for the dubious benefit of overfed seagulls—all occurring close enough for you to spot the plaque on the animal's two-inch incisor. If a 1,300-pound male swims by so close you could stretch out and grab an ear, don't.

From Kodiak, a few companies offer bear viewing, as well as flightseeing, drop-offs, and fishing charters. Uyak Air Service (Kodiak, 800/303-3407, 907/486-3407, www.alaskaoutdoors.com/Uyak/) is a company I've flown with. Others include Island Air Service (Kodiak, 800/504-2327, 907/486-6196), Sea Hawk Air Inc. (800/770-4295,

KODIAK

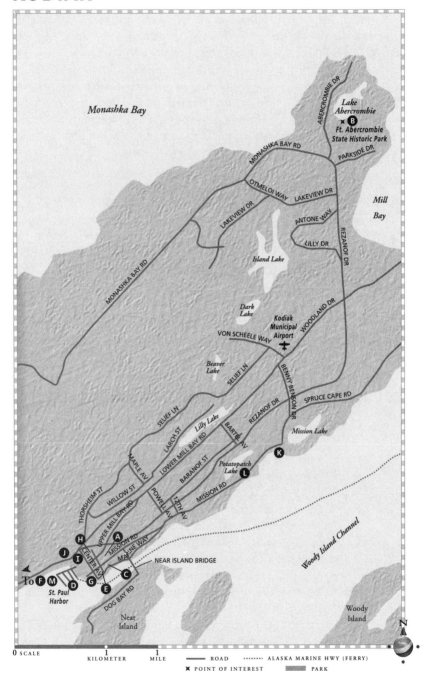

Monashka Bay

Mill Bay

Lake Abercrombie

✖ **B** Ft. Abercrombie State Historic Park

ABERCROMBIE DR

PARKSIDE DR

MONASHKA BAY RD

OTMELOI WAY

LAKEVIEW DR

LAKEVIEW DR

ANTONE WAY

LILLY DR

REZANOF DR

Island Lake

MONASHKA BAY RD

Dark Lake

Kodiak Municipal Airport ✈

WOODLAND DR

VON SCHEELE WAY

Beaver Lake

SELIEF LN

SELIEF LN

BENNY BENSON DR

SPRUCE CAPE RD

LARCH ST

Lilly Lake

LOWER MILL BAY RD

BARTEL AV

REZANOF DR

Mission Lake

MAPLE AV

BARANOF ST

K

WILLOW ST

POWELL AV

12TH AV

Potatopatch Lake

L

THORSHEIM ST

UPPER MILL BAY RD

MISSION RD

MISSION RD

A

MARINE WAY

H

CENTER AV

MARINE WAY

J

I

NEAR ISLAND BRIDGE

C

To ◄ **F** **M** **D** **G** **E**

DOG BAY RD

St. Paul Harbor

Near Island

Woody Island Channel

Woody Island

N

0 SCALE   1 KILOMETER   1 MILE   ▬▬ ROAD   ⋯⋯⋯ ALASKA MARINE HWY (FERRY)

✖ POINT OF INTEREST   ▬ PARK

907/486-8282), and Wilderness Air (Kodiak, 800/556-8101, 907/486-8101).

Details: (half day)

★★★ **ALUTIIQ MUSEUM/ARCHAEOLOGICAL REPOSITORY**
215 Mission Rd., Kodiak, 907/486-7004,
www.ptialaska.net/~alutiiq2
This nice new facility has been established to help preserve the language and culture of the native peoples on Kodiak Island. Local archaeologists are often on hand to interpret the excellent touring exhibits, as well as the fine and growing permanent collection.
Details: Open summer daily Mon–Fri 9–5, Sat 10–4, Sun 11–4; winter Tue–Fri 10–4, Sat 12–4. $2 adults, under 12 free. (1 hour)

★★★ **KODIAK BARANOV MUSEUM/ERSKINE HOUSE**
101 Marine Way, Kodiak, 907/486-5920
Built in 1808 as a secure magazine and storehouse, the Erskine House is one of the four original Russian structures remaining in the United States. The house is named for Wilbur Erskine, an officer of the Alaska Commercial Company. Today, it hosts the Baranov Museum with its collection of Aleut, Koniag, Russian, and American artifacts.
Details: Mid-May–Labor Day Mon–Fri 10–4, weekends 12–4; call for winter hours. (45 minutes)

SIGHTS

Ⓐ Alutiiq Museum/Archaeological Repository
Ⓑ Fort Abercrombie State Historic Site
Ⓒ Holy Resurrection Russian Orthodox Church
Ⓓ Guaranteed Bear Viewing
Ⓔ Kodiak Baranov Museum/Erskine House
Ⓕ Kodiak National Wildlife Refuge/Visitor Center
Ⓖ Liberty Ship Cannery

FOOD

Ⓗ Captain's Restaurant
Ⓗ El Chicano
Ⓘ Shire Bookstore

LODGING

Ⓙ Best Western Kodiak Inn
Ⓚ Shahafka Cove Bed and Breakfast
Ⓛ Wintel's Bed and Breakfast

CAMPING

Ⓜ Buskin River State Park
Ⓑ Fort Abercrombie State Park

Note: Items with the same letter are located in the same area.

★★ FORT ABERCROMBIE STATE HISTORIC SITE
Abercrombie Drive, 907/486-6339,
www.ptialaska.net/~kodsp/ftaber.html
The remains of a World War II military installation and a rugged coastline with several access trails are found at this popular, easily accessible park. A campground, group recreation site, and overflow parking for RV campers are available.

Details: *Located four miles north of downtown via Rezanof Drive. Public access. (2 hours)*

★★ HOLY RESURRECTION RUSSIAN ORTHODOX CHURCH
385 Kashavarof St., Kodiak, 907/486-3854
This Kodiak landmark is the oldest Orthodox parish in the state. Originally consecrated in 1794, the building underwent its fifth reconstruction in 1949–50. A replica of the first version can be seen at the seminary on Mission Road near Island Bridge. Drop by on your town walk, or call for a schedule of tours and services.

Details: *Call for hours and services. (30 minutes)*

★ KODIAK NATIONAL WILDLIFE REFUGE/ VISITOR CENTER
1390 Buskin River Rd., Kodiak, 907/487-2600,
www.r7.fws.gov/nwr/kodiak/kodnwr.html
Most of Kodiak Island is encompassed within the Kodiak National Wildlife Refuge, established in 1941 to preserve Kodiak brown bear habitat. While the peerless Kodiak brown bears are protected in certain areas, they are actively hunted in much of the refuge and thus are more skittish and usually harder to view than in Katmai. Recreational opportunities in the refuge include river trips, sea kayaking, and fishing.

The visitors center offers displays, films, information, and reservations for eight public-use cabins.

Details: *Open summer daily Mon–Fri 8–4:30, weekends 8–4; winter Mon–Fri 8–4:30. (30 minutes)*

★ LIBERTY SHIP CANNERY
Bottom of Marine Way near ferry dock, center of town
It's hard to miss this ship-turned-factory. After the 1964 earthquake, old World War II Liberty Ships were made available for emergency

© Paul Otteson

use. Take a look at this one from the outside. You'll have to talk your way in if you want to see how they process fish where once they hauled munitions and soldiers.

Details: *Walk by for a view. (10 minutes)*

SOUTHWEST SIGHTSEEING HIGHLIGHTS

★★★★ **ALEUTIAN ISLANDS/***M/V TUSTAMENA* **FERRY TRIP**
Alaska Marine Highway System, 800/642-0066,
www.dot.state.ak.us/external/amhs/home.html
About 10 times every summer, the A.M.H.S. ferry *Tustamena* travels from Homer out to Dutch Harbor/Unalaska and back, stopping at Kodiak and several Alaska Peninsula and Aleutian Islands towns. There is time in port for a brief walkabout before the *Tustamena*'s horn urges passengers back aboard. The route is exposed to the open ocean at many points. Those undaunted by rough seas can enjoy a fantastic and comparatively inexpensive experience.

Good places to link the ferry and flights include Cold Bay and Dutch Harbor/Unalaska. Both towns offer interesting activities for a stay of a day or more.

The chief community in the Aleutians, **Unalaska** (Convention & Visitors Bureau, 907/581-2612) is the name of both town and island, while Dutch Harbor refers to the port, air, and cannery facilities of adjacent Amaknak Island. Half of all fish harvested in Alaska are landed in Dutch Harbor—$160 million worth. Scheduled wildlife tours take visitors out and around the sheltered bays. While in town, walk the **Bunker Hill Trail** (0.75 mile, 421-foot gain) for a great view and some World War II history. Visit the **Holy Ascension Cathedral**, the unmistakable centerpiece of Unalaska built in 1825 and fully restored in 1996. Inside is one of the state's best collections of Russian artifacts, religious icons, and artworks.

Cold Bay was built around a now-defunct military base and today hosts a major runway that handles larger planes. It is also the gateway to the wonderful birding opportunities of **Izembek National Wildlife Refuge** (Cold Bay, 907/532-2445, www.r7.fws.gov/nwr/izembek/iznwr.html), featuring easy access via old military roads to Izembek Lagoon. Consult the refuge manager for options.

Details: Round-trip ferry from Homer is four days. Flights between Anchorage and Cold Bay or Dutch Harbor are offered by Reeve Aleutian Airways (800/544-2248), PenAir (800/448-4226), and Alaska Airlines (800/426-0333). (1 day minimum)

★★★★ BROOKS CAMP/KATMAI NATIONAL PARK
Headquarters, P.O. Box 7, King Salmon, AK 99613, 907/246-3305, www.nps.gov/katm/

Located where waters flow from Brooks Lake, over Brooks Falls, and into Naknek Lake, Brooks Camp is at the heart of Katmai National Park. Salmon struggle up the waters between the lakes to the benefit of fishing humans and brown bears. Rangers insist that visitors follow strict guidelines for behavior around the bears. Visitors typically fly from Anchorage to King Salmon, then shuttle by floatplane to Brooks Camp. **Brooks Lodge** (reservations, 800/544-0551) and **Brooks Camp Campground** (reservations, 800/365-2267) are the only accommodations. Only restaurant food is available. Reser-vations are necessary. Camping is $5; lodge stays $320 per room, up to four people per room.

Katmai concentrates 15 of the 70 active volcanoes in Alaska. In the last major eruption in 1912, Novarupta volcano dropped some 2 billion tons of ash, pumice, and debris over a 40-square-mile region. Thousands of vents and fumaroles sent steam plumes into the air, earning the region the nickname "Valley of Ten Thousand

Smokes." Since then, the ash has cooled and settled, putting an end to almost all steam activity. Brooks Camp visitors can take a shuttle over a 23-mile road to a viewpoint and short trail. Off-trail hiking and long-distance backpacking are options.

Flights to King Salmon from Anchorage and other points are offered by Alaska Airlines (800/426-0333), PenAir (800/448-4226), and Reeve Aleutian Airways (800/544-2248). Floatplane flights from King Salmon to Brooks Camp are offered by Branch River Air (907/246-3437, 907/248-2529 winter), C Air (907/246-6318, 907/688-3969 winter), Egli Air Haul (907/246-3554), and Katmai Air (907/246-3079, 907/243-5448). From Homer, Hughes Air (Homer, 888/299-1014, www.hughesair.com) flies to Brooks Camp and offers various fishing and flightseeing packages.

Details: (several days)

★★★★ **LAKE CLARK NATIONAL PARK AND PRESERVE**
Headquarters, 4230 University Dr., Suite 311, Anchorage, 907/271-3751
Field Headquarters, Port Alsworth, 907/781-2218,
www.nps.gov/lacl
Home to two impressive volcanoes, beautiful lakes, and glacier-shredded mountains, Lake Clark National Park and Preserve is a wilderness jewel. There are no roads in the park and only one trail, three miles long. Most visitors fly from Anchorage direct to a chosen drop-off. Facilities exist at Port Alsworth, including a designated camping area and small visitors center.

An excellent choice is a stay at **Alaska's Lake Clark Inn** (on Lake Clark within preserve, 1 Lang Rd., Port Alsworth, 907/781-2224, 907/781-2252). You can just relax and enjoy the views, or let the owner/pilot/innkeeper set you up for flightseeing, fishing, lake trips, and other adventures.

This is a wilderness park. All unguided visitors should be fully equipped and competent in outdoor skills. For flights from Anchorage to Port Alsworth contact Regal Air (4506 Lakeshore Dr., Anchorage, 907/243-8535, www.alaska.net/~regalair).

Details: (several days)

★★★★ **MCNEIL RIVER STATE GAME SANCTUARY**
The McNeil River flows from high cirques and glaciers in Katmai National Park down into Cook Inlet. In this valley dwells the greatest

seasonal concentration of brown bears in the world. The state has created a sanctuary, banning all hunting and fishing. Permission to visit the sanctuary is by lottery selection from all applications received. Applications are obtained via written or phone request to the Alaska Department of Fish and Game, Division of Wildlife Conservation (333 Raspberry Rd., Anchorage, AK 99502, 907/267-2182 for applications, 907/267-2137 for information, www.state.ak.us/adfg/wildlife/region2/refuge2/mr-home.htm). You must submit the application and a nonrefundable $25 fee before March 1.

Only 200 to 300 of the thousands who apply win the chance to go for a four-day stay. Non-Alaskan lottery winners must pay a $250 fee. Visitors cover all costs for transportation and supply their own food, camping gear, and waders for stream crossings. Rangers lead small groups on a two-hour hike from the camping area to a viewing pad by the falls, where as many as a hundred bears may congregate at a time (though usually fewer).

Details: *For more information, contact the Alaska Department of Fish and Game, Division of Wildlife Conservation, 907/344-0541. (4 days)*

★★★★ PRIBILOF ISLANDS/BIRDING TRIP
Town of Saint Paul, 907/546-2331,
www.seanet.com/~fowler/st_paul.htm
Two million seabirds make the Pribilof Islands home for the summer, most nesting among the cliffs. Fur seals also congregate here by the hundreds to bear their young. On Saint Paul Island is the town of Saint Paul, the largest community of Aleuts in the world (about 500). The town hosts most of the island's 700 annual visitors, the majority of whom come on a tour to observe some of the 225 bird species that have been identified. Arctic blue fox, fur seals, sea lions, whales, and reindeer are also commonly seen.

Details: *Tours and flights are offered by Reeve Aleutian Airways (800/544-2248). (1 day–several days)*

★★★★ WALRUS ISLANDS STATE GAME SANCTUARY
Alaska Department of Fish and Game, office in Juneau,
907/465-4100, www.state.ak.us/local/akpages/FISH.GAME/
wildlife/region2/refuge2/rnd-isl.htm
Round Island is the most important of the four islands and coastlands in the refuge. Up to 12,000 male walruses return here each spring,

gathering on the beach well into July. Steller's sea lions also come ashore and 450,000 seabirds nest on the rugged isles. Permits to visit the sanctuary are available from May 1 to August 15. Visitors typically pay about $200 for a Dillingham–Togiak round-trip flight, and $300 to boat to Round Island with a handful of other permit holders for a several-day stay. Contact the Department of Fish and Game for information and permits.

Johnson Maritime/Walrus Island Expeditions (Dillingham, 907-842-2102, www.alaskawalrusisland.com) offers up to six-day trips via a 50-foot motor yacht to view the walruses and other wildlife.

Details: *Reeve Aleutian Airways (800/544-2248), PenAir (800/448-4226), and Alaska Airlines (800/426-0333) have flights to Dillingham. (several days)*

★★★★ WOOD-TIKCHIK STATE PARK
Headquarters (May 15–Sept), Dillingham, 907/842-2375; headquarters (Oct–May 14), 3601 C St., Suite 300, Anchorage, 907/762-2654

Wood-Tikchik, the largest state park in the nation, features long, deep "finger" lakes nestled in steep valleys of the tundra-covered Wood River Mountains. The interconnected lakes afford pleasant stillwater paddling, though jetboats are commonly used for access. The park is reached via Dillingham, involving a $320-plus round-trip flight from Anchorage. Floatplane or boat shuttles can drop you where you like. Hiking the valleys and ridges of the Wood River Mountains is a great option from certain points.

Sportfishers often buy a lodge package, such as the one offered by the wonderful and pricey Tikchik Narrows Lodge (907/243-8450, www.tikchiklodge.com).

Reeve Aleutian Airways (800/544-2248), PenAir (800/448-4226), and Alaska Airlines (800/426-0333) have flights to Dillingham. Reel Wilderness Adventures (Dillingham, 800/726-8323) has fly-fishing packages into the park. Tikchik Riverboat Service (Dillingham, 907/842-4014) offers boat fishing trips up into the lower lakes.

Details: *(several days)*

FITNESS AND RECREATION
A walk about Kodiak is a fine choice. **Fort Abercrombie State Park** boasts a bike path and several hiking trails.

WILD SOUTHWEST

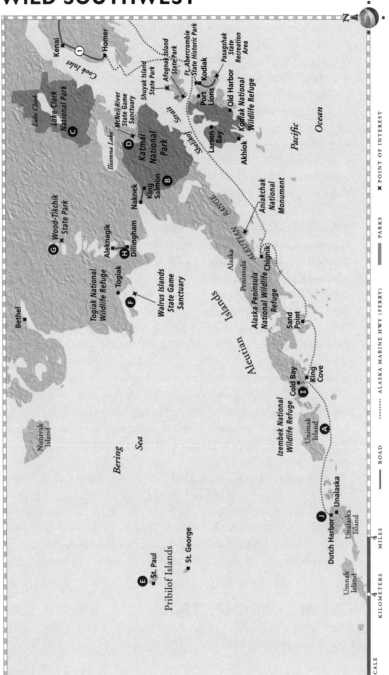

Kenai
Homer
Cook Inlet
Lake Clark
Lake Clark National Park
McNeil River State Game Sanctuary
Iliamna Lake
Afognak Island State Park
Shuyak Island State Park
Ft. Abercrombie State Historic Park
Pasagshak State Recreation Area
Kodiak
Port Lions
Old Harbor
Kodiak National Wildlife Refuge
Katmai National Park
King Salmon
Naknek
Larsen Bay
Akhiok
Shelikof Strait
Strait
Aniakchak National Monument
Wood-Tikchik State Park
Aleknagik
Dillingham
Togiak
Togiak National Wildlife Refuge
Walrus Islands State Game Sanctuary
Bethel
Chignik
Alaska Peninsula National Wildlife Refuge
Sand Point
Alaska Peninsula
ALEUTIAN RANGE
Aleutian Islands
Izembek National Wildlife Refuge
Cold Bay
King Cove
Unimak Island
Nunivak Island
Bering Sea
Pribilof Islands
St. Paul
St. George
Dutch Harbor
Unalaska
Unalaska Island
Umnak Island
Pacific Ocean

A
B
C
D
E
F
G
H
I
J
1

SCALE
0
KILOMETERS 4
MILES 4

- - - - ROAD
.... ALASKA MARINE HWY (FERRY)
PARKS
✕ POINT OF INTEREST

Area agencies book a variety of excursions, including bear viewing, flight-seeing, kayaking, fishing, remote lodge stays, and boat tours. They include **Custom Tours of Kodiak** (Kodiak, 907/486-4997) and **Kodiak Island Ultimate Adventures** (Kodiak, 907/487-2700).

Kodiak Kayak Tours (Kodiak, 907/486-2722) offers guided half-day kayak trips, as well as instruction and extended journeys. **Wavetamer Kayaking/Kayak Kodiak!** (Kodiak, 907/486-2604) sponsors some great sea-kayak trips, kayak bear viewing, birding, winter trips, and trip support.

Kodiak Treks (Kodiak, 907/487-2122) leads backpacking, hiking, and birding trips on Kodiak Island and in Katmai National Park.

FOOD

Some lodging options also include restaurants, notably the Best Western Kodiak Inn and all of the listings applying to remote destinations. See Lodging, below.

Kodiak has several good spots to grab a meal. **El Chicano** (103 Center Ave., Kodiak, 907/486-6116) offers a full Mexican menu and also steaks and burgers. It's open for lunch and dinner. A big and busy local favorite is **Henry's Great Alaskan** (512 Marine Way, Kodiak, 907/486-8844), opening at 11:30 for great lunches and dinners, and cold beer. I'm a big fan of the **Shire Bookstore** (104 Center Ave., Kodiak, 907/486-5001), open daily. You can browse the shelves, have coffee and snacks, and chat up the friendly owner and staff.

LODGING

Backcountry lodging associated with the remote destinations described above may be included with the listing. Specific tour providers have additional information.

SIGHTS

A Aleutian Islands/*M/V Tustamena* Ferry Trip
B Brooks Camp/Katmai National Park
C Lake Clark National Park and Preserve
D McNeil River State Game Sanctuary
E Pribilof Islands/Birding Trip
F Walrus Islands State Game Sanctuary
G Wood-Tikchik State Park

LODGING

H Bristol Inn
I King Eider Hotel
I Pavlov Services
J Grand Aleutian Hotel

Note: Items with the same letter are located in the same area.

The nicest hotel in town, the **Best Western Kodiak Inn** (236 Rezanof West, Kodiak, 800/544-0970, 907/486-5712), features a fine restaurant and lounge with great harbor views and comfortable rooms. Several tours can be booked at the convenient tour desk in the lobby. Rooms are $130 to $200. **Wintel's Bed and Breakfast** (1723 Mission Rd., Kodiak, 907/486-6935) offers rooms on the water for $65 to $100, within walking distance of all downtown attractions. Also on the water and similarly close to town is **Shahafka Cove Bed and Breakfast** (1812 Mission Rd., 888/688-6565 or 907/486-2409).

Visitors staying in Dillingham on the way to Walrus Islands or Wood-Tikchik can opt for the pleasant **Bristol Inn** (downtown Dillingham, 907/842-2240), featuring private baths, cable TV, continental breakfast, and airport shuttles.

Pribilof Island visitors will stay at the island's only accommodation, the **King Eider Hotel** (Saint Paul), and dine at the only eatery, the King Eider Restaurant. Rooms have shared baths. Some visitors complain of noise from the bar next door.

In Cold Bay, **Pavlov Services** (Cold Bay, 907/532-2437) operates the only hotel and restaurant, along with a store and pub.

Those who fly or take the *M/V Tustamena* to Dutch Harbor/Unalaska should stay at the **Grand Aleutian Hotel** (Airport Beach Road, Dutch Harbor, 800/891-1194, 907/581-3844), a surprisingly luxurious facility with all the amenities. Rates are $135 single, $150 double, $195 and up for suites.

CAMPING

In Kodiak, **Fort Abercrombie State Park** (see Sightseeing Highlights, above, 907/486-6339) has tentsites and an overflow lot where RV parking is permitted. South of town, **Buskin River State Park** (Rezanof Drive West, 4.5 miles south of town, 907/486-6339) has 15 sites.

Remote camping is possible in all of the destinations described above.

15
DENALI

Long before it was dedicated to President McKinley, the native people called North America's highest peak Denali (duh-NAH-lee), "the high one" or "the great one." While reaching only two-thirds the elevation of Mount Everest, at 20,320 feet Denali is actually the largest mountain in the world. With a base-to-summit height of 3.5 miles and an incomparable total mass, Denali is indeed "the great one." Some 3,000 climbers have reached its summit, and more than a few have died trying.

Denali National Park is the crown jewel of Alaska's public lands. The original, 1917 park boundaries now demark the designated wilderness area within the larger park and preserve created in 1980. Many visitors remember the park as the highlight of their Alaska trip, but a surprising number leave disappointed. If you are blessed by stellar vistas and thrilling glimpses of wildlife, fantastic. But you may find yourself on a bus for seven tedious hours with complaining tourists, and maybe see one bear a mile away and, instead of Denali, only the clouds that shroud it. Don't expect to be handed an experience on a platter; don't depend too heavily on a tourist-shuffling routine that all too often yields a canned and pale experience. Get off the bus and into the hills!

Three wonderful roads serve most travelers in the park and surrounding region. The George Parks Highway comes into its own as one of Alaska's most beautiful roads north of delightful Talkeetna. At Cantwell in Broad Pass,

DENALI REGION

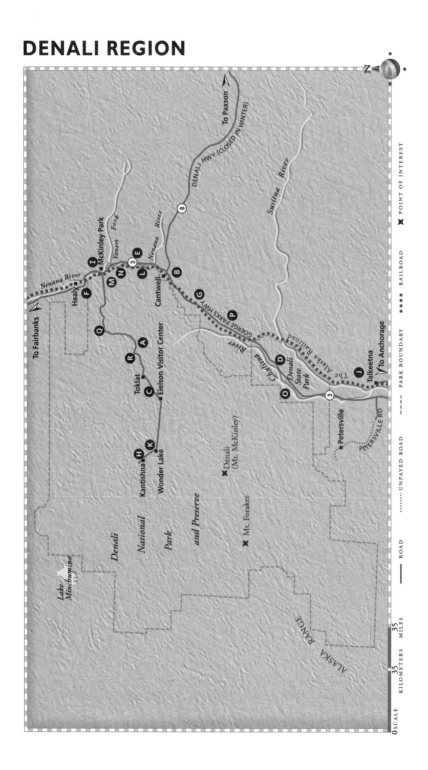

N

To Paxson

DENALI HWY (CLOSED IN WINTER)

Susitna River

8

McKinley Park

Yanert Fork

Nenana River

I

M N 3 E
L

F

Q

R

A

Eielson Visitor Center

Toklat

C

H K

Kantishna

Wonder Lake

Healy

Cantwell

B

G

P

GEORGE PARKS HWY

Chulitna River

The Alaska Railroad

D

O

Denali State Park

J

Talkeetna

3

To Anchorage

Petersville

PETERSVILLE RD

★ Denali
(Mt. McKinley)

★ Mt. Foraker

Denali

National

Park

and Preserve

Lake
Minchumina

ALASKA RANGE

To Fairbanks

Nenana River

0 SCALE

35 KILOMETERS
35 MILES

—— ROAD   ⋯⋯ UNPAVED ROAD   – – – PARK BOUNDARY   ▪▪▪▪ RAILROAD   ✖ POINT OF INTEREST

the rugged, gravel Denali Highway cuts east, staying above treeline for much of its 134 miles before linking with the Richardson Highway in Paxson. Best of all is the Denali Park Road, where thousands of visitors are treated to views of caribou, Dall sheep, moose, grizzly bears, and, perhaps, "the mountain."

A PERFECT DAY IN DENALI

Board your pre-booked, early-morning shuttle bus at the Denali National Park visitors center and head into the park. Sit near the front on the left side for the best views and a chance to more easily question the driver. Choose where to hike based on information you've collected about weather, bear sightings, and closed areas, perhaps along the Sanctuary River, in the hills above the Toklat River, or around Wonder Lake. Enjoy a day hike over the pathless terrain, following inspiration and whim, relaxing at high points to scan the landscape. Follow bear safety advice at all times. Head back to the road at day's end to catch a returning bus, then reminisce over pizza and beer at the Lynx Creek Pub.

SIGHTS

- **Ⓐ** Bus Tours
- **Ⓑ** Cantwell
- **Ⓒ** Day Hikes
- **Ⓐ** Denali Park Road
- **Ⓓ** Denali State Park
- **Ⓔ** Flightseeing
- **Ⓕ** Healy
- **Ⓖ** Hurricane Gulch
- **Ⓗ** Kantishna
- **Ⓘ** McKinley Park
- **Ⓙ** Talkeetna
- **Ⓚ** Wonder Lake

FOOD

- **Ⓛ** Lynx Creek Pub
- **Ⓘ** McKinley Deli
- **Ⓘ** McKinley/Denali Salmon Bake
- **Ⓞ** Perch
- **Ⓙ** Sparky's

LODGING

- **Ⓗ** Camp Denali
- **Ⓑ** Cantwell Lodge
- **Ⓛ** Carlo Creek Lodge
- **Ⓗ** Denali Backcountry Lodge
- **Ⓘ** Denali Crow's Nest
- **Ⓕ** Denali Dome Home Bed and Breakfast
- **Ⓜ** Denali National Park Hotel
- **Ⓘ** Denali Princess Lodge
- **Ⓝ** Denali River Cabins
- **Ⓗ** Kantishna Roadhouse
- **Ⓙ** Latitude 62°
- **Ⓘ** McKinley Chalet Resort
- **Ⓝ** McKinley Village Resort
- **Ⓞ** Mary's McKinley View Lodge
- **Ⓗ** North Face Lodge
- **Ⓛ** Rick Swenson's Carlo Heights Bed and Breakfast

LODGING (continued)

- **Ⓘ** Sourdough Cabins
- **Ⓟ** Sourdough Paul's Bed and Breakfast
- **Ⓖ** Stampede Lodge
- **Ⓙ** Swiss-Alaska Inn
- **Ⓙ** Talkeetna Motel
- **Ⓙ** Talkeetna Roadhouse
- **Ⓕ** Totem Inn

CAMPING

- **Ⓓ** Byers Lake State Campground
- **Ⓛ** Carlo Creek Lodge
- **Ⓝ** Denali River Cabins
- **Ⓠ** Igloo Creek
- **Ⓜ** Morino Campground
- **Ⓡ** Sanctuary River
- **Ⓓ** Troublesome Creek State Campground
- **Ⓚ** Wonder Lake Campground

Note: Items with the same letter are located in the same area.

PARK INFORMATION

For general area information, contact the Talkeetna/Denali Visitor Center (Talkeetna Spur Road at Mile 99 Parks Highway, 800/660-2688, 907/733-2688, www.alaskan.com/talkeetnadenali). It's open daily in summer from 8 to 8. For Denali National Park information, contact the visitors center (Mile 1 Denali Park Road, 907/683-2294, www.nps.gove/dena). For park weather, call 800/472-0391.

ORIENTATION

The Parks Highway and Alaska Railroad tracks run pretty much north-south between Talkeetna and Healy, cutting through the Alaska Range. The Denali massif rises to the north and east of both routes and is easily viewed from many points, weather permitting. From Broad Pass (Miles 195 to 210 Parks Highway, elevation 2,300 feet), road and tracks descend through the Nenana River valley. Moose are commonly seen near the river, while rafting parties are commonly seen on it. The Denali National Park entrance (Mile 237.3 Parks Highway) heads off to the west.

All towns and points of interest listed below are found on or very close to the road. The only exception of note is Talkeetna, which is at the end of the well-marked Talkeetna Spur Road.

VISITING DENALI NATIONAL PARK AND PRESERVE

Whether arriving by personal vehicle, train, or plane, nearly all visitors base their stays near the park entrance at Mile 237.3 of the Parks Highway. The visitors center, Denali Park Hotel, Alaska Railroad Station, Riley Creek and Morino Campgrounds, park airstrip, gas station, store, food service, bar, and post office are all within walking distance between Miles 0.2 and 1.6 of Denali Park Road. Park headquarters and the sled-dog kennels are further up, at Mile 3.5.

Unless you signed on to a package tour, getting organized can be confusing. Stop first at the visitors center to confirm procedures regarding campsites and park buses, both of which are best reserved *way ahead of time*. Free, frequent hotel buses shuttle people between the park hotel, visitors center, McKinley

Chalet Resort in McKinley Park, and McKinley Village Resort in McKinley Village. They also meet both daily trains.

If you plan to camp, backpack, or tour Denali, pay close attention to required reservations, permits, and procedures. During the peak months of July and August, dozens of visitors face serious disappointment due to poor planning:

Campground Reservations—Every vehicle site in park campgrounds is reservable by phone ahead of time! If you want a vehicle site but don't have a reservation, your chances of getting one are slim. See Camping, below, for specifics.

Backcountry Permits—The area on either side of the Denali Park Road is parceled out in roughly 100-square-mile sectors, or "units." Each can be used by only one or two small parties of backcountry campers on a given night. Permits are issued on a first-come, first-served basis, no more than one day in advance of your intended starting day (for example, Monday morning for a Tuesday first camping night).

Even if you're the first person in line, your chosen unit may already be taken by someone who filed an itinerary a week earlier and will be hitting that unit on the sixth day of their trip—the same day you wanted it. Some units are closed due to wildlife activity; others are very popular. It pays to be flexible.

Permits are free and are obtained at the visitors center. Rangers will provide your party with a bear-proof food container that must be used. You'll pay $15 for a camper bus ride to your drop-off.

Camper (Backpacker) Buses—Some park buses are reserved for those needing a shuttle to a backcountry drop-off or to Teklanika, Sanctuary, Igloo, or Wonder Lake Campgrounds. You can board any park bus to return. Unlike shuttle buses, camper buses don't stop for wildlife viewing—though most drivers won't pass up a good sighting. Tickets ($15.50 for adults, $7.75 for ages 13–16, under 13 free) are obtained when you get your backcountry permit or campground reservation, but no more than one day in advance. Note that only camper buses will carry bicycles.

Shuttle Buses—Since almost all private vehicles are forbidden past Mile 15 of the 91-mile Park Road, most visitors take a shuttle bus into the park. The not-too-comfortable buses leave from the visitors center. They cruise slowly, stopping for wildlife viewing. You are not permitted to get off the bus when wildlife is spotted near the road, but you may get off at all other points and catch another bus going in either direction. Pack snacks and fluids; there are no refreshment options.

Sixty-five percent of shuttle-bus seats are available for advance reservations (800/622-7275). Most sell out. Advance reservations are no longer taken within five days of intended use. Remaining seats are made available two days ahead of time (for example, Monday morning for a Wednesday shuttle ride); reserve by phone and at the visitors center. Buses travel one of four varying distances up the park road; tickets are priced accordingly:

Destination	Adult fare	Ages 13–16	Under 13
Toklat/Polychrome	$12.50	$6.25	free
Eielson	$21	$10.50	free
Wonder Lake	$27	$13.50	free
Kantishna	$31	$15.50	free

SIGHTSEEING HIGHLIGHTS SOUTH OF DENALI

★★★★ FLIGHTSEEING

About the best thing you can do with your extra cash is take a flight up into the Alaska Range from Talkeetna. Flying up 50-mile-long Ruth Glacier between the 5,000-foot walls of Great Gorge is unforgettable; only the occasional tiny dots of mountaineers' tents give perspective to the awesome scene. Coming out of the gorge, you'll see Denali rising opposite you across the 100-square-mile Don Sheldon Amphitheater. Your flight might continue on to the mountain, perhaps circling it. Many options include a glacier landing.

Four well-known and well-established companies operate from the Talkeetna airport just south of town: **K2 Aviation** (800/764-2291, 907/733-2291), **Doug Geeting Aviation** (800/770-2366), Hudson Air Service (907/733-2321), and **Talkeetna Air Taxi** (907/733-2218). Each has booking offices at the airport, in town, or along the Talkeetna Spur Road. Prices are always based on a per-person rate for groups of a certain size.

Details: Flights available year-round, weather and light permitting. (2–3 hours)

★★★★ TALKEETNA

Talkeetna/Denali Visitor Center, 800/660-2688, 907/733-2688

Located at the confluence of the Talkeetna, Chulitna, and Susitna Rivers, Talkeetna is the traditional base for Denali climbing expedi-

© Paul Otteson

tions. If you visit in late May or June, you're likely to meet sunburned climbers with stories to tell. The town's short, charming main street features cafés and shops, while a handful of motels, B&Bs, and the town campground offer accommodations.

One mile up the Talkeetna Spur Road from the Parks Highway junction is **Mary Carey's Fiddlehead Fern Farm** (907/733-2428), the only one of its kind in the world. Fiddleheads make a tasty, healthy Alaskan treat. Frozen, pickled, and fresh (in season) fiddleheads are for sale.

At the **Talkeetna Historical Society Museum**, stop for a look at the climbing displays and the 144-square-foot scale model of the Denali massif. It's located in the old railroad Section House (one block south of Main Street, just west of Talkeetna Spur/Airstrip Road, 907/733-2487), open daily in summer, 10 to 5 (call in winter). Admission is $1, under 12 free.

The **Museum of Northern Adventure**, located in the renovated, 70-year-old Alaska Railroad building (Main Street, 907/733-3999), offers a fun mix of "Alaskana" that includes life-size wax-figure dioramas. There's also a gift shop. The museum is open daily in summer, 11 to 7, winter afternoons and by request. Admission is $3.50 for adults, $3 for age 65 and over, $2 for kids under 12.

Details: *Visitor center located on Talkeetna Spur Road at Mile 99 Parks Highway. (2–4 hours)*

★★★ DENALI STATE PARK
MatSu area office, Wasilla, 907/745-3975,
www.dnr.state.ak.us/parks/units/denali.html
This often-ignored park is a wonderful appendage to its federal partner. Of particular interest to travelers are the views of Denali and the Alaska Range, and the trails that climb to the long, low Kesugi and Curry Ridges east of the Parks Highway. Byers Lake Campground is the best base for a day hike to outstanding views (see Fitness and Recreation, below).

Stop at Mile 135.2 of the Parks Highway for a good view of Denali. At this point you're about 35 miles from the mountain, which is as close as the road gets.

Details: Located at Miles 132 to 169 Parks Highway (drive-through or all day for hike)

★★ HURRICANE GULCH
Mile 174 Parks Highway
The bridge is 550 feet above Hurricane Creek. Take a walk out onto the bridge for a look, or find the unmarked trail on the east side of the road at the bridge's south end to walk along the gulch edge. Be careful with both choices: The bridge serves speeding cars and the trail is precarious in spots.

Details: (30 minutes)

★ CANTWELL
The settlement of Cantwell is situated near the junction of the Parks and Denali Highways where the Nenana River curves north out of Broad Pass. Turn left at the junction for the two-mile drive into town for a look. Highway services are available.

Details: (30 minutes)

DENALI NATIONAL PARK SIGHTSEEING HIGHLIGHTS

★★★★ DAY HIKES
Endless day-hike possibilities exist along river bars, across open tundra, and up ridges, though areas are sometimes closed for wildlife-related

---

reasons. The only official trails are found near the park entrance, but a few other routes are commonly used and offer clear, beaten paths. The best access to good ridge walks is near Savage River, Polychrome Pass, and Toklat River, though hills and low ridges are never far from the road. Just get off the shuttle bus and go—that is, after learning when the last inbound bus will pass your chosen pickup point.

Details: *Endless possibilities. (half to full day)*

★★★★ DENALI PARK ROAD

This 91-mile route follows a series of outwash lowlands, river valleys, and ridge flanks, affording many chances to observe wildlife and the mountain. Your park map will provide some details on mileage and highlights. The **Eielson Visitor Center** at Mile 66 offers water, rest rooms, film, maps, information, and a good mountain viewpoint—but no food.

If you're touring by bus, the driver will have the latest information on wildlife activity and the passengers' collective observation will ensure good spotting. If driving or cycling, talk to as many people as possible before hitting the road. Watch for the stopped buses and photographer "caravans" that indicate the presence of wildlife. Stop frequently and scan the land with binoculars. Look for grizzlies everywhere, but particularly around Sable Mountain, Sable Pass, and the Toklat River.

Details: *Accessible by camper bus, shuttle bus, bus tour, or bicycle. (all day)*

★★★★ WONDER LAKE

Picture-perfect Wonder Lake is near the end of the Denali Park Road at its closest approach to the mountain. If the mountain is "out," you'll find yourself in a living postcard. There's a campground here with reservable sites (see Camping, below). At the north end, you have the lake between you and the mountain—not the time to be out of film.

Details: *(2 hours or more)*

★★★ BUS TOURS

Denali Park Resorts, 800/276-7234, 907/276-7234, 907/683-2215 the day of the tour

The park concessionaire offers bus tours up the park road. Tour buses are more expensive than park shuttle buses; they depart from the hotels rather than the visitors center and they are narrated by a guide. The **Natural History Tour** (three hours, $35 adults, $20 under 12, includes snack) goes 19 miles into the park, while the **Tundra Wildlife Tour** (six to eight hours, $64 adults, $34.50 under 12, includes box lunch) turns around at the Toklat River, 53 miles into the park.

Be aware that on these tours, you cannot get off the bus at all except at designated rest areas. There is no day-hike or drop-off option. Note also that the Natural History Tour goes only four miles beyond the private vehicle limit, and that bear sightings in this area are uncommon. If you aren't part of a package-tour group, reserve your bus tour at least a month in advance. Reservations can be made up to the day before departure.

Remember that shuttle and camper bus drivers are well informed and will answer questions—narrative is not necessarily exclusive to tour buses.

Details: *(3¹/₂–8¹/₂ hours)*

★★★ KANTISHNA

Four fine, expensive backcountry lodges are located on private land within the park at road's end in the old mining district of Kantishna (see Lodging, below). If you're in the area, stop for a look at the original Kantishna Roadhouse on the grounds of the modern Kantishna Roadhouse. Walk possibilities are plenty, wildlife abounds, Wonder Lake is nearby, and Denali can seem close enough to touch.

Details: *Accessible by air, lodge transport, or park shuttle bus. (1 hour–several days)*

SIGHTSEEING HIGHLIGHTS NORTH OF DENALI

★ HEALY
www.ilovealaska.com/alaska/Healy
Alaska's wealthiest town (it's true!) offers all highway services and is the main town in the region. Most businesses are right on the highway. Take the Otto Lake Road one mile west at Mile 247 of the Parks Highway to reach little Otto Lake, which offers camping, fishing, swimming, B&Bs, a youth hostel, foothills access, and even a driving range. At Mile 248.8 of the Parks, the Healy Road leads east, past

the store and community center, past more B&Bs, and down to the rail tracks, airstrip, and Nenana River. Across the bridge over the Nenana is the eight-mile Sultrana Road, which leads to mining ruins along Healy Creek and good free camping.

Details: (drive-through or brief stop)

★ MCKINLEY PARK
Mile 238 to Mile 239

The main area of Denali travel services is located along a stretch of the Parks Highway a mile north of the park entrance. You can't miss the concentration of hotels, shops, cabins, parked buses, crawling RVs, strolling tourists, youthful workers, and outdoor adventurers. There is no more concentrated area of travel, tour, and seasonal employment activity in the state.

Several rafting companies offering Nenana River trips are based here, while ERA Helicopters offers flightseeing. Other diversions include occasional live music, primitive trails into the surrounding hills, and a half-dozen bars and restaurants. Most businesses can connect you with all of the above, as well as tours, lodging, shuttles, and advice. The **Northern Lights Theatre** (Mile 238.9 Parks Highway, 907/683-4000) offers splendid multimedia presentations on the aurora borealis or Denali National Park, as well as a gift shop; shows are at 9, 1, 5, 6, 7, and 8; tickets cost $6.50, $5 for children. The **Alaska Cabin Night Dinner Theater** (800/276-7234, 907/276-7234) at the McKinley Chalets offers two bright, hokey melodrama shows a night with all-you-can-eat family-style meals; tickets are $40.

Details: (gas stop or multi-day stay)

FITNESS AND RECREATION

Float trips on the Nenana River are exceedingly popular and well established. Several companies take groups in medium and large rafts for short and half-day floats. They include: **Alaska Raft Adventures** (Denali Park, 907/683-2215), **Denali Raft Adventures** (Denali Park, 907/683-2234), and **McKinley Raft Tours, Inc.** (Denali Park, 907/683-2392).

River trips are good options on the usually mild waters of the Tangle Lakes Canoe Trail and the Gulkana and Delta Rivers from the Denali Highway near Paxson. **Paxson Alpine Tours** (907/822-3330, 907/479-0765) offers options in various parts of the eastern Alaska Range. **Too-loo-ook River**

Guides (907/683-1542) sponsors trips statewide. **Canoe Alaska** (Fairbanks, 907/479-5183) has three- to five-day trips on the Delta and Gulkana, as well as on a number of great Interior Rivers like Birch Creek, Beaver Creek, Chena River, and Fortymile River.

In Denali State Park, the **Byers Lake Trail** (five-mile loop, no gain; seven miles to ridge, 1,500-foot gain) is a great route. The route to the ridge and back is a bit too long a day hike, but the views from above treeline are spectacular. From the campground, the lake loop trail provides access to fishing spots.

The Denali National Park pamphlet map details the few short trails in the immediate vicinity of the visitors center. These are the only official trails, but the best hikes are further up the park road. One nice unofficial trail climbs to **Primrose Ridge**, a couple hundred yards beyond the parking area at the end of the 15-mile segment open to private vehicles. Ask the ranger at the checkpoint how to get to the trailhead. It's about 1.5 miles up to the ridgecrest . . . unless a bear inspires you to detour.

FOOD

Most of the eating options in the Denali region are associated with hotels, roadhouses, and lodges. Make sure to check the Lodging listings below.

Talkeetna's Main Street, a great place to stroll about, hosts a variety of eating spots. The **McKinley Deli** (Main Street, Talkeetna, 907/733-1234) features the only pizza in town—and it's good. **Sparky's** (Main Street, Talkeetna) serves sandwiches and ice cream. What else do you need?

The closest thing to fine dining near Denali is the often excellent **Perch** (Mile 224 Parks Highway, 907/683-2523), which offers breakfast, lunch, and dinner. Very nice! The Perch also has cabins available for $65 to $95; open year-round. Call for winter dining hours.

A half-mile north of the Denali National Park entrance is the commercial strip known as McKinley Park, featuring several eating options. The **Lynx Creek Pub** (Parks Highway, McKinley Park) is perhaps my favorite spot in all of Alaska. If you like great pizza and good microbrews, you might enjoy it as well. The **McKinley/Denali Salmon Bake** (Parks Highway, McKinley Park, 907/683-2733) is a typical family-style salmon bake. Breakfast is served, and they also have tent-cabins for $70 to $110.

LODGING

Talkeetna makes a great base for exploring the area. The **Talkeetna Roadhouse** (Main Street, 907/733-1351) is a town fixture. At the restaurant you can enjoy homemade bread, good food, good music, and good company. Rates are $50 to $100. The **Latitude 62°** (Mile 14 Talkeetna Spur Road, 907/733-2262) is a decent motel with a restaurant and bar. Rooms start at $50. On the east side of town by the boat launch is the quiet **Swiss-Alaska Inn** (907/733-2424), where rates range from $80 to $110; there's a good restaurant on site. Look for the signs. The **Talkeetna Motel** (907/733-2323) features a restaurant and bar. Rooms go for $65 to $100.

A legendary spot along the Parks Highway is **Mary's McKinley View Lodge** (Mile 134.5 Parks Highway, 907/733-1555). While a reporter, area legend Mary Carey covered Mount McKinley by air and is still reputed to be "the only woman in the world to be on the nation's tallest peak in winter." She circled the world twice and authored 10 books. Though Mary herself has passed on, her lodge is still in business, offering some of the best southern views of Denali around. Rooms go for $75; the restaurant is open 8 to 8.

Sourdough Paul's Bed and Breakfast (Mile 193 Parks Highway, 907/768-2020) features a Finnish sauna, full breakfast, Denali view, and northern-lights viewing in winter. In the center of Cantwell by the train tracks is the **Cantwell Lodge** (two miles west of Mile 209.9 Parks Highway, Cantwell, 907/768-2512). Rates are $75 and up. This very basic roadhouse-style accommodation features a café, bar, and liquor store. The **Carlo Creek Lodge** (Mile 223.9 Parks Highway, 907/683-2576) offers creekside cabins for $11 and up, RV and tent sites, a store, and some very nice wooded campsites. **Rick Swenson's Carlo Heights B&B** (Mile 224.1 Parks Highway, 907/683-1615) is not just a nice place to stay, it's also a sled-dog school! Rick is an Iditarod champion.

Where the Parks Highway crosses the Nenana River between Cantwell and Denali, you'll find the enclave of McKinley Village. The **McKinley Village Resort** (Mile 231.1 Parks Highway, 800/276-7234, 907/683-2265) is one of Aramark's two big Denali resorts. Catering mainly to bus tourists, this lovely lodge features all the comforts, a good pub, and a fine restaurant. Rooms are $165 to $200. Nestled by the river is **Denali River Cabins** (Mile 231.1 Parks Highway, 800/230-7275, 907/683-2500), with very nice riverside cabins, a lodge, and a restaurant. Rooms are $150 and up.

The **Denali National Park Hotel** (Mile 1.5 Park Road, Denali National Park, 800/276-7234, 907/683-9214) is the only lodging in the park and is run by Aramark. It's not your classic, Yellowstone-style lodge, but the rooms are okay. The establishment includes a snack bar and the intriguing Spike Bar, which occupies two old rail cars.

Several options pepper the commercial stretch of the Parks Highway a half mile north of the park entrance. Perched high above the road on the

PLAN AHEAD!

Campsites at Denali National Park fill up fast. If you want to camp in the park with a vehicle, particularly in July and August, reserve months ahead of time. Reservations are taken beginning in February for the upcoming summer (800/622-7275, www.nps.gov/dena/campgrnd.htm).

east side is the **Denali Crow's Nest** (McKinley Park, 907/683-2723). Single or double cabins rent for $100 to $160. Both the cabins and the Overlook Bar & Grill offer great views over Nenana River valley. One of the two nicer hotels is the **Denali Princess Lodge** (Parks Highway, McKinley Park, 800/426-0500, rail tours 907/835-8907). Associated with Princess cruises and tours, it caters mainly to those who buy their packages. The hotel has a very good restaurant. Rooms are $140 to $280. The other top, full-featured resort is **McKinley Chalet Resort** (Parks Highway, McKinley Park, 800/276-7234, 907/276-7234), operated by Aramark, which also serves mainly bus and rail package tourists. Rooms go for $130 to $200. **Sourdough Cabins** (Parks Highway, McKinley Park, 800/354-6020907/683-2773) features nice $100 cabins amid the trees, not too close to each other.

Those with deeper pockets can stay at one of Kantishna's great lodges. All rates listed are per person, per night, based on double occupancy, and include all meals, guided activities, use of recreational equipment, and a guided tour/shuttle to and from the rail station and airstrip. The **Denali Backcountry Lodge** (Denali Park, 800/841-0692, 907/683-2594, winter 907/783-1342), located in the valley along Moose Creek, offers nice cabins clustered together. The rate is $300 with a two-night minimum stay. The original Kantishna Roadhouse, dating back to mining days, is preserved on the grounds of the new **Kantishna Roadhouse** (Kantishna, 800/942-7420, 907/479-2436). Located on Moose Creek, the roadhouse boasts nice cabins and a great lodge/restaurant. Rates are $280 with a two-night minimum stay. The plushest of the resorts is the **North Face Lodge** (Kantishna, 907/683-2290). It features Denali views (weather permitting) and excellent evening programs—splendid! Rooms are $325 with a two-night minimum. **Camp Denali** (Kantishna, 907/683-2290) is more rustic than partner North Face, but it is easily my favorite. Cabins are spread out on the hillside with the best Denali views! The rate is $325 per night with a three-night minimum stay, as opposed to two for the others. Within a dozen miles of the park entrance, Healy is a good place to get a room. The **Denali Dome Home Bed and Breakfast** (Healy Spur Road, Healy, 907/683-1239) occupies an interesting geodesic structure and is well kept and well run. The summer rate is $90. **Stampede Lodge** (Mile 248.8 Parks Highway, Healy, 800/478-2370, 907/683-2242) is a renovated historic lodge with a restaurant. Rooms start at $65. The main place in Healy is the **Totem Inn** (Mile 248.7 Parks Highway, Healy, 907/683-2384). Three classes of rooms range from $40 to $115. The bar and restaurant are favorites with the locals. A special glass-walled room has been built for winter northern-lights viewing.

CAMPING

A number of campgrounds are found along the Parks Highway, both public and private. In Denali State Park, **Troublesome Creek State Campground & Trailhead** (Mile 137.3 Parks Highway) has 10 sites at $6 each near a lovely, clear stream. Also within Denali State Park is **Byers Lake State Campground** (Mile 147 Parks Highway), with 66 sites at $12 each. Black bears are common here, so follow all bear-prevention advice. There is trail access around Byers Lake.

DENALI'S CAMPGROUNDS

	Park Rd. Milepost	Number of Sites	Vehicles Allowed	Advance Reservations
Riley Creek	0.5	102	Yes	All Sites
Morino	1.5 (hike-in)	60	No	No
Savage River	12	34	Yes	All Sites
Sanctuary River	22	7	No	No
Teklanika River	29	50	Yes*	All Sites
Igloo Creek	34	7	No	No
Wonder Lake	85	28	No	All Sites

*Visitors staying at Teklanika are permitted to drive 14 miles past the road-closed point, but must book at least a three-day stay and cannot drive back out any more than once for every three days of that stay.

Closer to Denali, **Carlo Creek Lodge** and **Denali River Cabins** both have campgrounds (see Lodging, above). **Denali National Park** operates seven campgrounds along Denali Park Road (see table on next page). All of the available sites in the three campgrounds that allow vehicles, campers, and trailers are reservable in advance, beginning in February for the upcoming summer. All **Wonder Lake Campground** sites are also reservable in advance, while **Igloo Creek** and **Sanctuary River** sites are available only on a first-come, first-served basis at the visitor centers. These campgrounds must be reached by camper bus (see Visiting Denali National Park, above). **Morino Campground** is a primitive backpacker campground with self-registration, reserved for walkins. Call 800/622-7275 for information and campsite reservations, or visit the Denali website at www.nps.gov/dena/campgrnd.htm. You can reserve by e-mail from the website.

In Healy, the **McKinley RV and Campground** (Mile 248.5 Parks Highway, Healy, 907/683-2379) is one of the nicer RV options and also has lawn tentsites near the highway. Tent sites are $18, RV sites range to $29.

Scenic Route: Denali Highway (134 Miles)

The all-gravel Denali Highway links Cantwell and Paxson, crossing the wide, remote land south of the central Alaska Range. The highlands it passes through are empty, exposed, and wild. Several small trails lead off to lakes and fishing spots. Three free BLM campgrounds and numerous roadside turnouts offer primitive places to stop and stay.

Paxson (Mile 0) is little more than a roadhouse at the junction with the Richardson Highway. From here, the road heads west through the **Tangle Lakes Archaeological District** (Mile 17 to Mile 35, information 907/822-3217), where some of the 400 identified sites show signs of human activity dating back 10,000 years. After winding past the lakes, fishing spots, campgrounds, and river put-ins of Tangle Lakes (Mile 21), the road climbs to its highest point at McLaren Summit (Mile 35.2, elevation 4,086 feet), the divide between the Yukon River and Cook Inlet watersheds.

Enjoy the one-lane, 1,000-foot-long **Susitna River Bridge** (Mile 79.3). The Susitna flows 260 miles from Susitna Glacier to Cook Inlet. Crossing up and over a gentle plateau, the road enters the Nenana River valley for a time before reaching the

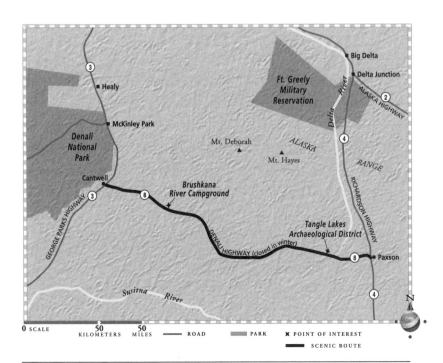

Parks Highway junction and Cantwell (Mile 133.7). *Some river runners like to put in to the Nenana at Mile 117.7, then float to McKinley Village or McKinley Park.*

You can stay at one of several remote lodges along the Denali Highway. The **Tangle River Inn** (Mile 20 Denali Highway, summer 907/822-3970, winter 907/895-4022) is a full-service roadhouse with gas, café, motel, showers, store, bar, canoe rental, and camping with RV hookups. Rooms start at $45. **Tangle Lakes Lodge** (Mile 22 Denali Highway, 907/822-7308) is known as a great choice for birders, thanks to the strong interest of the proprietors. Cabins go for $65; one larger cabin is $150. Near the Susitna River Bridge, you'll find the **Gracious House Lodge & Flying Service** (Mile 82 Denali Highway, 907/333-3148, 907/822-7307). In addition to cabins, a motel, bar, café, gas, and tentsites, you can arrange for direct air shuttles and flightseeing. Rooms range from $110 to $125, some with private baths.

Camping is available at three primitive BLM campgrounds. **Tangle Lakes Campground** (Mile 21.2 Denali Highway), 0.75 mile north of the road on the lakeshore, features good access to the Delta River Canoe Trail (see Fitness and Recreation, above). A half-mile further up the road is the **Tangle River Campground** (Mile 21.7 Denali Highway), with access to the Upper Tangle Lakes Canoe Trail (see Fitness and Recreation). The **Brushkana River Campground** (Mile 104.6 Denali Highway) offers stream access.

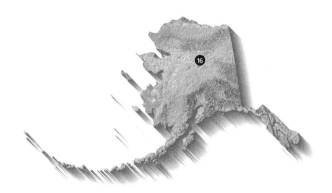

16
FAIRBANKS AND
VICINITY

Fairbanks is a randomly organized, somewhat confusing, not very attractive small city populated by hardy, friendly folks who live through winters that would kill normal people. It is those winters that constrain the architecture and landscaping that prettify warmer towns, and it's Fairbanks' role as the supply and services center for a vast region that contributes to its busy, haphazard feel. For Interior and northern Alaska, all roads lead to Fairbanks.

Fairbanks got its start when prospector Felix Pedro discovered gold in the area, setting off the "Pedro Dome gold rush" of 1902. Founding father E. T. Barnette set up shop as the town's chief merchant, convincing the miners to name the town after Charles Fairbanks, an Illinois senator who became Teddy Roosevelt's vice president. Barnette's reputation soured significantly when he absconded with his bank's deposits to California in 1911. The miners weathered that setback, however, just as they endured the frustrations of extracting gold buried under thick layers of gravel and frozen mud. The town was soon established as a center of trade and government.

Fairbanks visitors can enjoy a riverboat ride, an Alaskan theme park, a fine museum, lodging at one of countless B&Bs, transport into the bush via one of several air services, or road access to nearby mining sites, trails, river runs, and hot springs. The Parks, Richardson, and Steese Highways all reach the city, while the Elliott and Dalton Highways and Chena Hot Springs Road begin nearby. Fairbanks is a true crossroads—but let the roads tempt you as much as the crossing.

FAIRBANKS

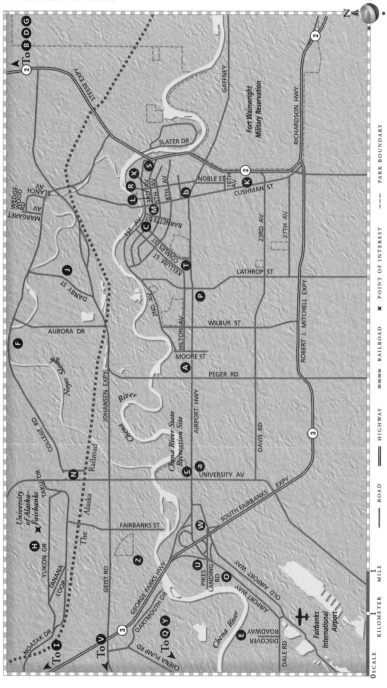

N

To B D G
2 To
STEESE EXPY
GAFFNEY
Fort Wainwright
Military Reservation
RICHARDSON HWY
2
SLATER DR
WEDGE-WOOD RD
BLANCH AV
MARGARET AV
S
X
R
L
C
M
3RD AV
5TH AV
8TH AV
BARNETTE ST
1ST AV
NOBLE ST
16TH AV
CUSHMAN ST
K 2
b
23RD AV
27TH AV
J
DANBY ST
KELLUM ST
COWLES ST
T
LATHROP ST
P
AURORA DR
2ND AV
HILTON AV
WILBUR ST
F
Noyes Slough
MOORE ST
A
PEGER RD
Chena River
AIRPORT HWY
DAVIS RD
ROBERT J. MITCHELL EXPY
3
COLLEGE RD
JOHANSEN EXPY
Chena River State
Recreation Site
a
c
UNIVERSITY AV
N
TAKU DR
Railroad
University
of Alaska–
Fairbanks
The Alaska
SOUTH FAIRBANKS EXPY
H
YUKON DR
FAIRBANKS ST
W
Tanana Loop
GEIST RD
Z
U
PIKES LANDING RD
O
OLD AIRPORT WAY
AIRPORT WAY
NOATAK DR
To I
To V
3
GEORGE PARKS HWY
DARTMOUTH DR
To Q Y
CHENA PUMP RD
E
Chena River
DISCOVER ROADWAY
DALE RD
Fairbanks
International
Airport

0 SCALE   KILOMETER   MILE

—— ROAD   ═══ HIGHWAY   ▬▬▬ RAILROAD   ✕ POINT OF INTEREST   --- PARK BOUNDARY

A PERFECT DAY IN FAIRBANKS

Make a day of it along the Steese Highway, visiting the Trans-Alaska Pipeline Viewpoint as you leave the metro area. Take a break at the Chatanika Lodge for that second cup of coffee, and stroll over to the old dredge across the road. Stop for a look at the Davidson Ditch turnout, then head up into the passes. Enjoy a day hike out onto the wonderful Pinnell Mountain Trail, then cruise down into Central. After a museum visit, head to Circle Hot Springs for a soak and a meal. If time allows, continue to Circle City, road's end, and the mighty Yukon River.

If it's a day in town you're looking for, piece together my top four recommendations. Take the morning cruise on the riverboat *Discovery*, hit the University Museum after lunch, explore Alaskaland as the afternoon wanes, and enjoy an evening with Mary Shields and the dogs.

ORIENTATION

The Chena River meanders from east to west through the heart of the city. Most of downtown lies on the river's south side. Numbered streets parallel the Chena, counting upward as you move south; First Avenue runs right along

SIGHTS

- Ⓐ Alaskaland
- Ⓑ Alaskan Tails of the Trail
- Ⓒ Alaska Public Lands Information Center
- Ⓓ Gold Dredge Number 8
- Ⓔ Historic Downtown
- Ⓕ Riverboat *Discovery*
- Ⓕ Tanana Valley Farmers Market
- Ⓖ Trans-Alaska Pipeline Viewpoint
- Ⓗ University of Alaska Museum
- Ⓘ Walk in the Woods

FOOD

- Ⓙ Cookie Jar's Garden Cafe
- Ⓚ Food Factory
- Ⓛ Fudge Pot
- Ⓜ Gambardella's Pasta Bella
- Ⓝ Hot Licks
- Ⓞ Pike's Landing
- Ⓟ Pizza Bella
- Ⓠ Pump House Restaurant
- Ⓡ Soapy Smith's
- Ⓢ Souvlaki

LODGING

- Ⓜ Bridgewater Hotel
- Ⓣ Captain Bartlett Inn

LODGING (continued)

- Ⓤ Fairbanks Princess Hotel
- Ⓥ Forget-Me-Not Lodge/Aurora Express
- Ⓦ Golden North Motel
- Ⓧ Northern Lights Hotel
- Ⓨ North Woods Lodge and International Hostel
- Ⓩ Seven Gables Inn
- ⓐ Wedgewood Resort
- ⓑ Westmark Fairbanks Hotel

CAMPING

- Ⓒ Chena River State Recreation Site

Note: Items with the same letter are located in the same area.

the water. Cushman Street, the main north-south artery through downtown, bridges the river. Airport Way/Gaffney Road is a major east-west commercial strip south of downtown. Where University Avenue meets College Road in the northwest corner of town, you'll find the University of Alaska. The airport is to the southwest at the end of Airport Way.

SIGHTSEEING HIGHLIGHTS IN FAIRBANKS

★★★★ UNIVERSITY OF ALASKA MUSEUM
University of Alaska campus, Fairbanks, 907/474-7505, www.uaf.edu/museum
This excellent museum tops my list as Fairbanks' finest attraction. Five distinct galleries house exhibits on the Trans-Alaska Pipeline, geology, natural history, native arts and cultures, and the northern lights. Displays of particular note include fine totem poles and a 36,000-year-old steppe bison mummy. Take University Avenue north from Airport Way, Geist Road, or College Road to the campus entrance and follow the signs.

Details: June–Aug daily 9–7; May and Sept daily 9–5; Oct–Apr weekdays 9–5, weekends 12–5. $5 adults, $4.50 seniors, $3 ages 12–17, under 12 free. (1 1/2 hours)

Information is available at the Fairbanks Log Cabin Visitors Center (First Avenue at Cushman, 800/ 327-5774, 907/456-5774, www .fairbanks.polarnet.com), open daily in summer 8 to 8, weekdays in winter 8 to 5.

★★★ ALASKALAND
Airport Way and Peger Road, on the south bank of the Chena River west of town, 907/459-1095, www.newsminer.com/Visitor/fairbanks/akland.html
This odd, very Alaskan, 44-acre theme park offers a fascinating blend of historic buildings, museums, gift shops, eateries, and theaters. Complete information is available from the staff at the entrance. Rides include an old carousel and the toy-sized Crooked Creek and Whiskey Island Railroad that makes 12-minute loops through the grounds. Admission is free.

Take a look at the **SS Nenana**, the second-largest wooden vessel in existence and the largest stern-wheeler ever built west of the

Mississippi, permanently moored in a large pond. Vintage aircraft and a history of Alaskan pilots are featured at the **Pioneer Air Museum** (907/451-0037), open Memorial Day to Labor Day. Admission is $2. Meals can be purchased at the food stands and enjoyed in picnic areas.

Besides several picnic areas and food stands, delicious and filling meals are available at the **Alaska Salmon Bake** (800/354-7274, 907/452-7274), offering a complete meal for $20, open 5 p.m. to 9 p.m. daily in summer. The nearby **Palace Theater & Saloon** (800/354-7274, 907/456-5960) hosts the Golden Heart Review nightly at 8:15. Stop in for an evening of happy melodrama, reservations recommended (ask about the 10 p.m. weekend "for adults only" show). The **Bear Art Gallery** (907/456-6485) features rotating exhibits with an Alaskan theme upstairs in the civic center building.

Details: *Public access to park, open Memorial Day to Labor Day daily 11 to 9. Free. Attractions have various hours. (1–2 hours)*

★★★ ALASKAN TAILS OF THE TRAIL
Call for reservations and directions, Fairbanks, 907/457-1117
Enjoy a personal, pleasant, and very informative evening with musher and author Mary Shields. She'll give you a close look at her dog team and tell tales of dogsledding in the northland. Call for reservations and information.

Details: *Presentations at 7:30 p.m. $25. (2 hours)*

★★★ RIVERBOAT *DISCOVERY*
1975 Discovery Dr., Fairbanks, 907/479-6673
Board Alaska's only operating stern-wheel riverboat for a four-hour trip on the Chena and Tanana Rivers. The boat stops at an Athabascan village site for a look around. Call for reservations and directions.

Details: *Sailings daily in summer at 8:45 a.m. and 2 p.m., 6:30 cruises on selected evenings. $40 adults, $37 teens and military, $30 ages 3–12. (4½ hours)*

★★ ALASKA PUBLIC LANDS INFORMATION CENTER
250 Cushman St., Suite 1A, Fairbanks, 907/456-0527,
www.nps.gov/aplic
Like its counterparts in Anchorage, Tok, and the Southeast, this center is the best one-stop source for information on all of Alaska's public

lands. If you're traveling on to Denali, stop here for up-to-the-minute information on shuttle bus and campsite availability.

Details: *Information center open Memorial Day–Labor Day daily 9–6; winter Tue–Sat 10–6. (1 hour)*

★★ GOLD DREDGE NUMBER 8
Mile 9.5 Steese Highway, Goldstream Road exit, Fairbanks, 907/457-6058

This developed tourist spot offers access to mining relics and buildings, gold panning, a mastodon and mammoth bone display, museum, gift shop, snack bar, RV parking, tours, and, of course, the gold dredge.

Details: *June–mid-Sep daily 9–6. $10 adults, 8 and under free. (1 hour)*

★★ WALK IN THE WOODS
University of Alaska Botanical Garden, 907/457-1117

The apt description in the literature reads, "Learn the northern niches of plants and wildlife . . . follow a quiet forest path and feel the spirit of the land." A two-hour tour starts in the botanical garden visitors center. Take Sheep Creek Road from Mile 355.8 of the Parks Highway; turn right on Tanana Loop Road to reach the garden.

Details: *2 p.m. daily. $20 adults, $15 kids. (2½ hours)*

★ HISTORIC DOWNTOWN
Visitor Center, First Avenue at Cushman, Fairbanks, 800/327-5774, 907/456-5774

Downtown Fairbanks' charms don't jump right out at you, so it pays to drop in first at the Log Cabin Visitor Information Center in Golden Heart Park to get information and pick up a walking tour map. Several buildings date back to the days of the Pedro Dome gold rush.

Details: *(1½ hours)*

★ TANANA VALLEY FARMERS MARKET
Tanana Valley Fairgrounds, Fairbanks

If you stop and browse, you might chance upon some of the state's famous giant cabbages, tomatoes, strawberries, and other biggies. Take College Road west from the Steese Highway or Johansen Expressway to the fairgrounds at Aurora Drive.

Details: *Open summer Wed 11–6, Fri 4–7, Sat 9–4. Free. (30 minutes)*

★ **TRANS-ALASKA PIPELINE VIEWPOINT**
Mile 8.9 Steese Highway,
information at 907/456-9391,
www.mosquitonet.com/~ranchmotel/transak.htm
This is a good place to take a long look at the pipeline. A visitors center is operated by Alyeska Pipeline. Tours are offered. **Details**: *Public access. Visitors center open Memorial Day–Labor Day daily 8–6. (30 minutes)*

SIGHTSEEING HIGHLIGHTS AROUND FAIRBANKS

★★ **NENANA**
Visitors Center, 907/832-9953
Nenana, situated at the confluence of the Nenana and Tanana Rivers, has long been an important transport center. Stop at the visitors center before touring the town.

See artifacts from the Alaska Railroad's early days at the **Alaska State Railroad Museum**, located in the old train depot where A Street meets the river (Front Street, Nenana, 907/832-5500), open late May through late September 8 to 6. Check out the Alaska Railroad bridge over the Tanana River—"the largest single span expansion bridge on rollers ever built"—which can actually be seen moving on its rollers when the temperature changes rapidly and the metal expands or contracts. Take a look at **St. Mark's Mission Church**, built in 1905 by early missionaries. Keep an eye out for traditional salmon-catching fish wheels along the riverbanks.

Nenana is famous for the **Nenana Ice Classic**, the annual contest to guess when Tanana River ice will break up. Local residents erect a large tripod on the ice in the middle of the river, attached by a pull cord to a clock that stops the moment the tripod has moved 100 feet and a device severs the cord. Entrants purchase $2 tickets, writing in the date and time they believe the big event will occur, then wait for the fateful moment. With prize money in the hundreds of thousands of dollars, they take this contest very seriously in the northland!

Details: *Visitors center, Mile 304.5 Parks Highway, open summer daily 8–6. Rail museum open summer daily 9–6, free. (1 hour)*

SIDE TRIPS: THREE CLASSIC HOT SPRINGS, THREE GREAT ROADS

Just north of Fairbanks from Mile 4.9 of the Steese Highway, Chena Hot Springs Road (60 miles long) heads eastward through lovely, historic mining country, climbing toward the divide between the Tanana and Yukon Valleys. Much of its length is within the Chena River State Recreation Area (Miles 26.1 to 50.7), popular with river runners and hikers.

At road's end, you'll come to **Chena Hot Springs** (Mile 56.5). Chena is the most popular of the three springs, though some find the sulfur smell a tad strong. There's an airstrip if you want to fly in. All springs access is via **The Resort at Chena Hot Springs** (Mile 56.5 Chena Hot Springs Road, Fairbanks, 800/478-4681, 907/452-7867). Rooms start at $105 in summer, $115 in winter, cabins range from $50 to $110, and campsites are $15 to $30. There are indoor and outdoor pools, whirlpools, soaking tubs, and a good restaurant. You can enjoy volleyball, bike rides, or cross-country skiing. A day pass is $8 for adults, $6 for seniors and kids ages 6 to 12, under 6 free.

At Mile 11 of the Steese Highway, the road splits and you can take the Elliott Highway (150 miles) northwest toward the Yukon River and the Far North. Two miles past the virtually abandoned mining community of Livengood (Mile 70.8), another junction (Mile 73.1) sends the Elliott back to the southwest while the Dalton Highway heads to the Arctic. The Elliott winds through forested hill country, past the road to the native settlement of Minto (Mile 110), through the mining center of Eureka, and to road's end at **Manley Hot Springs** (Mile 151.2 Elliott Highway).

Manley's waters are naturally cooler than Circle's but are not sulfurous like Chena's. Discovered in 1902, the springs became a famous local attraction after an Army telegraph station and trading post were built to support local mining activity and river trade. The original resort burned down in 1913. Today residents depend economically on a variety of jobs, subsistence, and barter. Many are active gardeners, and the fruits of their efforts are evident.

The last resort in Manley went bankrupt a few years ago. Today, the Dart family accommodates respectful bathers in three greenhouse tubs of varying temperature on their property. Call before visiting (672-3171), and check in upon arrival before you head to the tubs. A contribution may be expected. In business since 1906, the **Manley Roadhouse/Trading Post** is nearby (Mile 151.2 Elliott Highway, Manley Hot Springs, 907/672-3161) and offers food, bar, rooms, cabins, and an intriguing prehistoric and Alaskana artifact display. Rooms range from $65 to $95. A town campground has $5 sites.

Drivers who stay with the Steese Highway (160 Miles) will enjoy the best of the three roads. Heading north from Fairbanks, the Steese quickly turns northeast, past the monument to Felix Pedro (Mile 16.5), and climbs to the pass and ski slopes at Clearly Summit (Mile 20.3, elevation 2,233). From here, the road drops into the valley of the Chatanika River. Stop at the wonderful **Chatanika Lodge** (Mile 28.6, see Lodging, above). The Steese soon climbs again to two nice passes, first to Twelvemile Summit (Mile 85.5, elevation 2,982 feet), then later above treeline to Eagle Summit (Mile 108, 3,624 feet). Perhaps the Interior's nicest trail, the 27.3-mile **Pinnell Mountain Trail** connects the two passes via the high, open ridges of the White Mountains (see Fitness and Recreation, above).

After Eagle Pass, the Steese descends to the town of **Central** (Mile 127.8). Take a half-hour to visit the **Circle District Historical Society Museum** (Mile 127.7, Central, 907/520-1893), which features mining and area heritage exhibits. Ask about the great gold robbery of 1996!

Turn southeast at the junction in Central (Mile 127.8) for the eight-mile drive to **Circle Hot Springs Resort** (Mile 8.3 Circle Hot Springs Road, Central, 907/520-5113), my favorite of the three hot springs. The water here is hotter than Manley's and less sulfurous than Chena's. A very large, clean, outdoor pool invites soaking. The rustic, historic lodge is open year-round, as are the roads. An airstrip allows charter air access from Fairbanks. Rooms and cabins range from $50 to $110, floor space for sleeping bags is $20. Swimming for non-lodgers is $5.

After the rough and twisting final miles of the Steese, the road reaches Circle (Mile 162), the Yukon River, and road's end.

★ **ESTER GOLD CAMP**
Turn in at Mile 351.7 Parks Highway, Ester, 907/479-2500,
www.ptialaska.net/~akttt/ester.html
A hotel, buffet-style restaurant, and the Malemute Saloon are housed in some of the 11 historic structures in this old mining camp. Robert Service wrote some of his poetry in the Malemute. Visitors can enjoy Alaskan ales as they watch performances that mix comedy, music, poetry, and fun. Nearby in the Firehouse Theater, a 40-minute northern lights multimedia show entitled *The Crown of Light* plays through the summer.
   Details: *Musical comedy performances in summer daily Wed–Sun at 7 and 9 p.m., Sun–Tue at 9 only. $12 adults, $6 under 12. Crown of Light shows in summer daily 6:45 and 9:45 p.m., additional 6 p.m. daily show in July. $6 adults, $3 children. (3 hours)*

★ **NORTH POLE**
Visitors Center, Mile 348.7 Richardson Highway,
www.fairnet.org/npole/npole2.html
This little town milks its name for all it's worth in all the ways you might expect. Thousands upon thousands of letters from hopeful children arrive here every December, though no one claims that the genuine addressee ever arrives to collect his mail. Go ahead and check out the shops; it's never too early to start your Christmas buying.
   Details: *Various shops, open standard business hours. (30 minutes)*

FITNESS AND RECREATION

In town, consider a walk through **Creamer's Field Migratory Waterfowl Refuge** (Creamer Lane at College Road, 907/459-7307, www.state.ak.us/ local/akpages/FISH.GAME/wildlife/region3/refuge3/creamers.htm). You can enjoy about two miles of easy trails, as well as the Farmhouse Visitor Center, guided walks, and bird-banding demonstrations.
   The top out-of-town trails are accessed by the Steese Highway and Chena Hot Springs Roads. The best is the **Pinnell Mountain National Recreation Trail** (27.3 miles, up and down along ridge crests), one of the nicest backpack routes in the state (carry all water). Looping from Mile 85.6 to Mile 107.3 of the Steese Highway, the path follows a ridgeline route entirely above treeline. Closer to Fairbanks is the **Ski Loop Trail** (five miles, 500-foot gain). Sometimes muddy in places, the route begins and ends at Snowshoe Pass (Mile 28 Elliott Highway/AK 2), climbing to a summit.

FAIRBANKS REGION

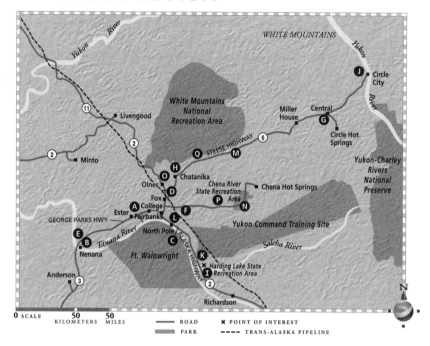

SIGHTS

Ⓐ Ester Gold Camp
Ⓑ Nenana
Ⓒ North Pole

FOOD

Ⓓ Fox Roadhouse
Ⓔ Monderosa
Ⓕ Two Rivers Lodge

LODGING

Ⓑ Bed & Maybe Breakfast
Ⓖ Central Motor Inn
Ⓗ Chatanika Lodge
Ⓐ Ester Gold Camp
Ⓘ Midway Lodge

LODGING (continued)

Ⓑ Nenana Inn
Ⓗ Old F. E. Gold Camp
Ⓙ Riverview Motel
Ⓚ Salcha River Lodge

CAMPING

Ⓛ Chena Lakes Recreation Area
Ⓜ Cripple Creek BLM Campground
Ⓝ Granite Tors Trail State Campground
Ⓘ Harding Lake State Recreation Area
Ⓞ Olnes Campground
Ⓟ Rosehip State Campground
Ⓠ Upper Chatanika River State Recreation Site Campground
Ⓞ Whitefish Campground

Note: Items with the same letter are located in the same area.

(Washington Plaza, Airport Way, Fairbanks, 907/479-8319) serves breakfast, lunch, and dinner, indoors and out. The eatery features fresh-baked cinnamon rolls in the morning; quiche, soups, and salads at lunch; "a delightful dinner menu"; and, of course, cookies.

On the highways out of town, you'll find some gems. **Two Rivers Lodge** (Mile 16 Chena Hot Springs Road, 907/488-6815) is a top-quality place for rustic fine dining. Halibut, salmon, and king crab are on the menu, as are pasta and meat entrées. The lodge offers a shuttle from town. The **Fox Roadhouse** (Mile 11 Steese Highway, Fox, 907/457-7461) serves seafood, steaks, prime rib, and lobster in the historical mining district of Fox.

Just outside of Nenana a couple of miles north of the river is the **Monderosa** (Mile 308.9 Parks Highway, Nenana, 907/832-5243), known far and wide as the place to get good, big burgers and more.

LODGING

The **Seven Gables Inn** (4312 Birch Lane, Fairbanks, 907/479-0751) is a wonderful B&B that occupies a huge, Tudor-style, converted frat house on Chena River. There's even an atrium with a waterfall. Rates range from $50 to $120. The **Forget-Me-Not Lodge/Aurora Express** (1540 Chena Ridge Rd., Fairbanks, 907/474-0949) features authentic Alaska Railroad cars refurbished in "Victorian splendor" with all the conveniences and private baths. Or you can stay in the modern lodge. Enjoy splendid views of the Tanana Valley. Rooms run $80 to $140, with full breakfast.

Typical of the chain, the **Westmark Fairbanks Hotel** (813 Noble St., Fairbanks, 907/456-7722) sets a standard for high-end comfort with all the amenities. Rooms range from $100 to $200. The tallest building downtown is the **Northern Lights Hotel** (427 1st Avenue, 907/561-5200). Rates range from $90 to $170; enjoy the views from the top-floor lounge and restaurant. The **Fairbanks Princess Hotel** (4477 Pikes Landing Rd., Fairbanks,

B&B TIPS
There are scores of B&Bs in the Fairbanks area. For information, contact the Log Cabin Visitor Information Center downtown (First Avenue at Cushman, 800/327-5774, 907/456-5774).

Rafting trips on the Chena River are offered by **Alaska Paddle Sports** (Fairbanks, 907/479-5183). Trips leave at 8 a.m. and return at 3 p.m., taking to the water on a lovely stretch of the Upper Chena an hour from town. **Circle City Charters** (Circle, 907/773-8439) offers motorboat trips up the Yukon River. Trips range from $50 for one hour to $150 for all day.

If you're around in winter, head to Nenana for a dogsled trip with **Mackey's Happy Dog Kennel** (Nenana, 907/832-1001). Day trips are $40. Be ready to miss being warm.

FOOD

Remember that, as throughout most of rural Alaska, eating places are often part of a lodging choice. Check the Lodging section, below, for several possibilities.

In downtown Fairbanks, **Souvlaki** (310 First Ave., Fairbanks, 907/452-5393) features eastern Mediterranean dishes, including several vegetarian options. Enjoy sandwiches, salads, souvlaki, seafood, and some good desserts; open Monday through Saturday. **Gambardella's Pasta Bella** (706 Second Ave., Fairbanks, 907/456-3417) serves good pizza and homemade bread along with fine pastas and amazing lasagna. The **Food Factory** (Cushman and 18th Avenue, Fairbanks, 907/452-6348) is a popular family place, serving cheese steaks, deep-fried halibut, ribs, burgers, and plenty more. There are two other locations in town. Named after the infamous gold-rush crime boss, **Soapy Smith's** (543 Second Ave., Fairbanks, 907/451-8380) features American cuisine such as steaks, seafood, and prime rib in a rustic atmosphere. If you're trying to stay trim, avoid the **Fudge Pot** (555 First Ave., Fairbanks, 907/456-3834), where pans of fresh-made fudge will tempt you.

Several good options are found elsewhere in town. A National Historic Site, the **Pump House Restaurant** (Mile 1.3 Chena Pump Road, Fairbanks, 907/479-8452) is a top choice for dinner. Built to supply Chena River water to gold-dredging operations in the early 1930s, the building was remodeled to house a restaurant and saloon in 1978. Take Geist Road west from the Parks Highway, then the first left. Enjoy dining on the deck. Another top, edge-of-town choice is the excellent **Pike's Landing** (Mile 4.5 Airport Road, Fairbanks, 907/479-6500). Open from 11:30 to 11, it features a huge deck on the Chena River and a nice Sunday brunch. **Hot Licks** (3549 College Rd., Fairbanks, 907/479-7183) is the place to go for great homemade ice cream, frozen yogurt, soup, and bread. Near Alaskaland and the movie theaters, you'll find **Pizza Bella** (1694 Airport Way, Fairbanks, 907/456-5657), featuring Italian, Greek, and American cuisine. The **Cookie Jar's Garden Cafe**

907/455-4477), one of several Alaska facilities operated by the huge cruise company, offers moderate luxury.

Three very nice Fairbanks hotels—**Sophie Station** (1717 University Ave.), the **Bridgewater Hotel** (201 First Ave., downtown), and the **Wedgewood Resort** (212 Wedgewood Dr.)—are served by the Hotel Hotline (800/528-4916, 907/479-3650). All have rooms starting in the $65 to $80 range and climbing well above $100.

The **Captain Bartlett Inn** (1411 Airport Way, Fairbanks, 800/544-7528 in Alaska only) is a big, decent, basic motel that features the hearty pleasures of Slough Foot Sue's Dining Hall and the Dog Sled Saloon. Rooms range from $85 to $130. Another basic entry is the **Golden North Motel** (4888 Old Airport Way, Fairbanks, 800/447-1910, 907/479-6201). Nice enough rooms run $80 and up.

Budget travelers can try the **North Woods Lodge & International Hostel** (Chena Hills Drive west of town, Fairbanks, 800/478-5305 in Alaska only, 907/479-5300). They offer free transport in town. Rooms and cabins are $65, bunks for $30, and campsites for $15.

Between Fairbanks and Delta Junction on the Richardson Highway, the **Salcha River Lodge** (Mile 322.2 Richardson Highway, Salcha, 907/488-2233) is a roadhouse with $50 rooms, restaurant open 7 to 9, and all services. Eight miles away is the **Midway Lodge** (Mile 314.8 Richardson Highway, Salcha, 907/488-2939), offering $40 to $55 rooms and a restaurant that's open daily 7 a.m. to 10 p.m.

Heading south on the Parks Highway is the **Ester Gold Camp** (see Sightseeing Highlights, above, Ester, 800/676-6925, 907/479-2500, www.alaskasbest.com/ester). The $50 to $80 rooms are in a renovated bunkhouse above the dining room; there are no phones or TVs, and every two rooms share a bath. Further west, Nenana offers the **Bed & Maybe Breakfast** (Front Street, Nenana, 907/832-5272). It's located upstairs in the old rail depot. Rooms are $65.

On the Steese Highway north of town between Fairbanks and Circle, the **Old F.E. Gold Camp** (Mile 27.9 Steese Highway, Chatanika, 907/389-2414) features food and lodging in a restored mining complex. They offer northern-lights viewing in the winter, taking visitors to viewing spots by snowmobile, then returning to the warm lodge. Basic room rates are

The Fairbanks Arts Association (Fairbanks, 907/456-6485) is a good source for information on arts and performance events going on in town.

$50 and up. One of my favorite Alaska roadhouse restaurants is at the **Chatanika Lodge** (Mile 28.6 Steese Highway, Chatanika, 907/389-2164). Rooms go for $50 and up. Central has the **Central Motor Inn** (central Central, 907/520-5228), with private bathrooms for $65, shared bath for $40. In Circle, the **Riverview Motel** (Mile 162 Steese Highway, Circle, 907/773-8439) has decent rooms with showers for $60 and up. This is a good base for Yukon River trips offered by the owner, who also runs Circle City Charters (same phone).

CAMPING

Forty miles east of Fairbanks on the Richardson Highway is the **Harding Lake State Recreation Area** (from Mile 321.5 Richardson Highway). Turn east here for the 1.5-mile road to a lakeside campground with $8 sites. Closer to town is the **Chena Lakes Recreation Area** (from Mile 346.7 Richardson Highway). Turn north to reach the swimming beach and campground; $3 day use, $6 campsites.

Right in Fairbanks is the surprisingly pleasant **Chena River State Recreation Site** (University Avenue north of Airport Way, Fairbanks). Nice $12 sites are on or near the Chena River, and you're right around the corner from Alaskaland.

Along the road to Chena Hot Springs, you'll find the **Rosehip State Campground** (Mile 27 Chena Hot Springs Road) and **Granite Tors Trail State Campground** (Mile 39.5 Chena Hot Springs Road). Both have pleasant sites along the river. Fishing, hiking, and river-running access are easy from the campgrounds.

Along the Elliott Highway are two campgrounds in the Lower Chatanika River State Recreation Area: **Olnes Campground** (Mile 10.6 Elliott Highway) has 50 campsites for $8 each one mile west of the highway, while **Whitefish Campground** (Mile 11 Elliott Highway) features $8 sites at the north end of the bridge.

The Steese Highway offers the **Upper Chatanika River State Recreation Site Campground** (Mile 39) with good river access and 25 sites for $8 each. Further up the road is **Cripple Creek BLM Campground** (Mile 60) with 21 sites.

NIGHTLIFE

The choice for a happy Alaskan evening is to head to **Alaskaland** to dine at the Alaska Salmon Bake, then catch the Golden Heart Revue at the Palace

Theatre and Saloon. For details, see Alaskaland in Sightseeing Highlights, above. Some of the regularly active arts organizations include the following. The **Fairbanks Summer Arts Festival** (907/474-8869) offers two weekends of performances. The **Fairbanks Concert Association** (907/474-8081) sponsors top touring shows and performers. The **Fairbanks Light Opera Theatre** (907/456-3568) serves up community musical theater. Professional, resident, and local amateur dancers perform with the **North Star Ballet** (907/451-8800). **Theatre UAF** (907/474-7751) is the university theater. The local **Fairbanks Symphony** (907/ 479-3407) offers concert series. Community performances and children's theater is on the playbill of the **Fairbanks Drama Association** (907/456-7529).

17
FAR NORTH

The Far North is my favorite region in the state, in part because it is so wild, but also because of the strange potency of Arctic light and the intensity of the short growing season. The region encompasses the largely treeless Brooks Range, northernmost extension of the Rocky Mountains, and the tundra hills and plains of the North Slope. Located entirely north of the Arctic Circle, residents experience up to two months a year when the sun doesn't rise at all. Wildlife is thoroughly adapted to the challenge of long, bitter winters. Tundra plants burst into life with early summer's thaw, and animals birth, feed, and mate during the intense months of life before trying to survive another winter.

The opening of the Dalton Highway to general traffic makes it possible to drive a standard car or RV all the way to Prudhoe Bay. That thread of civilization is all you might need to sample the Far North on your own.

The Far North supports only nine permanent settlements; a combined population of about 9,300 dwells in an area nearly the size of Montana. All of these souls live in the North Slope Borough, the world's largest municipality and Alaska's least populated. Located just south of North America's northernmost point, Barrow is the only town used to receiving tourists, most of whom come on a tour to experience the midnight sun and native culture. The other "town" of particular interest to travelers is Deadhorse, the central area of services for the Prudhoe Bay oilfields.

FAR NORTH

Chukchi Sea

Arctic Ocean

■ Barrow

B

NORTH SLOPE

■ Kaktovik

Prudhoe Bay
■ Deadhorse
D

DALTON HIGHWAY

G **C**

11

Arctic National Wildlife
Refuge and Preserve

A
■ Arctic
Village

Venetie
Indian
Reservation

RANGE

BROOKS

Anaktuvuk
Pass

Coldfoot
L

Nolan
I **H**
Wiseman ■

Bettles ■

Yukon Flats National

Yukon River

K

11

Kanuti
National
Wildlife
Refuge

J
Livengood

2

Manley
Hot Spring ■

Fairbanks ■

STEESE HIGHWAY

6

Fort Yukon ■

Circle City ■

ALASKA

CANADA

Yukon-Charley Rivers
National Preserve

White Mountains
National
Recreation
Area

Wildlife Refuge

2

3

Gates of the
Arctic National Park

E

F

Koyukuk National
Wildlife Refuge

Noatak National Preserve

Kobuk Valley
National Park

Noorvik
Indian
Reservation

Selawik National
Wildlife Refuge

Cape Krusenstern
National Monument

Kotzebue ■

Bering
Land Bridge
National
Preserve

ARCTIC CIRCLE

Seward

Peninsula

Nome ■

0 SCALE
150
KILOMETERS
150
MILES

━━━ ROAD   - - - - TRANS ALASKA PIPELINE   ✕ POINT OF INTEREST   ▬ PARKS

A PERFECT DAY IN THE FAR NORTH

A perfect day? Doesn't work this time. The Far North isn't a place for a day, it's a region for an adventure. Only Barrow offers a semblance of packaged tourist attractions that can be sandwiched between two fast flights in more or less of a day. If you decide to do Alaska's arctic wilds justice, block out several days or more on your travel calendar.

ORIENTATION

The Dalton Highway and Trans-Alaska Pipeline cut through the absolute wilderness of the Yukon Valley, Brooks Range, and North Slope to reach the drilling pads of Prudhoe Bay and the town of Deadhorse. In the Brooks Range, the Arctic National Wildlife Refuge is to the east of the road, while Gates of the Arctic National Park is to the west. Barrow is about 220 miles east of Prudhoe Bay.

SIGHTSEEING HIGHLIGHTS

★★★★ **ARCTIC NATIONAL WILDLIFE REFUGE**
Headquarters, Room 266, Federal Building and Courthouse, 101 12th Ave., Fairbanks, 907/456-0250, www.r7.fws.gov/nwr/arctic/r7arctc.htm
America's northernmost and second-largest wildlife refuge is commonly known by its acronym, ANWR (pronounced "AN-wahr"). The refuge is larger than the state of West Virginia and encompasses

---

SIGHTS
- Ⓐ Arctic National Wildlife Refuge
- Ⓑ Barrow
- Ⓒ Dalton Highway Drive
- Ⓓ Deadhorse (Prudhoe Bay)
- Ⓔ Gates of the Arctic National Park and Preserve
- Ⓕ Midnight Sun

LODGING
- Ⓖ Arctic Wilderness Lodge
- Ⓗ Coldfoot Services and Arctic Acres Inn
- Ⓓ Prudhoe Bay Hotel
- Ⓑ Top of the World Hotel
- Ⓘ Wiseman Bed & Breakfast
- Ⓙ Yukon Ventures Alaska

CAMPING
- Ⓚ Arctic Circle Wayside
- Ⓛ Marion Creek BLM Campground

Note: Items with the same letter are located in the same area.

---

virtually the entire northeastern corner of Alaska. Famous as the calving grounds of the Porcupine caribou herd, Arctic National Wildlife Refuge (ANWR) is home to at least 180 species of birds and 36 species of land mammal, including all three bear species. Nine marine mammal species frequent the coasts. With good reason, ANWR is sometimes known as the "American Serengeti."

ANWR is strictly a wilderness refuge; access is difficult and expensive. Most visitors charter a bush pilot to fly them in. Planes land on gravel bars for drop-offs, then return to a designated rendezvous days later. Coastal access via kayak and extended trekking through the Brooks Range from the Dalton Highway are also possible approaches. Kayak and raft outfitters have identified several river routes within the refuge, including a couple that run from the Brooks Range all the way to the Arctic Ocean. Flightseeing from Deadhorse or elsewhere is always an option.

The Athabascan Indian town of Arctic Village (Arctic Village Traditional Council, 907/587-5990) and the Eskimo town of Kaktovik (Barter Island, City of Kaktovik, 907/640-6313) are the only two settlements in close proximity to the refuge, though only Kaktovik has lodging and neither is often used as a travel base.

Arctic National Wildlife Refuge has no roads or facilities of any kind. Visitors should be competent in outdoor skills and fully equipped. Check the Gates of the Arctic National Park and Preserve and Deadhorse listings below for tour providers and air companies.

Details: Flightseeing or extended adventure. (1 day–several days)

★★★★ DALTON HIGHWAY DRIVE (413 MILES)
Paralleling the Trans-Alaska Pipeline and long known as the "Haul Road," there is no wilder drive in America. You may see grizzlies

bounding across a tundra whitened by a summer snow, or glimpse a herd of musk ox munching contentedly. When you reach the store in Deadhorse and ask about a bar or restaurant, you'll find that there are none. The North Slope is officially dry, and the only fixed-menu meals are served at the hotels.

The Dalton begins at its junction with the Elliott Highway near Livengood, 85 miles north of Fairbanks. It's good, graded gravel for its entire length; slow down and stay far to the right when approaching oncoming vehicles to minimize damage from flying stones. You'll find services at key points, though there's no gas until the end for the final 240 miles.

Passing first through hilly, forested country, the Dalton drops steadily down to the Yukon River Crossing (Mile 55.6), the only bridge over the Yukon in Alaska. From here, the road begins a very gradual climb out of this vast watershed. Stop at the **Arctic Circle Wayside** (Mile 115.3), where an overlook marks the Arctic Circle. Undeveloped campsites are found here.

Coldfoot (Mile 175) bills itself as "the farthest north resort in the world." While Barrow residents might argue with that claim, Coldfoot certainly boasts the farthest north bar in America. This is also your last chance to gas up until Prudhoe Bay. Stop at the Coldfoot Interagency Visitor Center (Mile 175 Dalton Highway, Coldfoot, 907/678-5209, aurora.ak.blm.gov/arcticinfo) for information on the public lands of the Far North, open June 1 to September 10, daily from 10 to 10. Evening slide programs are offered.

The settlements of Wiseman and Nolan (Mile 188.6) are reached via a short road that meets the Dalton. Along with Coldfoot, they were centers of mining activity a century ago. Today, **Wiseman** hosts a hearty group of residents glad to live the frontier life. A small B&B, store, museum, and public phone are found here, though there is no gas.

Soon after Wiseman, the road leaves the forest behind for good, climbing into the Brooks Range and up to Atigun Pass (Mile 244, elevation 4,739 feet), the highest year-round road pass in Alaska and the farthest-north road pass in the world. This is also the continental divide between the Pacific and Arctic Ocean watersheds. The pass can be snowy and icy at any time, so use caution.

Enjoy your 175-mile descent from the Brooks, onto the North Slope, and down the valley of the Sagavanirktok River (Sag River). If you wish, stop for a look at the Toolik Lake Research Camp (Mile

284.3). There are no services or public reception facilities, but someone might be around for a talk. Soon, you'll see the industrial landscape of Prudhoe Bay looming on the horizon. Follow the signs to Deadhorse; it's just north of the airport. **Details**: *Graded gravel road, can be rough, services spread out. (3- to 4-day round trip)*

★★★★ **GATES OF THE ARCTIC NATIONAL PARK AND PRESERVE**
Headquarters, 201 First Avenue, Fairbanks, 907/456-0281; Bettles Ranger Station, 907/692-5494, www.nps.gov/gaar
Lying entirely north of the Arctic Circle, Gates of the Arctic is second only to Wrangell–St. Elias National Park in size. Encompassing most of the central Brooks Range, the park features rugged peaks, lonely valleys, wild rivers, and pretty lakes. Forests reach to the 2,000-foot level on the southern slopes of the Brooks, but the high country and northern slopes are treeless, falling from barren ridges to sheltered brushlands and tundra. Parts of six National Wild Rivers are within the park and preserve.

Anaktuvuk Pass (City Office, Anaktuvuk Pass, 907/661-3612), home to about 300, is the only year-round settlement in the Brooks Range. Mountaineers and wilderness explorers can base trips here. Flights are possible from Fairbanks, Bettles, and elsewhere. In town, visitors can stay at the **Nunamiut Corporation Hotel** (Anaktuvuk Pass, 907/661-3220) for around $170 (includes three meals). Here, check out the **Simon Paneak Memorial Museum** (Anaktuvuk Pass, 907/661-3413). Billed as America's farthest-north museum, it displays Nunamiut Inupiat Eskimo heritage items.

Bettles (City Office, Bettles Field, 907/692-5191) is the most commonly used base for enjoying the park. Small planes shuttle many summer visitors to the area, most on their way to the Brooks Range or a river drop-off. You can stay at the **Bettles Lodge** (Bettles, 800/770-5111, 907/692-5111), a historic lodge with modern conveniences like Jacuzzis, a restaurant, and tavern.

Gates of the Arctic is strictly a wilderness park, and travelers leaving the settlements should be fully equipped and competent in outdoor skills. Guides should provide you with a list of necessary gear. Contact the Bettles Ranger Station (907/692-5494) before beginning any hikes or river runs. Reservations are recommended for all flights and lodging.

ARCTIC CIRCLE WAYSIDE

© Paul Otteson

The following companies offer some or all of guided backpacking, hiking, kayaking, canoeing, rafting, and fishing in both Gates of the Arctic N.P.P. and ANWR: ABEC's Alaska Adventures (Fairbanks, 907/457-8907), Alaska Fish and Trails (Fairbanks, Bettles Field, 907/479-7630), Arctic Treks (Fairbanks, 907/455-6502, www.gorp .com/arctreks/), Nature Alaska Tours (Fairbanks, 907/488-3746), Sourdough Outfitters (Bettles Field, 907/692-5252), and Wilderness: Alaska/Mexico (Fairbanks, 907/479-8203).

Air tours are offered to Anaktuvuk Pass from Fairbanks by Northern Alaska Tour Company (Fairbanks, 907/474-8600). Drop-offs and flightseeing are available in Bettles from Bettles Air Service (Bettles Field, 907/692-5111) and Brooks Range Aviation (Bettles Field, 907/692-5444).

Details: *Air tour or extended adventure. (1 day–several days)*

★★★ BARROW
City Office, Barrow, 907/852-5211,
www.wintersolstice.com/barrow.html
Named for Sir John Barrow of the British Admiralty, this traditional Inupiaq Eskimo village is the chief settlement in the Far North. Ukpeagvik is the native name for the town, which means, roughly,

"a high place for viewing," so named because Cape Smythe achieves the lofty local elevation of about 30 feet. Barrow made the news in 1935 as the place where Wiley Post and Will Rogers died in a plane crash. Visitors come to Barrow because it's the northernmost point in the United States. At 71 degrees north latitude, Barrow enjoys 84 continuous days of sunlight in the summer while suffering 67 sunless ones in the winter. Some visitors erroneously believe that they must go to Barrow to experience the midnight sun, which occurs anywhere north of the Arctic Circle, or the aurora borealis, which is actually better viewed at the Fairbanks latitude. Even so, there is something special about standing at the tip of Point Barrow and looking toward a North Pole that doesn't seem so far off.

Tundra Tours (Barrow, 800/882-8478, 800/478-8520 in Alaska) teams with Alaska Airlines (800/468-2248) to provide a package tour. Visitors can enjoy a trip to the tip of it all at Point Barrow, featuring the Arctic Ocean, excellent Inupiat cultural program, area tour, and the midnight sun (early May–July). Off-season trips feature northern-lights viewing.

Details: *(overnight tour or longer)*

★★ **DEADHORSE (PRUDHOE BAY)**
The newer oil-extraction facilities of Prudhoe Bay are designed to protect the tundra and exist in harmony with wildlife. Yet one glimpse reveals how many square miles are given over to industrial sprawl. Take a look, then take a plane, puzzling over the ironic fact that the ugliness is required to fuel the freedom.

Deadhorse exists almost solely to meet the needs of the oil business. Repair shops, rental yards, and subcontracting businesses are scattered along the haphazard roads. A general store/post office serves the workers. Two hotels, built of "Atco units," host business visitors and contractors. There are no bars or any other civic entertainments. Prepared food can be purchased in the hotels, but you'll find no menus, only the chef's special of the day (which can be delicious; see Lodging, below).

The store and hotels that comprise Deadhorse are located near the moderately busy airport a few miles inland of the coast. To visit the Arctic Ocean, you must take a $25 van tour from one of the hotels. Your best choice is to head to the airport for some flightseeing.

Details: *Flightseeing and drop-offs are offered by 40-Mile Air*

(Prudhoe Bay Airport, 907/659-2344) and Alaska Flyers (Prudhoe Bay Airport, 907/659-2544). (overnight typical)

★ MIDNIGHT SUN

The Arctic Circle marks the point where the midline of the sun just reaches the horizon at midday of the winter solstice and just dips to the horizon at midnight of the summer solstice. North of the line, summer brings the "midnight sun," while winter brings sunless days. The further north you go, the more sunless winter days and dark-free summer days you get.

I think the midnight sun is an iffy thrill, not enough to justify an expensive excursion. You can enjoy 10 or 11 p.m. sun in more accessible points in Alaska, remembering that a bright twilight lingers in the short hours of "darkness." Consider the phenomenon to be a small bonus on trips to the amazing Far North.

Details: Observable north of the Arctic Circle, up to two months in summer. (1 night)

FITNESS AND RECREATION

There's not an official trail to be found anywhere. Along the Dalton Highway, just head out from the side of the road whenever you're so inspired. If you are on a guided adventure, it's comfort and relaxation you'll treasure after long days of walking, fishing, or paddling.

FOOD

Virtually all dining options are associated with lodging. Check the listings below.

LODGING

Don't expect much along the Dalton Highway. **Yukon Ventures Alaska** (Mile 56 Dalton Highway) is a typical full-service highway center that has it all: gas, food, information, lodging, car service, showers, and towing. Inquire about river cruises and floats. Another example is **Coldfoot Services and Arctic Acres Inn** (Mile 175 Dalton Highway, 907/678-5201), with lodging, gas, bar, restaurant, gift shops, and frontier attitude. Rooms start at $135. If you make your way into the enclave of Wiseman, you'll find the absolutely Alaskan **Wiseman Bed & Breakfast** (from Mile 188.6 Dalton Highway, Igloo #8, follow the signs, Wiseman, 907/678-4456). It's as rustic and frontiersy as they get, possibly my favorite lodging in the state ($90 includes breakfast). The **Arctic Wilderness Lodge** (Mile 334 Dalton Highway, 907/659-2955, winter 907/376-7955) is a bare-bones B&B with $85 rooms that may or may not be open when you call. There's an airstrip and flying service. Raft rentals, fishing and viewing packages, and wilderness drop-offs are all available, starting at about $300.

Deadhorse has the **Prudhoe Bay Hotel** (Prudhoe Bay, 907/659-2449), offering very basic rooms for $110 single, $180 double (private bath) and $75 single, $130 double (shared bath). For both, the price includes three meals, which are also available for purchase to non-guests (call for times).

Barrow's one and only option is the **Top of the World Hotel** (Barrow, 800/882-8478, in Alaska 800/478-8520, 907/852-3900), a modern, full-service hotel with a restaurant. Tourist-rate rooms are $160–$180.

CAMPING

An undeveloped campground is found at the **Arctic Circle Wayside** (Mile 115.3 Dalton Highway). Near Coldfoot, the **Marion Creek BLM Campground** (Mile 180 Dalton Highway) has developed but primitive sites with fire rings, tables, and restrooms for $6.

Remember that it is against the law to block any of the numerous short roads that allow access to the pipeline, though some of these are wide enough to allow room for a big emergency truck to get by your parked camper.

18
NOME AND THE
SEWARD PENINSULA

"There's no place like Nome!" proclaims the city's motto, and it's true. This historic town of 5,000 was born in 1898 when gold was discovered in the beaches along Norton Sound. By the turn of the century, 20,000 miners were sluicing the rich sands; their numbers represented one-third of Alaska's non-native population at the time. Inevitably, the rush faded and the population declined, but Nome's boom years left behind a legacy and character that makes this somewhat remote destination an excellent choice for a visit.

The town isn't much to look at, which is typical of communities in zones of permafrost and bitter cold. The people, however, are about as steeped in Alaskan character as you'll find anywhere, and they are generally glad to make your acquaintance.

Three wonderful roads branch out from Nome, enabling exploration of the Seward Peninsula by rented pickup. One follows the coast northwestward past gold dredges and reindeer herds to the native village of Teller. The northbound Taylor or Kougarok Road passes through the lovely, barren Kigluaik Mountains, past beautiful Salmon Lake, to the Kougarok River bridge. The third follows the historic gold coast eastward, past the rusting "Train to Nowhere" at Solomon, and on to the vacation hamlet of Council. Renting a vehicle to explore the peninsula is a must.

On the north shore of the Seward Peninsula is Kotzebue, the region's other chief town. Largely a native community, Kotzebue has a good hotel and

NOME

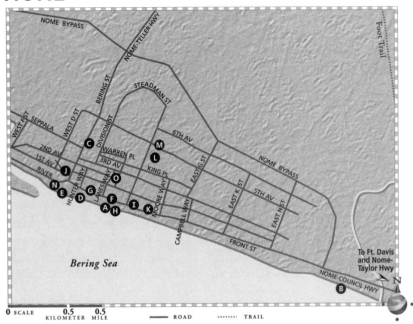

SIGHTS

- Ⓐ Carrie M. McLain Memorial Museum
- Ⓑ East Beach
- Ⓒ Largest Gold Pan in Alaska
- Ⓓ Visitor Information Center

FOOD

- Ⓔ Fat Freddies
- Ⓕ Nacho's Restaurant
- Ⓖ Pizza Napoli
- Ⓗ Polar Cub Cafe
- Ⓘ Twin Dragon

LODGING

- Ⓙ Aurora Executive Suites
- Ⓚ Aurora Inn
- Ⓛ Golden Sands Guest House
- Ⓜ No Place Like Nome Bed-N-Breakfast
- Ⓝ Nugget Inn
- Ⓞ Ponderosa Inn

restaurants and serves as base for regional bush flights. Try a rafting trip on the Noatak River, a visit to Serpentine Hot Springs in the Bering Land Bridge National Monument, or a flightseeing loop over the Kobuk Sand Dunes.

A PERFECT DAY IN NOME

Climb into your rented pickup and head out of town on the eastbound Council Highway. Stop at the site of Fort Davis for a walk on the beach. Strike up a conversation with a miner sluicing beach gravel or a native fisherman relaxing by his beach hut. Back on the highway, enjoy the coastal scenery, stopping once in a while for a headlands view or to scan the skies for migrating trumpeter swans. As you climb up a bridge approach about 34 miles out, look to your right to find the famous "Train to Nowhere," three, small, rusting locomotives once used to haul goods on a now-defunct rail line. Finish your excursion with a walk into the sleepy village of Council, enjoying the trees that are absent everywhere else in the region. Head home with an eye out for swans and gold-rush artifacts, including Swanberg's Dredge, just north of the road a mile east of town. A hearty dinner at Fat Freddies completes the day.

THE IDITAROD SLED DOG RACE

In 1925, Nome was struck by a diphtheria epidemic and in desperate need of medicine. When news of the situation reached Palmer, a group of mushers and their dogs picked up the needed serum at the railhead in Nenana, then traveled by dogsled to Nome, covering 674 miles in 127.5 hours. Their valiant journey inspired the creation of the Iditarod Sled Dog Race.

City maps are available at kiosks in the identical airport terminals. Road guides and maps are available at the visitors center on Front Street.

Today the annual race runs from Anchorage to Nome, following much of the historic Iditarod route that brought miners to the region during the Nome gold rush. It takes from 10 to 12 days for the lead racers to complete the grueling course, still 99 percent wild. In Nome, rooms for the race period in March are booked well in advance and the town comes alive with celebration. Other events staged during the same period include the Bering Sea Ice Golf Classic, in which competitors hit orange balls toward Astroturf "greens" on the frozen ice of the Bering Sea.

ORIENTATION

Nome and the Seward Peninsula are easy to reach and navigate. Alaska Airlines has twice-daily loop flights from Anchorage to Kotzebue and Nome and one Nome flight a day from Fairbanks. Both Nome and Kotzebue are just a few blocks long and wide. Both have long, straight waterfronts, with the main street of interest running along the water. The airports in both towns are a moderate walk or quick taxi from the centers and all accommodations. The only road system on the peninsula is centered in Nome, with three gravel highways heading out like spokes to the northwest, north, and east—all of them less than 90 miles long.

NOME SIGHTSEEING HIGHLIGHTS

★★★★ ROAD EXPLORATION
The best choice in Nome is certainly to rent a pickup from one of the two outlets and to explore the countryside via the three Seward Peninsula roads. Descriptive road guides and maps are available at the visitors center on Front Street and are supplied with your vehicle. It's impossible to get lost. The good, graded gravel roads can sustain speeds of about 45 miles per hour. Allow at least five hours for a round trip to the ends of any of the roads, though shorter round trips are possible to highlights like the "Train to Nowhere" and Salmon Lake. See Around the Seward Peninsula, below, for destination specifics.

Vehicles can be rented at Stampede Rent-A-Car (907/443-3838) and Alaska Cab Garage (907/443-2939). The cost is $75 to $85 per day; gas costs about $2 a gallon.

Details: *(5 hours or more)*

LAST TRAIN TO NOWHERE

© Paul Otteson

★★★ AREA TOURS
907/443-5535, tourinfo@ci.nome.ak.us
While I certainly recommend renting a pickup for a day or two to explore, you'll learn a lot more by joining one of the excellent tours of the area. Opportunities include remote fishing and mining camps, boat and kayak trips, and taxi tours. The best option might be **Nome Discovery Tours** (907/443-2814, discover@dwarf.nome.net), operated by local character and enthusiast Richard Beneville. You'll get an unforgettable taste of the real Nome on a custom tour that might include a historic loop, gold panning, exploring the tundra, visiting an Eskimo village, an ivory carving demonstration, or Pilgrim Hot Springs.
Details: *Various options. (half day)*

★★ CARRIE M. MCLAIN MEMORIAL MUSEUM
Kegoayah Kozga Library, Front Street,
907/443-2566
Located in the basement of the library, the museum collection includes natural history and native and gold-rush artifacts, including a good display of gold rush–era photographs.
Details: *Mon–Sat 1–7 (closes at 6 Sat). Call to confirm hours. Free. (30 minutes)*

★★ DOGSLED RIDES
907/443-2958
Hungry for a taste of traditional winter transport in the Alaskan bush? The Burmeister family in Nome offers dogsled rides, both winter and summer. Call for an appointment for this exhilarating and educational experience. And when the ride is done, imagine doing it for 10 long days through the dark and cold Alaskan wilderness in the Iditarod.
Details: *By appointment. (2 hours)*

★★ EAST BEACH
The waterfront east of town
Take a stroll on the beach east of downtown to get a feel for Nome life past and present. You're likely to see a couple of miners, perhaps operating one-man floating dredges just offshore to reach the remaining gold-bearing sands. The motley assortment of huts and shelters along the strand are the miners' shacks, fish camps,

summer escapes, and sometimes seasonal homes. Just remember that, though it's a public beach, structures and property should be respected.

Details: *Beach east of town center. (1 hour)*

★★ **VISITOR INFORMATION CENTER**
Front Street at Division, 907/443-5535,
tourinfo@ci.nome.ak.us
A friendly, knowledgeable staff is the best feature here. Scrapbooks, photo albums, and historic displays are a bonus. Look for the gazebo on Front Street across from City Hall.

Details: *Open daily, hours vary. (30 minutes)*

★ **LARGEST GOLD PAN IN ALASKA**
Bering Street and Airport Road
You can't miss it. A sign explains a bit of history, and the nearby statues of the "three Swedes" immortalize the lucky trio who first stumbled onto Nome's golden secret.

Details: *Outdoors in church green. (5 minutes)*

SIGHTSEEING HIGHLIGHTS AROUND THE SEWARD PENINSULA

★★★ **KOTZEBUE**
Information, 907/442-3760
At the tip of the narrow Baldwin Peninsula that juts into the Chukchi Sea sits the town of Kotzebue. Long before German lieutenant Otto Von Kotzebue discovered it for the Russians in 1818, the settlement of Kikiktagruk was a center of Arctic trade. Featuring a largely native population, Kotzebue serves as the regional trade, transport, and government center. It is perhaps the best base for float trips on the famous Noatak River in Noatak National Preserve (headquarters, Kotzebue, 907/442-8300, 907/442-3760 for information, www.nps.gov/noat).

If you fly Alaska Airlines to Nome from Anchorage, it's worth it to stop over a day or two in Kotzebue. NANA, the regional native corporation, sponsors Tour Arctic (907/442-3301) tours and operates the fine **NANA Museum of the Arctic** (Second Street, 907/442-3301, open summer daily 8:30–5:30, $20). Tours include interpretive museum programs, native dancing and blanket toss, a town tour, and tundra drive. You can book a complete package through the Alaska Airlines Vacation Desk (800/468-2248). On your own, you can stroll the gravel streets and long waterfront road of this busy, working town. Check out the displays at the National Park Service Visitor Center (Second Avenue near Lake Street, 907/442-3890) for the National Parks of the northwest, which include Cape Krusenstern National Monument, Noatak National Preserve, and Kobuk Valley National Park. Stroll over to the airport and book a seat on a bush flight for a flightseeing adventure with village landings. Baker Aviation (Kotzebue Airport, 907/442-3108) is one of several offering regular and charter runs.

Details: 551 air miles northwest of Anchorage. (1–2 days)

★★★ **SALMON LAKE**
Mile 38 Taylor Road
North of town along the Taylor Highway is beautiful Salmon Lake. It's a perfect place to hike, picnic, or camp, and to enjoy the beautiful high hill country of the Kigluaik Mountains. Near the long lake's north end is a marked turnout to the BLM campground and picnic area.

Details: 38 miles from Nome on Taylor Road. (3 hours round trip–overnight)

★★★ **"TRAIN TO NOWHERE" AND SOLOMON**
Three small, rusting steam locomotives and a few flatcars are all that's left of the Council City and Solomon Railroad. Built in 1881 and transported to Nome in 1903, the engines served the waning days of the region's gold boom before being abandoned to the elements in 1907. You can't miss them as you drive east on the Council Highway, about 34 miles from Nome. Look for them to the right as the road swings up onto a bridge approach.

Near Mile 36, you'll pass the remnant structures of the old mining town of Solomon. You can poke around a bit if you wish, but respect all private property signs and be aware that a few buildings are still in use.

Details: 34 miles from Nome on Council Road. (3 hours round trip)

★★ **SERPENTINE HOT SPRINGS**
Bering Land Bridge National Monument,
www.nps.gov/bela

These pleasant springs are certainly the main attraction in the monument. There is a primitive bunkhouse at the springs, located north of Taylor. Charter flights are available from Kotzebue and Nome. Consult the ranger for details (240 Front St., Nome, 907/443-2522).
Details: *Remote hot springs, charter flight from Nome or Kotzebue. (2 days)*

★★ **TELLER**

After passing through tundra-covered hill country, the Teller Road drops quickly to sea level and road's end, affording marvelous views of the village and its harbor. Once a gold-boom town of 5,000, Teller now shelters about 180 residents and is oriented towards commercial fishing and subsistence wildlife harvesting. A herd of some 1,000 reindeer grazes in the area. Walk out onto the spit for a long bay view. Stop in at the store for a snack and conversation. There are only three streets, so you can't get lost.
Details: *73 miles from Nome on Teller Road. (5 hours round trip)*

★ **COUNCIL**

If you follow the road east from Nome to the end, you'll come to the Niukluk River, across which is the community of Council. Once home to as many as 15,000 miners, only a few folks live here today, though about 30 families have vacation property in the area. Turn right at the river to reach the vehicle ford and boat crossing where, with luck, you can catch a ride across for a closer look at the place, including access to some cabin ruins that date to the turn of the century. Chancing the ford is not recommended unless you can closely follow a local who knows the shallow path.
Details: *72 miles from Nome on Council Road. (5 hours round trip)*

FITNESS AND RECREATION

Hiking and walking are the obvious choices for a Seward Peninsula adventure, with three main areas to pick from. Ridge and tundra hikes are particularly good in the well-drained high country around **Salmon Lake**. The endless sand and gravel beaches are perfect for explorations during the lingering twilight; try the coast along the **Council Road** or where a spur of the Teller Road allows access to the beach at **Cape Wooley**. The lanes and streets of Nome, Kotzebue, Teller, and the villages are great places to stretch your legs.

SEWARD PENINSULA

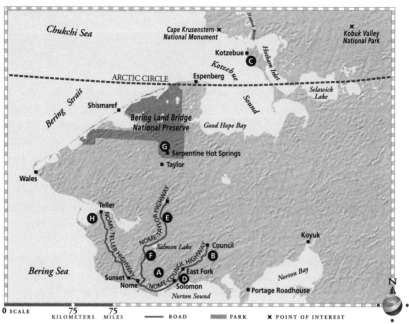

SIGHTS

A Area Tours
B Council
C Kotzebue
D The "Last Train to Nowhere" and Solomon
E Road Exploration
F Salmon Lake
G Serpentine Hot Springs
H Teller

FOOD

C Bayside Restaurant
C Ice Cafe
C Nullagvik Hotel

LODGING

C Nullagvik Hotel

CAMPING

F Salmon Lake BLM Campground

Note: Items with the same letter are located in the same area.

Raft trips on the **Noatak** and other rivers can be scheduled with the help of the ranger in Kotzebue (907/442-3890) or a flying service. Kayak trips are offered in Nome (907/443-4994 for information).

FOOD

Several good eateries are found along Front Street in the heart of Nome. **Fat Freddies** (Front Street east of Bering Street, 907/443-5899), right on the water, features a big menu with tasty seafood offerings. It's connected by a long hallway to the Nugget Inn, which can be nice for inn guests when the weather is rough.

A block east is a basic pizza joint called **Pizza Napoli** (Front Street at Lanes Way, 907/443-5300). It's just what you'd expect, pretty good and not expensive.

Moving east again and across the street is **Nacho's Restaurant** (Front Street between Lanes and Federal, 907/443-6836) and, in the same building, the **Twin Dragon** (Front Street between Lanes and Federal, 907/443-5552). Other ethnic selections mixed in with the Mexican and Asian offerings make this pair the center for international cuisine in town.

Just across the street is a local favorite and my choice for grabbing a Nome breakfast: the **Polar Cub Cafe** (Front Street and Federal Way, 907/443-5191).

In Kotzebue, you can't do better than the dining room in the **Nullagvik Hotel** (see Lodging, below), but there are a couple of other good choices just a block to the south on Shore Avenue. The **Bayside Restaurant** (303 Front St., 907/442-3600) is a cozy spot with a good mixed menu, while the **Ice Cafe** (Shore Avenue between Tundra and Lagoon) serves delicious ice cream, desserts, and fast food.

LODGING

The classic place in Nome is the **Nugget Inn** (Front and Bering Streets, 907/443-2323), offering ocean-view rooms in the heart of town. It's clean and has character, with an entertaining lobby and a waterfront lounge. Rooms range from $85 to $95.

For a longer stay, you might consider the new **Aurora Executive Suites** (Second and West D Streets, 907/443-3838), which features studios with kitchenettes starting at $100 and big two-bedroom apartments for $125. The new **Aurora Inn** on Front Street may be complete when you arrive.

The **Ponderosa Inn** (Spokane Avenue and East Third Street, 907/443-2368) has a homey feel, with singles, doubles, and full-kitchen suites ranging from $64 to $120.

A handful of B&Bs are found around Nome, including the **No Place Like Nome Bed-N-Breakfast** (Steadman and East Fifth Streets, 907/443-2451). Located five blocks from the lights and cars of Front Street, singles go for $60, doubles $70. A full sourdough-pancake breakfast is included.

Another B&B choice is the **Golden Sands Guest House** (411 Alley Way, 907/443-3900). A continental breakfast comes with the $55 single and $65 double rooms. "Sleeping-bag space" is available for $25.

In Kotzebue, the **Nullagvik Hotel** (Front Street and Tundra Way, 907/442-3331) is the best of the few options in town. The rooms are modern and comfortable, and there's a good restaurant and excellent gift shop. It's right on the water.

CAMPING

Free camping is possible on the beach or roadside turnouts, though most visitors base themselves in Nome. The one official campground of note is the **Salmon Lake BLM Campground** (Mile 38, Taylor Highway).

APPENDIX

Consider this appendix your travel tool box. Use it along with the material in the Planning Your Trip chapter to craft the trip you want. Here are the tools you'll find inside:

1. **Planning Map.** Make copies of this map and plot out various trip possibilities. Once you've decided on your route, you can write it on the original map and refer to it as you're traveling.

2. **Mileage Chart.** This chart shows the driving distances (in miles) between various destinations throughout the state. Use it in conjunction with the Planning Map.

3. **Special Interest Tours.** If you'd like to plan a trip around a certain theme—such as nature, sports, or art—one of these tours may work for you.

4. **Calendar of Events.** Here you'll find a month-by-month listing of major area events.

5. **Resources.** This guide lists various regional chambers of commerce and visitors bureaus, state offices, bed-and-breakfast registries, and other useful sources of information.

PLANNING MAP: Alaska

ALASKA

1. Ketchikan and the Southern Panhandle
2. Wrangell and Petersburg
3. Juneau
4. Sitka
5. Skagway and Haines
6. Tanana Valley and the Alaska Highway
7. Copper River Valley
8. Prince William Sound/Valdez, Cordova, and Whittier
9. MatSu
10. Anchorage and Vicinity
11. Seward and the Eastern Kenai Peninsula
12. Western Kenai Peninsula
13. Homer and Kachemak Bay
14. Kodiak and the Wild Southwest
15. Denali
16. Fairbanks and Vicinity
17. Far North
18. Nome and the Seward Peninsula

Arctic Ocean

Bar▪

Chukchi Sea

RUSSIA

Arctic Circle

RUSSIA U.S.A.

▪Point Hope   *Brooks Rang*

▪Kotzebue

Bering Land Bridge National Preserve

Taylor▪
Teller▪

Seward Peninsula

Nome▪ ⑱ ▪Council   Galena▪

International Date Line

Bering Strait

St. Lawrence Island

Norton Sound

Yukon River

Kuskowim Mountain

Bering Sea

Hooper▪ Bay

Kuskokwin

Nunivak Island

Bethel▪

Alaska Ra

Dillingham▪

Katmai National Park

Pribolof Islands

Bristol Bay

Alaska Peninsula

Aleutian Range

Aleutian Islands
Unalaska▪
Unalaska Island

O SCALE

| 400 | 400 |
| KILOMETERS | MILES |

—— ROAD

- - - - AREA OR PARK BOU
✕— POINT OF INTEREST

You have permission to photocopy this map.

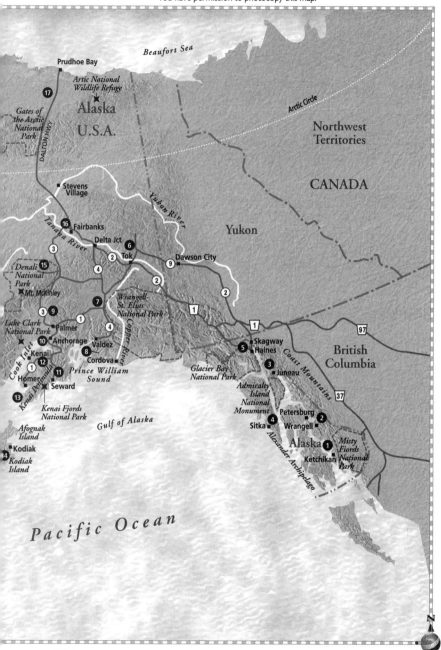

Beaufort Sea

Prudhoe Bay

Artic National
Wildlife Refuge

17

Gates of
the Arctic
National
Park

Arctic Circle

Alaska
U.S.A.

Northwest
Territories

CANADA

DALTON HWY

Stevens
Village

Yukon River

Tanana River

16 Fairbanks

Yukon

Delta Jct

3

6

2 Tok

9 Dawson City

Denali
National
Park

15

4

2

Mt. McKinley

7

Wrangell-
St. Elias
National Park

2

3 9

1

1

Lake Clark
National Park

Palmer

4

Copper River

1

97

Cook Inlet

10

Anchorage

Valdez

8 Cordova

5

Skagway
Haines

British
Columbia

Kenai

12

11

Prince William
Sound

Glacier Bay
National Park

3 Juneau

Coast Mountains

37

Homer

Seward

Admiralty
Island
National
Monument

Petersburg

2

13

Kenai Fjords
National Park

Kenai Peninsula

Sitka

4

Wrangell

Afognak
Island

Gulf of Alaska

Alaska

1

Misty
Fiords
National
Park

4

Kodiak

Ketchikan

Kodiak
Island

Alexander Archipelago

Pacific Ocean

N

— · ·— **INTERNATIONAL BOUNDARY**
— ·— **PROVINCIAL BOUNDARY**

	Anchorage	Deadhorse	Denali	Fairbanks	Haines	Homer	Seattle, WA	Seward	Skagway	Tok	Valdez
Anchorage											
Deadhorse	847										
Denali	239	614									
Fairbanks	358	489	125								
Haines	775	1142	790	653							
Homer	226	1073	464	584	1001						
Seattle, WA	2435	2802	2438	2313	1962	2661					
Seward	126	973	365	484	901	173	2561				
Skagway	832	1199	835	710	359	1058	1819	959			
Tok	328	695	331	206	447	554	2107	454	504		
Valdez	304	853	543	364	701	530	2361	430	758	254	
Whitehorse	724	1091	727	602	251	950	1711	850	108	396	650

DRIVING MILEAGE CHART

	Prince Rupert	Ketchikan	Petersburg	Juneau	Haines	Skagway
Bellingham	30	36	39	48	52.5	53.5
Prince Rupert		6	15	24	28.5	29.5
Ketchikan			9	18	22.5	23.5
Petersburg				9	13.5	14.5
Juneau					4.5	5.5
Haines						1

SOUTHEAST FERRY HOURS

	Anchorage	Fairbanks
Anchorage		265
Fairbanks	265	
Juneau	570	620
Kodiak	250	
Unalaska/Dutch	800	
Pribilof Islands	800	
Nome	530	510
Bettles		180
Barrow	720	490
Deadhorse	625	380
Fort Yukon		140

AIR MILEAGE

SPECIAL INTEREST TOURS

With *Alaska Travel•Smart* you can plan a trip of any length—a one-day excursion, a getaway weekend, or a three-week vacation—around any special interest. To get you started, the following pages contain six tours geared toward a variety of interests. For more information, refer to the chapters listed—chapter names are bolded and chapter numbers appear inside black bullets. You can follow a suggested itinerary in its entirety, or shorten, lengthen, or combine parts of each depending on your starting and ending points.

Discuss alternative routes and schedules with your travel companions—it's a great way to have fun, even before you leave home. And remember: don't hesitate to change your itinerary once you're on the road. Careful study and planning ahead of time will help you make informed decisions as you go, but spontaneity is the extra ingredient that will make your trip memorable.

ARTS AND CULTURE TOUR

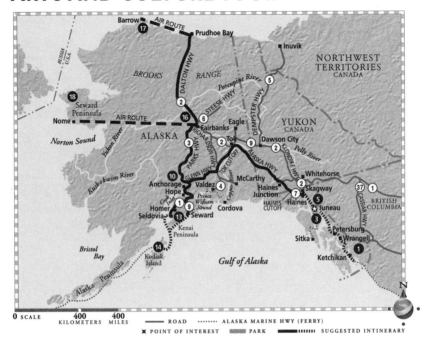

Enjoy performances, exhibits, and sights that express the artistic and cultural heritage of Alaska's diverse peoples.

❶ **Ketchikan and the Southern Panhandle** (Totem Heritage Center, Saxman, Metlakatla, Hydaburg)

❸ **Juneau** (Alaska State Museum, Naa Kahidi Theater)

❺ **Skagway and Haines** (Haines galleries, Chilkat Center for the Arts, Chilkat Dancers)

❿ **Anchorage and Vicinity** (Anchorage Museum of History and Art, Eklutna Village Historical Park)

⓭ **Homer and Kachemak Bay** (Homer galleries, Seldovia, Halibut Cove)

⓮ **Kodiak and the Wild Southwest** (Alutiiq Museum)

⓰ **Fairbanks and Vicinity** (University of Alaska Museum)

⓱ **Far North** (Barrow)

⓲ **Nome and the Seward Peninsula** (Nome, NANA Museum)

GOLD RUSH HISTORY TOUR

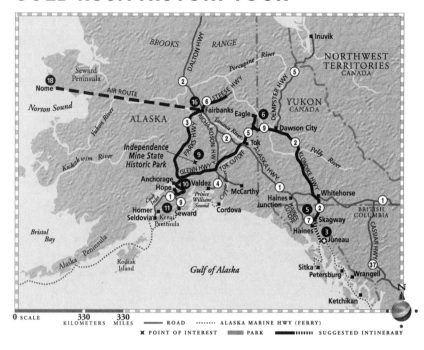

Evidence of gold mining past and present is found in many parts of the state. Try these areas for the best of it.

- **3** **Juneau** (Last Chance Mining Museum)
- **5** **Skagway and Haines** (Klondike Gold Rush National Historic Park, Yukon and White Pass Route, Chilkoot Trail)
- **6** **Tanana Valley and the Alaska Highway** (Dawson City, Eagle, Chicken, Fortymile valley)
- **9** **MatSu** (Independence Mine, Hatcher Pass)
- **10** **Anchorage and Vicinity** (Alaska Gold Mining Museum, Crow Creek Mine)
- **11** **Seward and the Eastern Kenai Peninsula** (Hope)
- **16** **Fairbanks and Vicinity** (Ester Gold Camp, Gold Dredge #8, Steese Highway, Chatanika, Central)
- **18** **Nome and the Seward Peninsula** (East Beach, Largest Gold Pan in Alaska, Solomon, Train to Nowhere)

WILDLIFE VIEWING TOUR

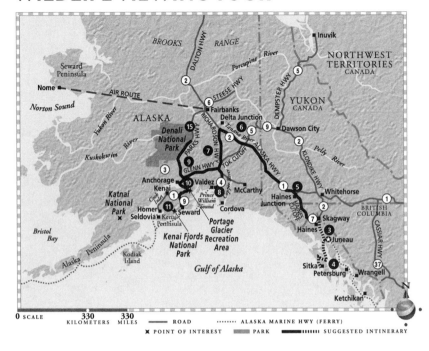

Wildlife can be seen throughout the state. Here are a few areas where observers are all but assured of successful viewing, including a few sites where wildlife is artificially concentrated.

- ❸ **Juneau** (Glacier Bay cruise, Tracy Arm cruise, Point Adolphus whale watching)
- ❹ **Sitka** (Alaska Raptor Rehabilitation Center)
- ❺ **Skagway and Haines** (Alaska Chilkat Bald Eagle Preserve)
- ❻ **Tanana Valley and the Alaska Highway** (Delta Junction Bison Range)
- ❼ **Copper River Valley** (Sheep Mountain)
- ❽ **Prince William Sound** (cruises, Crooked Creek Salmon Viewpoint)
- ❾ **MatSu** (Musk Ox Farm, Williams' Reindeer Farm)
- ❿ **Anchorage and Vicinity** (Alaska Zoo, Potter Marsh, Beluga Point, Big Game Alaska)
- ⓫ **Seward and the Eastern Kenai Peninsula** (Alaska SeaLife Center, Kenai Fjords tour)
- ⓯ **Denali** (Park road tours, day hikes)

BEAR VIEWING TOUR

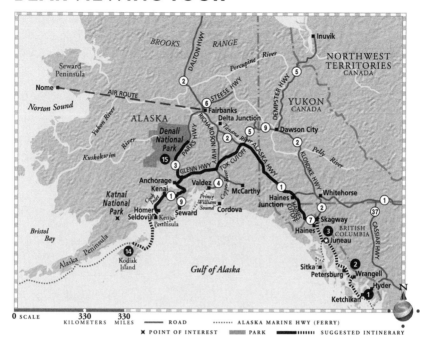

Want to see grizzlies? If you get to any of these renowned areas, your chances are excellent.

❶ Ketchikan and the Southern Panhandle (Fish Creek)

❷ Wrangell and Petersburg (Anan Bear Observatory)

❸ Juneau (Pack Creek)

⑭ Kodiak and the Wild Southwest ("Guaranteed" Bear Viewing from Kodiak, Brooks Camp, McNeil River)

⑮ Denali (Park road tours, day hikes)

GLACIER TOUR

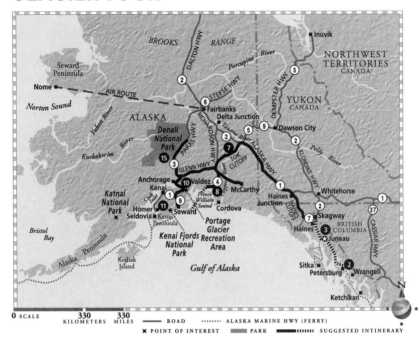

When you're in the mountainous regions of Alaska, it's hard not to see a glacier, but a few areas feature close access to large glaciers that terminate on land or to "tidewater" glaciers that calve bergs into the sea.

- **❷ Wrangell and Petersburg** (LeConte Glacier)
- **❸ Juneau** (Mendenhall Glacier, Tracy Arm cruise, Taku Lodge excursion, Glacier Bay cruise)
- **❼ Copper River Valley** (Kennicott and Root Glaciers, Worthington Glacier)
- **❽ Prince William Sound** (Blackstone Glacier, Harriman Fjord, College Fjord, Columbia Glacier, Childs Glacier, Matanuska Glacier)
- **❿ Anchorage and Vicinity** (Portage Glacier Recreation Area)
- **⓫ Seward and the Eastern Kenai Peninsula** (Kenai Fjords tour, Exit Glacier)
- **⓯ Denali** (Ruth Glacier flight)

RUSSIAN HISTORY TOUR

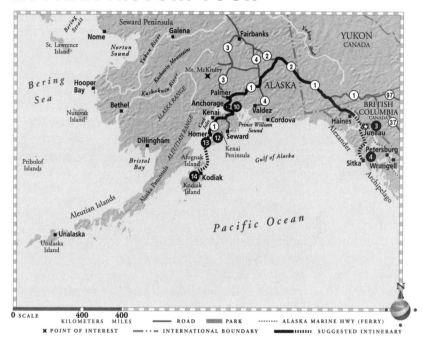

Though hard on both wildlife and Alaska's native peoples, Russian explorers and settlers made a lasting impression in many communities.

- ❸ **Juneau** (Saint Nicholas Orthodox Church)
- ❹ **Sitka** (Sitka National Historic Park, Russian Bishop's House, Castle Hill State Historic Park, Isabel Miller Museum, Sheldon Jackson Museum, Saint Michael's Russian Orthodox Church, Russian Cemetery and Blockhouse)
- ❿ **Anchorage and Vicinity** (Eklutna Village)
- ⑫ **Western Kenai Peninsula** (Historic Kenai, Ninilchik)
- ⑬ **Homer and Kachemak Bay** (Seldovia)
- ⑭ **Kodiak and the Wild Southwest** (Kodiak Baranov Museum, Holy Resurrection Church, Holy Ascension Cathedral)

January
Alcan 200 Road Rally Snowmachine Race, Haines
Copper Basin 300 Sled Dog Race, Glenallen
Great Alaska Beer Festival, Anchorage
Polar Bear Jump Off Festival, Seward
Russian New Year & Masquerade Ball, Kodiak
Tustamena 200 Sled Dog Race, Kenai

February
Cordova Ice Worm Festival, Cordova
Fur Rendezvous, Anchorage
Homer Winter Carnival, Homer
International Ice Climbing Festival, Valdez
Taku Rondy at Eaglecrest, Juneau
Tent City Winter Festival, Wrangell
Yukon Quest Sled Dog Race, between Fairbanks and Whitehorse; events in
    Fairbanks, Eagle, Dawson, Circle, and Whitehorse

March
Bering Sea Ice Classic Golf tournament, Nome
Festival of Native Arts, Fairbanks
Iditarod Trail Sled Dog Race, Anchorage to Nome; events in Anchorage,
    Wasilla and Nome
Nenana Ice Classic Tripod Raising, Nenana
North Pole Winter Carnival, North Pole
Winter Carnival, Fairbanks
Winter King Salmon Tournament, Homer
World Ice Art Championships, Fairbanks

April
ACTFEST Theater Festival, Haines
Alaska Folk Festival, Juneau
Alyeska Spring Carnival, Girdwood
Garnet Festival, Wrangell
Jazz Week, Anchorage
Whale Fest, Kodiak
World Extreme Ski Championships, Valdez

May
Buffalo Wallow Square Dance Festival, Delta Junction
Celebration of the Sea, Ketchikan
Copper River Delta Shorebird Festival, Valdez
Great Alaska Craft Beer Festival, Haines
Juneau Jazz and Classics Music Festival, Juneau
Kachemak Bay Shorebird Festival, Homer
Kachemak Bay Wooden Boat Festival, Homer
Kodiak King Crab Festival, Kodiak
Little Norway Festival, Petersburg
Miner's Day Celebration, Talkeetna
Polar Bear Swim, Nome

June
Alaska Mardi Gras, Haines
Big Lake Regatta Water Festival, Big Lake
Colony Days, Palmer
Homer Summer Fair, Homer
International Rodeo, Hyder, Stewart
Kenai River Festival, Kenai
Midnight Sun Festival, Nome
Salmon & Seafood Festival, Cordova
Sitka Summer Music Festival, Sitka
Summer Solstice Festivals, Haines, Fairbanks, Moose Pass

July
Bear Paw Festival, Eagle River
Cantwell Music Festival, Cantwell
Deltana Fair, Delta Junction
Golden Days, Fairbanks
July 4th Celebrations, many locations
Kodiak Bear Country Music Festival, Kodiak
Mount Marathon Run/July 4th Celebration, Seward
Soldotna Progress Days, Soldotna
World Eskimo-Indian Olympics, Fairbanks

August
Alaska State Fair, Palmer
Blueberry Festival, Ketchikan
Discovery Days Festival, Dawson City, Yukon

Kenai Peninsula State Fair, Ninilchik
Gold Rush Days, Valdez
Silver Salmon Derby, Seward
Southeast Alaska State Fair, Haines
Talkeetna Bluegrass Festival, Talkeetna
Tanana Valley State Fair, Fairbanks

September
Discovery Days Celebration, Valdez
Kodiak State Fair and Rodeo, Kodiak
Make It Alaskan Festival, Anchorage

October
Alaska Day Celebration, Sitka
Kodiak State Fair & Rodeo, Kodiak
Oktoberfests, Fairbanks, Homer and Kodiak
Quiana Alaska Native Dance Festival, Anchorage

November
Alascattalo Day Parade, Anchorage
Alaska Bald Eagle Festival, Haines
Athapaskan Old-Time Fiddling Festival, Fairbanks
Top of the World Classic/NCAA Division I Basketball, Fairbanks

December
Bachelor Society Ball, Talkeetna
Barrow Christmas Games, Barrow
Nutcracker Performance and Art Fair, Homer
Talkeetna Winterfest, Talkeetna
Winter Solstice Celebrations, various locations

RESOURCES

Alaska Public Lands Information Centers
Anchorage, 907/271-2737
Fairbanks, 907/451-7352
Ketchikan (Southeast Alaska Visitor Center), 907/228-6214
Tok, 907/883-5667

Bureau of Land Management
Anchorage, 907/271-5960, www.ak.blm.gov/
Anchorage District Office, Anchorage, 907/267-1246
Arctic District Office, Fairbanks, 907/474-2300
Glenallen District Office, Glenallen, 907/822-3217
Kobuk District Office, Fairbanks, 907/474-2330
Steese/White Mountains District Office, Fairbanks, 907/474-2350

National Forests
Alaska Region: Juneau, 907/586-8863,
    www.fs.fed.us/recreation/states/ak.html
Forest Service Information Center, Juneau, 907/586-8751
Chugach National Forest
    Main office, Anchorage, 907/271-2500
    Glacier Ranger District, Girdwood, 907/783-3242
    Seward Ranger District, Seward, 907/224-3374
    Cordova Ranger District, Cordova, 907/424-7661
Tongass National Forest
    Ketchikan Area, Ketchikan, 907/225-3101
    Chatham Area, Sitka, 907/747-6671
    Stikine Area, Petersburg, 907/772-3841
National Park Service, Anchorage, 907/257-2690,
    www.nps.gov/parklists/ak.html
U.S. Fish & Wildlife Service, Anchorage, 907/786-3357

Alaska State Government
Alaska Department of Fish and Game, Anchorage, 907/344-0541, www.state.ak.us/adfg
Alaska Division of Tourism, Juneau, 907/465-2012,
    www.state.ak.us/tourism/
Alaska Mainstreet Visitor Center, Tok, 907/883-5775

Alaska Office of History and Archaeology, Anchorage, 907/762-2622

Alaska State Parks, Department of Natural Resources/Division of Parks & Outdoor Recreation, Anchorage, 907/762-2617

Alaska Native Information
Alaska Native Tourism Council, Anchorage, 800/544-0552, 907/265-2494

Best Local Information Contacts
(chambers of commerce, visitors bureaus, etc.)
Anchor Point, 907/235-2600
Anchorage, 907/274-3531
Barrow, 907/852-5222
Bethel, 907/543-2911
Big Lake, 907/892-6109
Copper Valley (region), 907/822-5555
Cordova, 907/424-7260
Delta Junction, 907/895-9941 (summer), 907/895-4628 (winter)
Dillingham, 907/842-5283
Eagle River (and vicinity), 907/696-4636
Fairbanks, 907/452-1105
Funny River, 907/262-7711
Gustavus, 907/697-2358
Haines, 800/458-3579
Healy, P.O. Box 907/437, Healy AK, 99743 (no phone)
Homer, 907/235-5300
Hyder, 604/636-9148
Juneau, 907/586-1737
Kenai, 907/283-1991
Ketchikan, 907/225-6166
King Salmon, 907/246-4250
Kodiak, 907/486-4782
Kotzebue, 907/442-3760
MatSu Region, 907/746-5000
Metlakatla, 907/886-1216 or 907/886-4161
Nenana, 907/832-5541
Nome, 907/443-5535
North Peninsula (Kenai), 907/776-8369
North Pole, 907/488-2242

Palmer, 907/745-2880
Petersburg, 907/772-3975
Prince of Wales Island, 907/826-3870
Prince William Sound Region, 907/344-1693
Seldovia, 907/234-7890
Seward, 907/224-8051
Sitka, 907/747-5940
Skagway, 907/983-2854
Soldotna, 907/262-9814
Sutton, 907/745-4527
Talkeetna, 907/733-2330
Tok, 907/883-5775 (summer), 907/883-5887 (winter)
Unalaska/Dutch Harbor, 907/581-1483
Valdez, 800/770-5954
Wasilla, 907/373-9071
Whittier, 907/472-2379, 907/472-2327
Wrangell, 907/874-2010

Alaska Information Web Sites
Alaska One, www.AlaskaOne.com/travel
Alaska Science Forum, www.gi.alaska.edu/ScienceForum/asf.html
Alaska Tourism and Travel Guide, www.alaskan.com
Alaska Volcano Observatory, www.avo.alaska.edu
Alaska Wild and Scenic Rivers,
      www.nps.gov/ccso/wildriverslist.htm#ak
State of Alaska, www.state.ak.us/

INDEX

261

MAP INDEX

Guidebooks that really *guide*

City•Smart™ Guidebooks

Pick one for your favorite city: *Albuquerque, Anchorage, Austin, Calgary, Charlotte, Chicago, Cincinnati, Cleveland, Denver, Indianapolis, Kansas City, Memphis, Milwaukee, Minneapolis/St. Paul, Nashville, Pittsburgh, Portland, Richmond, Salt Lake City, San Antonio, San Francisco, St. Louis, Tampa/St. Petersburg, Tucson.* US $12.95 to 15.95

Retirement & Relocation Guidebooks

The World's Top Retirement Havens, Live Well in Honduras, Live Well in Ireland, Live Well in Mexico. US $15.95 to $16.95

Travel•Smart® Guidebooks

Trip planners with select recommendations to *Alaska, American Southwest, Arizona, Carolinas, Colorado, Deep South, Eastern Canada, Florida, Florida Gulf Coast, Hawaii, Illinois/Indiana, Kentucky/Tennessee, Maryland/Delaware, Michigan, Minnesota/Wisconsin, Montana/Wyoming/Idaho, New England, New Mexico, New York State, Northern California, Ohio, Pacific Northwest, Pennsylvania/New Jersey, South Florida and the Keys, Southern California, Texas, Utah, Virginias, Western Canada.* US $14.95 to $17.95

Rick Steves' Guides

See *Europe Through the Back Door* and take along guides to *France, Belgium & the Netherlands; Germany, Austria & Switzerland; Great Britain & Ireland; Italy; Scandinavia; Spain & Portugal; London; Paris;* or *Best of Europe.* US $12.95 to $21.95

Adventures in Nature

Plan your next adventure in *Alaska, Belize, Caribbean, Costa Rica, Guatemala, Hawaii, Honduras, Mexico.* US $17.95 to $18.95

Into the Heart of Jerusalem

A traveler's guide to visits, celebrations, and sojourns. US $17.95

The People's Guide to Mexico

This is so much more than a guidebook—it's a trip to Mexico in and of itself, complete with the flavor of the country and its sights, sounds, and people. US $22.95

JOHN MUIR PUBLICATIONS
5855 Beaudry Street • Emeryville, CA 94608

Available at your favorite bookstore.

PAUL OTTESON

ABOUT THE AUTHOR

Paul Otteson has traveled throughout western North America, camera in hand, for more than two decades. He has covered thousands of miles on foot, exploring scores of parks and wilderness areas and more than a quarter-million miles on the highways and backroads of the West. He has spent many months in Alaska, traveling by land, air, and sea, immersing himself in the Alaskan experience while maintaining a traveler's eye.

Otteson's international journeys led to his first book, *The World Awaits: A Comprehensive Guide to Extended Backpack Travel*, which is fast becoming a classic for those planning independent travel overseas. His other works include *Alaska: Adventures in Nature, Northern California Travel•Smart, and Kids Who Walk on Volcanoes*, a children's book on the lives of kids in the Central American Highlands. Paul is the managing editor of Hostels.com, the premier hostelling site on the web.

Paul and his wife, Mary, currently reside in San Francisco—though Alaska, where they met, will always be their second home.

alaskajourney.com—To check on the latest updates to the information in this book, visit the author's Alaska website: www.alaskajourney.com. The site also features an indexed collection of Paul's photographs from all over the state, as well as related content, opinions, and links.